The Dark Face of Marxism
Rites of Passage of a Master Spy
Based on a True Spy Story

Dr. Julio Antonio del Marmol
The Cuban Lightning

© Copyright 2017 Dr. Julio Antonio del Marmol.
All rights reserved. No part of this publication may be reproduced, stored in a retrieval system, or transmitted, in any form or by any means, electronic, mechanical, photocopying, recording, or otherwise, without the written prior permission of the author.

ISBN: 978-1-68588-013-2 (sc)
ISBN: 978-1-68588-012-5 (hc)
ISBN: 978-1-68588-014-9 (e)

Because of the dynamic nature of the Internet, any web addresses or links contained in
this book may have changed since publication and may no longer be valid.

Any people depicted in stock imagery provided by Thinkstock are models, and such images are being used for illustrative purposes only.
Certain stock imagery © Thinkstock.

Cuban Lightning Publications, Int rev. 01/26/2017

Introduction

At the age of twelve, the author, Julio Antonio del Marmol, found that his destiny had taken him through extraordinary circumstances that happen only a few times in history during widespread social chaos—like those seen in the deranged turmoil of the Cuban Revolution in 1959. The supreme leader, Fidel Castro, nominated this young boy to be the Commander-in-Chief of the new army for the future.

As Fidel Castro went through his own changes of heart at the start of this tumultuous time, the youth went through his own conflict as he watched his childhood friends abandon the island, discontented with the complete disruption of democratic establishment and the institution of Marxist ideology by the new leaders. Julio Antonio del Marmol, the Young Commander, sadly remained behind and daily observed the freedom of the Cuban people evaporate as promise after promise was broken. In spite of the commitment to equality for all without distinction based on political or religious belief, the Castro brothers and Che Guevara ruthlessly hunted down and exterminated all opposition. His admiration towards the leaders turned into disappointment and frustration, as he watched the Castros' forces execute their enemies and commit the most horrendous crimes humanity had ever seen in their ambition to maintain power.

He concluded that this is not what the Cuban people had fought their revolution for and decided, before sharing these horrible experiences with anyone, including his father, to abandon the country as his friends had done. When he did share these intentions with his uncle, he received the most shocking surprise: his relative was a veteran master spy. His uncle proposed that he be trained to be the next in line, and Julio Antonio del Marmol became the youngest spy in modern history at the age of thirteen.

In this story, the reader will find seemingly unbelievable and undoubtedly controversial details about the blueprints to create communist revolutions, spread corruption, and commit assassinations so outrageous that nobody ever could create this as a fiction. We are transported back to 1961, where the youthful master spy Julio Antonio del Marmol continues his dance with the sinister Cuban G-2, avoiding the traps laid by their head, Manuel Piñeiro, who doubts the Commandantico's loyalty to the Revolution. All the while, he continues penetrating the puzzling maze of duplicate men, eventually meeting face-to-face the original: Lee Harvey Oswald!

The author tells the story not merely as a narrator; he was an active participant in these events as part of his first steps in his life as a thirteen-year-old spy, as he tried to retrieve what he felt to be important documents for his friends in his intelligence network. He perceived the relevance and import of what he had obtained. Readers will draw their own conclusions and put the facts together. Only when the author's friends reviewed the data did he realize the sheer magnitude of what he had accomplished as he exposed in this one act what really lies behind the dark face of Marxism.

The Cuban Lightning

Volume III of Rites of Passage of a Master Spy

Acknowledgements

I am a very lucky man because I have a great group of people by my side that I not only consider my friends but also who are the most capable, sacrificing professionals equal to the ones I've risked my life with over the past 50 years in their dedication and values. This group has made possible the publication of this book. To them, with all my heart today, I give the best of my love, gratitude, and sincerest thanks to every one of these fantastic warriors. In order of seniority, I would especially like to thank O'Brien: a great friend, a great individual with extraordinary values, thank you for your contributions you have made in many different ways to this project, as well being loyally by my side and watching my back for almost all of my career. I know for a fact you have never done that before for anyone. To my right arm and great friend, Tad Atkinson: for your dedication to every detail in research and many hours of hard work with me, never hesitating to sacrifice even your personal and private family time in order to make this happen. To Steve Weese: thank you for the many pieces of computer and graphic work as well professional enhancement of photos to improve the quality of the book. To Carlos Mota: my thanks for your dedication and multiple contributions and sacrifices you have made in order to make this happen. To Gervasin Neto: for your constant loyalty and many hours standing on your feet or hiding between cars in order to maintain our security with your group of people you've coordinated to watch our backs, continually keeping us informed of any suspicious activity that occurs in our surroundings. To Chopin: for your great companionship, loyalty, and support for the last 50 years with me in our fight for freedom and that beautiful, generous letter you wrote in behalf of the project. To our editor, Jen Poiry-Prough: who managed to make this book as easy to read, using her magic touch to polishing this piece of coal and bring to you, the readers, what I consider to be a very rare diamond. It makes all of us very proud to be involved in this project. Your professionalism, vast knowledge, and dedication, has made this book a great piece for future generations. To all of you, my friends who remain in the shadows, who contributed in one way or another in making this book and help me to bring the truth to the public, you have given the best of yourselves, putting forth your best effort to educate future generations. God bless you all. I embrace you as the Christian warriors that you all are.

Dr. Julio Antonio del Marmol

Poverty Is Not a Disease

Being poor is not a disease and nothing to be ashamed of. For a good, hard-working man it's only a challenge he faces as he goes through life's ups and downs. What is truly shameful is to try to get out of that poverty using arbitrary political tricks and laws to steal by force the wealth that others labored so hard to earn. That is worse than shameful, it is criminal! Whoever takes this path or agitates for it should be universally repudiated by society, no matter who those people are. Such agitators should be condemned and sent to jail for many years, forced to work while incarcerated until they learn by their own sweat how unfair their doctrines were and not to be abusers of others. Only then can they truly realize the depths of their crimes and repent for the path they took in life.

Dr. Julio Antonio del Marmol

Prologue: Arbitrary Rip-offs

I had returned to my house in Pinar del Rio. Mima had tears in her eyes, and the house filled with long-faced strangers.

As I walked into the living room, I passed by my father's office and library. The large old safe he kept in the corner had been opened. A few individuals I had never seen before stood there, and my father was handing them envelopes filled with bills.

This caught my attention, even though it was by no means unusual to see my father paying people. Normally, however, those were familiar faces. I thought I may have been away from home too long and these were new business acquaintances.

What concerned me even more was that it was the middle of the week. I wondered what important event could be occurring that would keep my father from going to his business in Guane as he had for so many years.

I entered the sitting room, where more strangers sat waiting for my father to complete his business with the others. More strangers came in through the front door. Mima, in spite of her distress, very politely tried to welcome and accommodate the newcomers in the already-crowded space.

A strange, sad feeling developed inside me at the sight of all this extremely unusual activity. The look on my father's face as he handed those people the envelopes, combined with Mima's expression, told me they were going through a very difficult moment.

On the route I had taken through the city as I drove towards my home, I had noticed long lines of people waiting at the local banks and other financial institutions. This hadn't really surprised me, because it had become very usual to see long lines everywhere, even to buy a simple loaf of bread. As I later discovered, this was not a localized event; it was happening everywhere on the island.

Mima nodded sadly to me as I walked through, and she tried to muster a smile for me. All she was able to manage, however, was a half-smile. She stood up from where she had been sitting and apologized to those waiting. She hugged me and kissed me on the cheek. I nodded and cordially greeted everyone present, but every single one of those people looked me up and down with a blend of discontent and distrust, taking in my uniform and sidearm. The latter especially seemed to occupy their attention. I was a little worried and so tried to avoid meeting any of their eyes or their rude stares.

Mima put her arm around my shoulders. "Don't worry," she said apologetically. "This is my son."

She led me towards the back of the house. We walked through the long hallway to the kitchen in silence, far away from the prying eyes and ears of those visitors. Mima hugged me once more and started to cry in a fashion I had never before seen, not even when I returned home after she had thought me dead during my recent disappearance. Tears welled up in my eyes as I gently tried to get her to sit down.

"What's wrong Mima?" I asked worriedly. "Why are all these people in the house? Why are you crying? Calm down, you know this is not good for your heart."

She composed herself and at last answered between sniffles, as she dried her tears with a small handkerchief that was already soaked in her tears. I could see the torment as she looked in my eyes. Her face changed from an expression of sorrow to one of anger.

"I've been telling your father for a long time," she said, "even before these bandits took power in our country, that we would lose everything we've been working and sweating for over the last twenty years." She wiped at her eyes again. "This morning, this arbitrary Revolutionary government declared on the radio and the official newspaper that no one citizen of Cuba can have more than a thousand pesos in the bank. They've been secretly printing new money which has no international value at all. This new currency has their own pictures on the bills, since we now have a new kingdom here. Every person has to bring all the legitimate money they currently have in their possession for exchange within the next twenty-four hours, because it will no longer be accepted anywhere in the country."

She pointed to my father's office. "This is what your father is doing right now with some of the people he knows and their friends. This has to be done very quietly, because this constitutes what the government calls an illegal breaking of Revolutionary law, punishable by ten years in jail. But your father is offering fifty percent of whatever they can offer in exchange for some of the money he's been saving all his life. Some of those people have no business or savings, so they have no objection, as they're only making money."

She raised her arms in distress and frowned sorrowfully.

"Whatever will be left we will probably have to burn, because it won't even be good for use as toilet paper. What a disaster! Giving away that money is like giving away years of sacrifice, sleepless nights, when I was working virtually without stop, twenty-four hours a day for days on end. When I was working so hard to embroider sheets and pillows for people about to get married. That is the sweat and sacrifice of our work."

She pointed out towards the living room. "This didn't take me by surprise, even though it did your father. I listened to that Marxist bandit Fidel Castro continually refer to the rich millionaires as 'fat cats' and 'enslavers of the proletariat.' I told Leonardo, 'This man is not only a lazy bandit but a resentful idiot, and he won't stop with the rich and the millionaires. He will continue to the middle class and on to anyone who has any achievement in their lives in order to fill his pockets. Not to help the poor and the underdogs, as he announces in his lying demagogical speeches. He will turn all of us to the poor and homeless, destroy Cuba, and convert the Princess of the Caribbean into the Cinderella of the American Continent."

I could not help the knot of frustration that formed in my throat. Two tears rolled down my cheeks. I embraced

The Dark Face of Marxism

Mima harder than I ever had in my life as I felt her pain sympathetically in my own chest.

I said in her ear, "This is what these unscrupulous bandits don't tell the poor: that at the same time they're robbing people like you and Papi, they're robbing the impoverished of their dreams and hopes for the remotest possibility to rise up out of poverty. If they told the poor the truth, no one would sympathize or applaud them. Unfortunately, Mima, this is the dark face of the Marxists."

Dr. Julio Antonio del Marmol

Chapter 1: Blowing Smoke and the Devil's Distrust

March 25, 1960

Che Guevara smirked as he watched Jack Ruby leave with Marcelino and Alfonzo Machi. He waited for a few moments to make certain they were well out of earshot before speaking again. He looked at me and waved me back to my chair.

"Sit down, sit down," Che said. He gestured to the guards around us. "Go and bring a big jar of orange juice. I know the Commandantico likes it."

"No, no, it's OK," I said. "We just ate."

"No, it's good to have it around. We'll be here for a while."

"But I'm full to here," I joked, pointing at my throat.

Che leaned back in his seat. After he took a deep puff from his cigar and exhaled the smoke, he shook his head slightly. "I don't think it's necessary to remind you that whatever we talk about here is strictly confidential."

"Every time we meet, I consider everything said as completely in confidence," I replied. "Whatever we don't repeat to others we don't have to repent, especially when we're not authorized to repeat it."

He looked at me and nodded in satisfaction. He leaned on the table and clasped his fingers together.

The Dark Face of Marxism

"Unfortunately, we cannot maintain that loyalty and absolute confidentiality with everybody. Even though we're all on the same team and have the same ideology, we can only be loyal to one person. The ego in every individual usually gets in the way and tries to control, for jealousy or some other reason, what others do. This creates division between us.

"I told you before and will repeat more explicitly to you now, because you've earned my complete trust, that Fidel has an ego the size of the Eiffel Tower. Believe it or not, that ego is his worst enemy, because he feels that everyone is like him, and therefore everyone around him is trying to take away his crown. He then creates not only division, he creates an atmosphere of distrust between everyone, including us. In other words, no one trusts anyone anymore.

"That is the reason that every single enterprise or project the Revolution takes the reins on goes wrong. The directors of each enterprise act out of fear and indecision because they don't know who might be watching them with a plan to take them down and replace them." He tapped his chest. "I told him many times, *que no me ande rompiendo los huevos*[1]. I also told him that I don't want his crown and I have no fear of him or anyone. If he doesn't want me here in Cuba, all he has to do is tell me to go, and I will go to any country and make my own Revolution. I don't need him or anyone else to do it; I've got my own people."

---

[1] *Don't break my balls.*

He was speaking very calmly, though his voice was slightly elevated. He was more fed up about the situation than angry about it. He paused, and I looked at him seriously while he took another puff off of his cigar.

I asked, "Has something bad happened between you and Fidel?"

He pulled his cigar away in his right hand and with his left wiped his face from forehead to beard. "You know, the same old shit and stupidities. These two brothers think they know everything. They are identical, a pair of *boludos*[2], what we call in Argentina someone who is very difficult to deal with because they think they are the professors and everyone else the student. They never listen to anyone."

He tapped the ash off of his cigar agitatedly. "I already told them that if they want me to be the architect of this plan, they need to leave me alone and let me work in complete freedom and tranquility. Even if they have any doubts about the results, I know in the end this will be bigger than ten or twenty revolutions. It will change the political course in not just one country but possibly the entire world."

He leaned back once more and smiled. "We will cut off the head of the serpent with perhaps only two or three bullets. We will collapse the Mecca of the capitalist system and bring them to their knees, leading to the new era in which our Socialist revolutions take over." He raised his left index finger high. "The best part is that after

---

[2] *Idiots*

maybe fifty or a hundred years pass, the real architect of this master plan will be revealed."

I smiled this time and scratched my neck. "That will probably be the most difficult accomplishment. My mother says that a secret is no secret after two people have knowledge of it."

He smiled and nodded in agreement. He replied, "That is very true. Your mom is a very intelligent woman. No wonder you are the way you are. You have solid genes behind you.

"But there is a remedy for every single disease. The remedy here is to very carefully create several credible versions of that secret. This will protect this secret, even though it is in the mouths of several others. It will remain protected for a very long time—even the rest of your life.

"At the heart of it is the desire for the person who created it to bring the truth out so he can bask in the glory of the accomplishment, to go down in history, so that someone else doesn't take the credit away from him. Even when the truth of his masterpiece is eventually revealed, which ultimately cannot be avoided, it will still be covered by a fog of doubt in history. Unfortunately, that is the risk every superior mind takes—to never receive the accolades for his masterpiece, for the truth to be buried in history forever."

He looked at me and leaned to one side in his chair. "Maybe you don't understand all of what I'm saying. But the day is not too far off when I will be able to explain everything to you. By that time, it won't have to be a secret anymore, and you can be my witness in the future."

I said, "I might not completely understand what you're talking about, but I have a pretty good idea of what you're implying. Remember, my friend Che: for those with great understanding, a few words are sufficient."

If you only knew how much I truly understood, I thought.

I paused. "You know how when someone tells you a tale, and they never mention the name of the saint, but when you go and visit the church a bell rings and you realize which one they were talking about. I know you're not precisely talking about any saint," I added with a cynical smile. "It's a man, nothing more."

He smiled. "Absolutely, I assure you one hundred percent that the man we're talking about is far away from being a saint: he's responsible for the deaths of many people around the world, including those dying right now in Vietnam." He nodded. "I like to talk to you; even though you're very young, you are intelligent, loyal, and tight-lipped. I like those qualities very much in you."

"Thank you," I replied. "The feeling is mutual."

He stayed quiet for a moment, enjoying his cigar. Then he broke the silence. "You already know Yuri and Marko, and now you've met Marcelino. You have yet to meet the fourth and final leg of the table. The table will be prepared to receive all the weight and the consequences of my plan."

He nodded his head, looking quite pleased with himself. "What do you think of the resemblance between these men?"

I shook my head and said, "Absolutely extraordinary. I think, each time I meet the next one, that I had already met him the time before."

He smiled proudly in satisfaction. "Yes, I see how you wouldn't know the difference between any of them. That

The Dark Face of Marxism

is precisely the objective of the entire plan. When one of them comes into a place and another one leaves, everyone thinks it's the same person. He could even seem to be in different places at the same time that way."

I nodded, but I had yet to meet this fourth person. I only knew them as A, B, C, and D—there were no names in the outline I had read from the portfolio. Until I met D, I wouldn't be able to completely piece it all together. I knew that whatever Che had in mind must be very diabolical, like all the other plans these people hatched.

Suddenly he asked me, "Did you know that Silvano died?"

"Yes," I said, "I'm sorry. I know he was very close to you."

"Well, another martyr for our Revolution," he shrugged in complete indifference. He might have felt more emotion at the death of a dog. "All historical events have their consequences. Sometimes it's good to have martyrs, so that other men will feel more passion for what they're doing—especially when we can blame our enemies for the death. Why do you think Lazaro left that note using your name as a witness if something adverse happened to him?"

I immediately went into gear mentally. He had timed this question in the middle of all this conversation as a way to catch me off guard. I knew this was the main reason he had sent for me, and he had been trying to distract and relax me with incidental conversation. Now he was going to carefully scrutinize my reaction to this most crucial question that I had long prepared for.

I kept my expression serious as I shifted in my chair comfortably. I gave the demeanor of complete tranquility and confidence. I said in a surprised voice, "He did what?" I made the appearance of thinking that through and said slowly, "I have no idea. No one had told me about that. Although ultimately, it doesn't surprise me, considering the conversation he and I had in his house a few nights before he died. He made a series of confessions of remorse that he was having that, according to him, kept him from sleep for weeks."

Che opened his eyes in surprise. Full of curiosity, he moved forward. "What? He made confessions to you?" I had his complete and undivided attention now. Clearly I had touched a nerve. "How is that? What kind of confession did he make?"

"Well, for example, he told me that Silvano and other powerful forces behind him were planning the sabotage of the ship *La Coubre*. He said it had three purposes." I pretended to think back on the conversation, to remember the words carefully. "First, to break diplomatic relations between Cuba and the USA and all the formal compromises between the two countries. Second, to get rid of all the obsolete weapons, because the recent secret treaty between the USSR and the Cuban government would keep us supplied with modern weapons. And the third and most important one, to create a tremendous influx of the *divisas*[3] Cuba needs so badly from the insurance company paying for the loss of all those weapons. Since the Belgian government wasn't going to permit a refund of the money to the Cuban government, the insurance money would provide that refund to us. For

---

[3] *Foreign currency*

The Dark Face of Marxism

the perfect alibi, we have as a scapegoat the Yankee imperialists. The insurance company would have no choice but to conclude that there was no fraud from the Cuban government involved."

Che removed his beret from his head and vigorously scratched his hair with both hands in obvious discontent, confusion, and frustration blended together. This time, he asked in an exasperated tone, "Will you explain to me why Lazaro had all this confidence in you in particular? Why you?"

I looked at him gravely in displeasure at his tone. I rubbed my eyebrows with my index and middle fingers. I drew strength from that memory and asked Che, "Are you upset with me or something?" Without waiting for a reply, I continued, "Maybe for the same reason that you told me a little while ago that Fidel has an ego the size of the Eiffel Tower."

Che's eyes bulged in astonishment.

"Maybe," I continued feigning hurt feelings, "I inspired in Lazaro the same trust I've inspired in you. He knew very well, as you know, that unless death comes between us, I will never—never—betray a confidence. Whatever he said to me in utter trust would die with me, no matter what."

He looked me straight in the eyes for a few seconds. "I'm sorry, it wasn't my intention to put you in doubt. I'm pissed, but it's not with you; it's with Lazaro. To know that Lazaro had so little discretion—it really pisses me off. It's very disappointing."

I leaned back and said, "Remember what I told you before—what I learned from my mother about secrets?"

He looked at me seriously and with worry in his face. "Did Lazaro tell you anything else?"

"Yes," I replied.

"What did he tell you?" he asked quickly.

"He said that Silvano and these powerful forces promised him that there would be two explosions, not simultaneous. The first would be a small one to alert him and give him time to get his men out of danger. The second would make sure the ship went to the bottom of the sea."

I paused to observe Che's reaction. He was scratching his beard in agitated concern, anxiously waiting for what I was going to say next. I leaned back in my chair and kept my silence for a few more seconds just to make him sweat a little more.

"Is that everything?" he finally asked.

"No," I said. "He said he had completely lost his confidence in Silvano, and he didn't feel he was being told the entire truth. He had changed his mind and wanted to stop his part in the plot. His worse fear was that he would be betrayed and blown up with all his men so that no witnesses of this sabotage would be left."

Che leaned forward, placed both elbows on the table, and clutched his forehead with both hands. "That is what that son of a bitch told you? Now I understand. Until now, none of this made logical sense to me." He laced his fingers together. "Now it all meshes." He shook his head in obvious stress and disappointment. He called for one of the escort and said to him, "Bring me my usual sedative, please."

We remained silent for several minutes while he puffed more often than usual on his cigar. The soldier brought a

The Dark Face of Marxism

glass with ice and a yellow liquor that looked like tequila. There was a lime on the bottom of the glass. He grabbed the glass and emptied it in several gulps. He took the lime and bit into it, sucking the juice into his mouth before discarding it.

He looked at me and tried to smile but only managed to summon a wan grimace. "Did Lazaro ever mention to you who the 'powerful forces' behind Silvano were?" He still held the glass to his chest as he asked.

I moved forward as though I wanted to whisper so that the escort about twenty feet away wouldn't hear me. "Yes, he told me that it was you and Fidel who had been planning everything."

Lazaro hadn't actually said that, but I wanted to see his reaction. I also wanted to let him know that I knew all of the details, even though all of the information from his own briefcase that I had stolen. I would die before he would ever know about that.

He leaned back and scratched his ear nervously. Without admitting anything, he asked, "Have you told this to anyone else?"

I shook my head. "Absolutely nobody. As I told you before, the only reason I'm telling you this now is because Lazaro is dead. If he were still alive, I would never even be repeating to you what I know, since it was said to me in complete confidence. Besides, if you were in fact involved, you wouldn't need to know."

He sighed in relief. "I really admire your qualities, but remember what I told you before: we can only be loyal to one person. I hope I can earn the privilege of your loyalty. I guarantee you I will never betray you for any reason whatsoever."

I looked at him incredulously. "You have my loyalty—you know you've got it. That is the only reason I shared all of this with you today."

"What are you going to tell the French ambassador tomorrow when he asks you about what Lazaro left behind in that note?"

"I will keep it short and simple," I replied. "I don't have the slightest idea why he left that note."

Che smiled.

"I will add that I'd been a great friend of his son," I continued, "who was my driver for a long time in the Commandos. But I hardly knew Lazaro and only spoke to him very briefly. He would occasionally visit Pinar del Rio, and I was invited to have dinner with the family. That is the full extent of my relationship with Lazaro, nothing more." I spread my hands. "I know nothing about anything else."

We were sitting close to each other, and he leaned over to pat me on the shoulder. "You are a real man, kid."

"Thank you very much," I said. "But I have a little question to ask you."

He raised his arms, assuming I wanted to question him about the sabotage of the ship. "Believe me, things almost never completely come out how you planned them," he said. "That is the reason I always include alternatives—Plan B, Plan C, and so on. I want you to remember for the Internationalist Revolutionaries, there are no obstacles to our goal. For the hundred that die today a thousand will live better tomorrow. We have to do what we have to do, and the ends justify the means."

I raised my right arm to stop him. "I agree with you, sure. I'm not going to recriminate you in any way or form for the sabotage. My question is personal. In the last twenty-four hours, I've had two attempts on my life. The first was in Pinar del Rio's central park, in front of hundreds of people, when a few individuals shot at me from rooftops. They killed, I assume by accident, one of my friends. The other attempt was more insidious. Someone sent a code over the secure police radio frequency to not only the local police, but also the DTI and other covert patrols. They described the license plate of the Volga you gave me as having been stolen by counterrevolutionaries, and they listed the occupants of the car as armed and dangerous. They gave an order to shoot to kill. Fortunately, I drove to the nearest police station where one of my brothers-in-law works, and my persecutors were eluded, even after they blocked the road. It seems extremely strange to me, because they were driving a brand-new Buick like the ones the government uses. It almost cost the lives of my companion and me." I paused. "This is my question: do you know who could be behind all of this? This started after I came back from the trip we took to Santa Clara."

He jerked back in surprise, his expression one of shocked astonishment. "No, I haven't the slightest idea. The first thing that crossed my mind is that it must be the counterrevolution."

I squeezed my chin. "That was also in my mind, until the second attempt occurred. I understood then it had to be somebody inside the government and not the counterrevolution. Even if they had managed to steal our radios, only the armed forces, the police, and the DTI know the codes for 'armed and dangerous.' How in the hell would these people have them in their hands?"

He looked at me and nodded. "Who do you think it is?" he asked. "Do you have any information?"

"Now this is in complete confidence," I replied, "from me to you."

"Of course."

I frowned. "According to my information, both Piñeiro and Raul Castro have a special interest in creating an excuse to list me as a primary suspect in the theft of your portfolio from the Regiment. Apparently Piñeiro has serious doubts about me. I don't think, though, that this is the reason to kill me. It must be because I'm getting too close to you and detaching a little bit from Fidel. It doesn't make any sense in my mind as to why Raul would be so stupid as to allow Piñeiro to convince him of something that has no substance to it. There can be no other reason—it must be you."

He leaned back in his chair and stroked his beard, deep in thought.

I continued, "Not too long ago, I read a book that said that if you want to know why anybody would want to hurt or eliminate you, dig deeply and analyze, and you will find out that the main reason is fear. Fear of you or fear of those around you."

He nodded in agreement. "I think you're right—that is a great possibility. I will make some phone calls tonight. First to Piñeiro to see his reaction to that whistle. Then to Raul. I will tell him my people are already following a solid lead for that theft and that I have fresh information that elements from the G-2 are directly involved in the attempts on your life. If this is true, I will personally inform Fidel of these criminal plots. If either or both of them are remotely involved as your sources tell you, Raul will

The Dark Face of Marxism

immediately pick up the phone and give Piñeiro orders to bring his dogs, and I believe we will then be able to resolve that problem. I will testify to Fidel that men of my personal confidence were crossing with those cars and Piñeiro's men in Pinar del Rio when they went to pick you up for your declaration to the ambassadors and the insurance investigator tomorrow. They will assure me that one of those cars is very similar to the Buick you described to me driven by one of your persecutors."

Raising my hand, I said, "Thank you."

He looked at me seriously. "You're welcome. We have to be on the same page, you and I. How can we win the war against the capitalists around the world if we let this egomaniac wage a war between us?"

I leaned back in my chair and replied, "I want to make something clear. I'm not completely sure who was persecuting us or on whose behalf they were acting. But I'm extremely alarmed and suspicious." I raised both hands. "As I said, it was the radio situation that really made me wonder."

"If Fidel asks you, don't tell him that. No matter that I'm not very sure, either, we have to be on the same page. I will tell Fausto and the other members of my team that traveled to pick you up so that they say the same thing. This way, you don't have to reveal from where you have the information you just relayed to me. We'll both of us get Raul and that ass-kisser Piñeiro off of our backs." He grunted a laugh. "These people have some nerve—using me and my portfolio as an excuse to harm you and take you away from my side! These people are really bad!"

You're no better than they are, I thought. I wonder how you feel, dealing with people who have the same nature as yourself.

He picked up his empty glass and held it up. The escort rushed to take it. "Bring me another one, please."

The man took the glass and left without a word. After he left, Che rubbed his forehead with his left hand as he held up the cigar in his right. He clucked his tongue. "This Piñeiro, I never liked this guy. He's always got his nose up everyone's ass. He is old lady's gossip and he kisses Raul's butt so much—that is the only reason Fidel gave him charge of the G-2. As the state security, the G-2 is the official organ of authorized gossip in Cuba. They whisper some rumor in Fidel's ear and someone is ruined. None of the armed forces or government bureaus like them or their instigators. We all despise them. I believe Piñeiro has feminine inclinations. That is why he gets along so well with Raul—birds of a feather flock together."

The soldier returned with the glass and handed it to Che.

"Thank you."

The soldier walked to the other side of the terrace where the rest of the escort was sitting around a glass table under an umbrella.

Che took a long sip from the glass. He squeezed some lime juice into his mouth. "I wanted to give you a warning with the French ambassador. You don't have to worry about him—he is on our side.

"The one you have to really be careful with is the Belgian ambassador. He is a rabid anti-communist. He may even be an informant for the CIA. This ambassador visited too frequently with Lazaro, and we think Lazaro

The Dark Face of Marxism

was informing him constantly whatever was going on with us. Silvano suspected he was the one responsible for changing Lazaro's heart. That is why he betrayed us. If it happened the way Silvano assumed, Lazaro was never completely dedicated to our cause. He wasn't strong enough ideologically. He was an easy target for conversion by the ambassador.

"I'm telling you all of this because it's absolutely necessary that you are prepared with this man. He is extremely intelligent, and he will be there with the insurance investigator. He might try to trip you up in his questioning, seeing if he can get you to contradict yourself. The ambassador might pretend to like you and be cordial and in sympathy with you. Don't be fooled by that—he is not your friend. He might pretend to be very affected by the death of your friend Lazaro to try to get information he can use against us. He is very good at this game—I wouldn't even be surprised if he sheds some tears, knowing that you're very young and that might create a hole in your heart he can work through."

Che leaned back and put the glass on the table. He took a long puff from his cigar and tapped the ashes into the ashtray.

I stretched back in my seat and yawned, long enough for Che to smile. He asked, "Are you tired?"

"Yes, a little. I've been on an adrenaline rush all day long, and as natural, after the storm you get the calm."

He smiled again. "I like those comparisons and sayings you always have. Who taught you all this?" He didn't wait for my answered and continued, "Whoever it was, they did a great job with you."

I smiled this time. "Thank you," I said once again. "Books. I like to read a lot. And my mom and dad, who I admire, love, and respect very much."

He nodded appreciatively. He stayed silent for a few seconds. I put some ice in one of the glasses and poured some orange juice from the jar that had been placed on the table. I started to take a sip. I glanced at him from the corner of my eyes as I drank. He was smoking his cigar, and I thought of several things. I had been learning from his conversation over the past hour. I started to form a plan, and I was going to proceed with it immediately.

I asked myself if I would prefer it to be Raul and Piñeiro who were behind those attempts in my life. Perhaps the dark hand was Che himself. Even though he had always been pleasant and respectful with me, today he had been a little extreme in his compliments and was making a great effort to show me his friendship. I considered it suspicious. I had enough evidence of what Che could conceive of and knew he had a criminal mind. Perhaps he had no reason. Perhaps he feared I would expose before the Belgian ambassador the entire sinister plot.

Fausto had been around town in Pinar del Rio very early in the day, and I knew for a fact that he was the one behind the robbery and shooting at the jewelry store. He had shot the owner in the brain and left him for dead. Perhaps some of his accomplices were members of the escort that had accompanied him to my house to pick me up. I squeezed my lower lip with my index and thumb as I remembered what Mima had told me when I arrived at the house—that Fausto had been waiting for me for a long time.

The Dark Face of Marxism

I realized then that it would be difficult for Fausto to have perpetrated the attempt in the park. I shook my head dismissively.

Che noticed the motion and looked at me. "Are you OK?"

"Just a little headache," I said in partial truth. I did have a headache as a result of the stresses of the day.

He raised his arm and motioned to the escort. "Bring two aspirin to the Commandantico." Without saying a word, the soldier nodded his head and left with a pleasant smile to comply with the order.

I said, "I would like to ask you a small favor that I believe will help me get better results in the interview tomorrow."

He asked, "What do you need?"

"Two things," I replied. "First, a handful of Habanos cigars, like the ones you smoke, the good quality."

He looked at me in puzzlement, but then nodded. "Of course, not a problem at all. I didn't know you smoked."

"No, no," I said, "those are just to offer to the ambassador and the investigator as a distraction and to break the ice. And if it's OK with you, I'll use your name, since those are the ones you smoke. That way, they'll think it an honor to smoke one of your Habanos cigars and will be even more disarmed."

He shook his finger at me knowingly. "You are a little devil." He smiled and nodded in satisfaction. "You're going have those guys wrapped around your fingers. I have no doubt about that!"

I smiled. "I might even light one of those cigars, although they stink like hell and I probably won't be able to finish it, but they'll look at me with more respect and astonished surprise. It will create a double distraction," I concluded.

Che stroked his beard and shook his head. "You know what? That is a magnificent idea! I had been a little worried about that interview, but now I have no doubt that it will go very well."

"Thank you. I appreciate your confidence." The soldier returned with the aspirin. As usual, I put it into my mouth and chewed it, washing it down with a couple of sips of orange juice. The soldier grimaced at the sight and immediately offered to refill my glass. I accepted and drank a little more.

Che smiled and said to the soldier as he pointed at me, "That is how you should take aspirin! Who taught you that?"

"My uncle—he's a gynecologist and an obstetrician."

Che smiled and nodded again. The soldier, shaking his head, retreated without saying a word. He looked nauseous.

"The other thing I wanted to ask you," I went on, "is if I could borrow one of your cars. I want to go back to the city and make sure that the girl who was with me today got home safe and sound. I also want to run an errand before I go to bed tonight."

"Of course—as soon as Fausto gets back, I'll tell him to take you to the garage and give you one of the cars. Believe me, we have plenty. And you can coordinate with him when you plan to leave tomorrow, because you're going to spend the night here tonight. I'll leave him and two of my most trustworthy men to escort you to the meetings tomorrow."

"Thank you very much."

"Stop thanking me. You're too polite!"

"You can never be too polite."

"Yes, you're right—I was just joking with you." He stood up. "Follow me. Let's go inside, and I'll give you those cigars you intend to smoke tomorrow. Good luck!"

"Yes," I said, putting my hand on my stomach, "that will be another sacrifice for the Revolution."

He laughed deeply and loudly at that.

I walked behind him through that magnificent residence. Both structurally and in décor, it reminded me of a medieval castle. We crossed a large salon with swords and other arms decorating the walls. We entered a massive library. I smiled as I looked around, and he smiled in understanding at my joy at being in there with so many books.

"Any time you want to borrow a book from here, feel free. It's your house. This is actually one of my hiding places. I go to my family's house only two or three times a month. I'm here more frequently, working. This is one of my safe-houses."

"You have more books here than in the National Public Library!"

He smiled and opened a large cabinet. It was full of boxes of different brands of refined Habanos cigars. He took one wooden box that was about 8½ by 11 inches. "My God, I don't need that many cigars! I only need a handful."

"You take only as many as you need for your target—the rest, take home to your friends and family for them to enjoy."

"OK, if that's what you want. Thank you."

Dr. Julio Antonio del Marmol

Fausto knocked on the door to the library and asked respectfully for permission to enter. Che replied, "Yes, yes—come in, come in. We're waiting for you. Take the Commandantico with you to the garage and give him one of the cars there. He will go into the city on an errand tonight, but arrange with him when you'll leave tomorrow for the meetings. I'm going to bed now, since I have leave early in the morning with the rest of the guys for Santiago de Cuba."

We said goodbye, and Che went upstairs to his room.

Chapter 2: The Luxuries of the Proletariat

Cars "stored" in Che's garage

I went downstairs with Fausto to the garage. It was a surprise when he switched on the lights. The garage was vast, and had about twenty-five beautiful, expensive cars. It looked like a showroom for a high-end car dealer: Bugattis, Maseratis, Ferraris, Daimlers, and so many other brands filled the room.

Fausto looked at me and said, "What do you think? One more gift from the capitalists to our Revolution. Pick whatever you like best."

I shrugged in bewilderment. "Any one of them is fine. I'm only going to use it to go to Havana and come back in a few hours."

Fausto smiled again. This time, he shrugged. "Well, Che said to give you one of the cars, but he didn't say which one. Whatever you want to choose, it's fine with me. Now, you decide what you want. I can't decide for you."

He started to take me among the cars, patting them, and identifying them by year and make: "Here is a 1936 Bugatti . . . here is a 1946 Maserati . . . a 1950 Aston Martin . . . there is a 1960 Ferrari, brand new—what do you want?"

One of the cars he put his hand on was red and white, and caught my attention. When he opened the door, I was taken by how it opened up, not out. It was a Mercedes roadster, and I said, "I like this one. It will be fine!"

Fausto grinned. "You've got great taste—this is a twelve-cylinder, fifty-thousand dollar car! Do you know how to drive standard with clutch?"

I smiled. "Claro! I learned to drive one of those in my father's Ford."

"Well, this is a big step up from a Ford. It's a Mercedes classic, a 300SL. Let's go upstairs. I'll show you your room and get you the key."

After he showed me my room—where they had already put my travel bag—he gave me the keys and said goodbye. "Watch out," he cautioned, "don't do the same thing that you did with the Volga!"

"Hey, man!" I protested, holding my arms out. "It wasn't my fault!"

"I was just joking with you," Fausto said. "Whatever you do with the car, it's OK. If you wreck it, you call us and we'll pick you up in a helicopter."

The Dark Face of Marxism

I left the house in that beautiful, flaming Mercedes. Heaven knew whom they had stolen it from.

I hit the wide highway towards the capital and put my foot on the accelerator. I wanted to know for certain if that car really could get up to the maximum speed of 220 miles per hour marked on the speedometer.

Two hundred twenty miles, I thought. That's a lot of kilometers!

The freeway was almost empty, and I said aloud, "Show me what you're capable of."

I stepped down on the accelerator. Slowly, I sped up to one hundred, and then to 110, 130, 135, and suddenly I noticed something ahead on the highway. It wasn't clear, and I couldn't determine what it was, but I immediately took my foot off of the accelerator. I didn't want to slam on the brakes, because I had been told that at high speeds, you can flip when you do that.

As I grew close to the object, I first saw men and women crossing the highway with what looked like a raft on top of their heads. Behind them were several children. The children had belongings on their heads. Even though I had been gradually decelerating, my speed was still too great, and I slammed on the brakes.

The car started to swerve all over the highway, and I could see smoke rising from behind me on the pavement. The people ran, trying to get out of my way. I turned my wheel frantically in an attempt to regain control of the car while avoiding hitting all of these people and their children.

They had been lying in the ditch beside the highway, having left their car on the left side, inland. They were now crossing to the right side and towards the ocean. In my erratic path across the road, I swept by them, managing to avoid hitting any of them. In the midst of all of this, the men and women who were dragging the large raft dropped it to one side as they rushed back to help the children out of danger.

I could no longer hold the wheel. The car hopped up over the cement divider and flew off of the road. I went through the grassy field for around three hundred feet, desperately trying to avoid the trees but nearly hitting one of the large ones. Finally, I was able to stop a few feet from the trunk of a large Poinciana, the front bumper nearly touching the tree.

The Mercedes 300 SL

I breathed a sigh of relief. My heart was pounding. My worst fear had been that the car would flip, but I managed to safely stop without even scratching it. With the engine still running and the lights on, I reclined the seat. I tried to pull myself back together—my leg was trembling violently, and my heart was still beating rapidly. I wondered how those people had come to be there and crossing at that exact spot, while at the same time I took myself to task for driving so fast. I put my hand on my forehead, and in the same way my mother would recriminate me, I said aloud, "Julio Antonio Marmol!"

I calmed myself down, put my arm over the back seat, and tried to see if I could back out of there. Before I could put it in gear, however, I could see not far off the two couples with their kids approaching me. Something else caught my attention—both men had something in their hands that looked like machetes. One of them had also had what could be a handgun in his other hand. Both were approaching with arms upraised. The women were coming behind with the children. I started to worry about this. Without thinking twice, I opened the door and stepped out. I unsnapped the peace bond on my holster. I rested my hand on the butt of my pistol and stayed by the side of the Mercedes, watching them approach.

When they got about twenty feet from me, one of the men yelled, "Are you OK?"

"Yes," I called back, "I'm fine. Thank you."

They stopped. The man who had called out to me lowered the object in his hand. "We were just going to do some fishing. We saw your car coming from very far away. We thought we would have enough time to cross the highway without any major problem. Evidently we miscalculated the speed."

"Yes, maybe because I was in a rush to reach the capital, I was driving at a high speed, and you guys didn't take that into account."

A little girl, about five years old, listened to us speaking in such a friendly manner, asked me, "Do you want to come with us to Miami?"

A boy of about seven said to her, "Shut up, Cristina! Can't you see that he's a communist?"

The two men and women looked at each other and said to another kid, about ten, "Paco—go ahead and take your brother and the rest to the other side of the highway where we left the raft."

Paco said, "Why do we have to go?"

"Shh!" the man said abruptly. "Go! *Carajo*! Do what I tell you!"

The adults looked at me with hostility and fear. One of the women pointed her finger at me and directed a flashlight into my face. "Oh, I know who you are! You are the Commandantico, the kid who is by Fidel on television all the time."

I raised my left hand to protect my eyes from the light and replied, "Yes, please, can you take that flashlight out of my face?" She complied with my request. When she did so, I noticed that the object the man was holding next to his leg was indeed a revolver—a little two-shot Derringer. He was trying to hide it from view. I cleared my holster to make a drawing of my pistol much easier. They noticed that and looked at me in fear. I was expecting the worst, since I realized that they were on their way to leave the country.

"Listen, we don't want to hurt you," the man said. "Will you please say you won't tell anyone what you saw here tonight?"

"What did I see?" I replied. "All I know is that I spun out of the road, almost killing myself and all of you in the process. I didn't see anything else."

The first man asked his friend, "Do you trust him? What are we going to do?"

The second man said, "Well, we are four—we can put him down, if you think it's absolutely necessary."

"No, please," one of the women said. "We don't want that on our conscience. We've got our kids with us."

The first man pulled his revolver out and said, "If we let him go, he'll report us to the authorities and we'll get arrested. I think we should put him down. Look at him, he's with the militia or some military organization."

I pulled my pistol out. "I think you guys are forgetting something, and I will repeat it to you once more—that's it. It's true that you are four, but I can see you've got that tiny little two-shot revolver. If you point that thing at me, I will shoot each one of you and those kids will be orphans. I told you I didn't see anything, and I can't do anything if I didn't see anything. I'm not what you think I am. Just a few days ago, I helped a family like you to leave to safety because they couldn't live here anymore. That is your choice. You want to walk away, let me reverse my car and leave in peace. Or do you want to start something that will end badly?"

One of the women started to cry hysterically. "For God's sake, what are you doing? Are you crazy? Look at him, he's got a gun. He's just a kid, and he doesn't want to hurt us!"

The other woman nodded and said, "I think we'd better go. Eleanor, let's go." She grabbed the other woman. "You guys do what you want, but I'm not leaving my children here alone. You're both crazy!" She tapped her finger against her temple. "You're both stupid and irrational!" Both women started to walk away towards the highway.

The man with the revolver pulled it down and put it in his pocket. He said, "Please, kid—don't say anything. We didn't do any harm to anyone. All we want to do is leave this country in peace, where we—"

I interrupted him, "Ah, ah! I don't want to know any more. You go with your wives and your kids, and leave me alone. And if I hear even my muffler backfire behind me, I swear I will shoot you guys."

"No, we're not going to shoot you. Good night—do you need any help?"

"No," I said. "I'm fine." They had given me no reason to trust them, and I just wanted them gone. I watched them disappear into the dark.

I decided to turn the car around rather than reverse it. I turned the lights on them and watched them leave. I sat there and waited for a while, until I saw them reach the highway and disappear on the other side. Once I was certain they weren't going to be able to take a shot at me, I slowly drove across the grass to get back on the highway and continued on my way to Havana. I thanked God that this area was very flat—only trees and grass—so that I was able to navigate adequately and avoid scratching that beautiful car. It would have been the ultimate embarrassment to me after what had happened to the Volga.

It only took a little while after that to reach the city of Havana, and I drove to the *Malecón*. I turned onto 23rd Street and took that all the way to L Street. I went around the block to ensure that I was not being followed. I found a parking space by the CMQ radio and television station and walked a short distance to a public telephone booth

The Dark Face of Marxism

outside the building. I locked myself inside one and dialed Chandee's number.

Mrs. Xiang answered. "Hello?"

"Hello, it's me," I replied. "Julio Antonio."

"Oh! How are you doing?" she asked in a friendly voice. "Thank you for the things you sent to us."

"You're welcome. I'm glad you liked them. Is Chandee or Mr. Xiang at home?"

"My husband is not at home," she said in her thick Chinese accent, "but Chandee is. I'll get her for you."

"Thank you." I heard the sound of the receiver being put down.

A few seconds later, Chandee's voice said, "Oh, God! You called right away! Yes, OK, I'm fine. Thank you very much for your call."

I smiled and replied, "I'm very glad you reached your home safe and sound. Did you have a good trip?"

"Yes, yes, I had a great trip, without any problems. I stopped in the middle in a small town, and had the most delicious chicken soup I've ever eaten. By the way, I already have the handkerchiefs to replace the ones you promised your brother-in-law, Canen, as well as a few other little things I have to give you when I come back to Pinar del Rio next week. We can talk then, unless you come to the capital before then. If you do, please call me, because we could perhaps go to the movies like we did last time. I had a great time with you."

I smiled again, understanding what she was telling me in this disguised fashion, just in case the line was tapped. "Well, I don't think I should make you wait too long, sweetie. For me, your wishes are my commands. I'm right here in Havana at the corner of L and 23rd in La Rampa, right in the center of *Radiocentro*."

"No!" she exclaimed in disbelief. "You're joking!"

"No, I'm not. I'm serious. I'm right here. Che sent for me not even an hour after I said goodbye to you at the bus station. There's something extremely important I have to attend to tomorrow afternoon."

"If you want, why don't you stop by in a little while? My father has a business meeting and took the car."

"How much time do you need to get ready?" I asked.

"I'm ready now. You can come anytime."

"Very well. I'll just jump in the car, and I'll be there in a few minutes."

"Ciao," she said, "I'll be waiting for you."

"Ciao." I hung up and looked around to see if I could see anything strange around the booth or sitting in any of the cars. Everything was quiet. I walked over the Mercedes and was surprised to see ten people gathered around it, looking at it as if it were some alien spaceship.

When they saw me, so young, long-haired, and dressed in military clothes walking towards that car, they couldn't believe their eyes. Since it was in front of the station, they must have thought it was some famous actor brought into the country from the U.S. to work on something. I said hello and received several compliments from the crowd. I opened the door, jumped in, and made sure to squeal the tires as I left, as a way to brag a little.

One of the kids in the crowd yelled, "Burn the rubber; Papa Fidel paid for it!"

I smiled at that but then felt guilty about it. It wasn't really my car, and so I really shouldn't have done that.

The Dark Face of Marxism

When I arrived at Chandee's house, she was waiting outside for me but didn't recognize the car. I blew the air horn at her. She jumped a little. Then she saw me and shook her head, putting her hand to her mouth in embarrassment.

I got out of the car and opened the passenger's door for her. Her eyes widened in awe as she watched the door open upwards like the wings of a bird. "What did you do this time to deserve this?" she asked. "You pull Che out of the water when he was drowning?"

"Maybe you're joking," I replied, "but that is what he's thinking—I'm his life saver, and I might be his life saver tomorrow."

"I think you woke up the entire neighborhood with that horn!"

"It's still early—" I began. I looked at my watch. "Oh, it's ten-thirty. I'm sorry, I didn't realize it was so late. But when I saw you standing there looking so beautiful, I wanted to announce my joy to everyone."

"I know," she said, "that is the effect I always have on the opposite sex."

I shook my head as I closed the door. "Ah, *chinita*, you are something." I walked around and got in the driver's side. "You know, you must have been royalty in another life. You at least believe so."

I pulled away slowly and noiselessly to avoid further harassment from Chandee.

She looked at the dashboard. "What a beautiful car!" she said. "It must have cost a fortune. Seriously, what have you done? Heaven knows how much hard sweat some poor devil put in to be able to buy this car before the Revolution stole it."

"Ha!" I said. "This is one of the toys Che has in an underground garage in the house where I'm supposed to stay. He's got twenty or thirty more in his collection. Take into consideration the famous speech Fidel made at the beginning in the Plaza de la Revolución, when he said, 'Why should we tolerate the social injustice of some people not having a bicycle, while at the same time others have three luxury cars?' They think that those of us who have too much should redistribute our wealth to share it with those who are less fortunate. He forgot to put it one way in that speech—that we should redistribute the wealth of other people by taking it for ourselves. But the rest of you shouldn't touch our wealth."

Chandee shook her head in obvious distress and clucked her tongue. "Before this Revolution, I thought I knew hypocrisy, jealousy, and lies—but how wrong I was! These communists have truly shown the face of hypocrisy, jealousy, and lies—completely naked."

"That is nothing," I said. "You have to see the house on the beach where I'm supposed to stay tonight. It's not a house—it's a mansion! I didn't see any poor or black people living in there. I saw Che, by himself, using it as one of his meeting places. What a fraud!" I finished with a disgusted shake of my head. "Some of those cars I've never seen on the street before in my life."

I removed my beret and put it on the divider between the seats. "Changing the subject, I need your help. Che informed me a little while ago that the Belgian ambassador is not only an anti-communist, he's a 'rabid' anti-communist. He also told me that he and his people are under the impression that the ambassador is working with the intelligence community—in the best scenario, with the North American CIA." I massaged my forehead with the fingers of my left hand. "This gives me what I think is a great idea. The investigator for the insurance company that was covering *La Coubre* will also be present at the meeting."

Chandee had a mischievous smile on her face, as she imagined what I had in mind. "Be careful," she cautioned me. "You can be absolutely sure that Che won't send you to that interview alone. He could be the craziest man in the world, but he's not an idiot."

I smiled and replied, "Of course. I never underestimate my enemy, even though I think I convinced him he has nothing to worry about with me. He will be relaxing on the other side of the island. Of course, he's sending the best of his dogs—the one who replaced Silvano, a man named Fausto—to keep his eyes on me. He'll make sure I don't say anything that could jeopardize their scam, even by accident, or make any mistake in my testimony. That could not only ruin his reputation but it could create a major problem for the claim for millions of dollars that they're waiting impatiently to receive as a result of this Machiavellian sabotage."

"What do you have in your head this time?" Chandee asked. "How are you planning to ditch Fausto in order to ruin his claim with the insurance company without putting yourself in jeopardy or blowing your cover?"

I smiled and replied, "That is what I need your help for."

She looked at me unhappily but nodded. "OK. What can I do for you?"

"Thank you," I said. "It's not really complicated. I only want you to stay in the car when I leave it in front of Lazaro's house. Blow the horn if you see anything suspicious so I don't get caught with my hand in the cookie jar. I'm going to try and break in, because I think that I might find in there what I'm looking for."

Chandee shook her head violently and raised her arm. "This is too dangerous, especially considering all the things that have happened recently. Besides, what do you expect to find in that house? By now, any evidence that could be useful for us, even assuming Lazaro left anything behind, will already be in the hands of the G-2 or Che by now. They probably combed that house from corner to corner in order to prevent somebody like you from getting his hands on anything that could in any way implicate them."

"I know, I know. But there is still a small possibility that Daniel, may he rest in peace, might have hidden some evidence to protect both himself and his father. He was very savvy, and I know he would find a way to hide something like that without anyone being able to find it."

Chandee looked at me in frustration. "Even professionals like the G-2?" She shook her head in disagreement again. "This is a shot in the dark and in the darkest of rooms. The risk is too high. If you get caught in there and arrested inside that house, you'll have no excuse to save yourself or explain what you were doing in there. Let's suppose that you get what you're looking for. How are you going to get it into the hands of either the investigator or the ambassador? Remember—Fausto won't leave you alone for one minute. You don't even know what Che told him about you, since Che tells everyone something different. He must have told him something to make sure Fausto keeps his nose to your butt."

The Dark Face of Marxism

I smiled. "Let me worry about that. I told you I have a plan. We might complete it at your house later on, if I find what I'm looking for. But let's not waste any time."

Chandee shook her head in frustration again and looked me in the eyes. "OK, if you think it's worth the risk, at least let me be the one breaking into the house."

"Oh, no!" I said. "You must be kidding me! I know you have the training, but you've never been in that house. I have. If it would take me two hours, it would take you four, and I'll be sitting here listening to the rooster singing before you're out of there."

"Listen," she said in an attempt to convince me, "no one knows who I am. If I'm arrested, it will be of no importance, since I can invent any number of excuses to get them to let me go."

I patted her shoulder with a gentle smile on my face. "Thank you very much. I really appreciate your offer. But I will have greater odds of finding what I'm looking for. I only ask you for one thing. If I get arrested inside that house, you leave this Mercedes here as if you have nothing to do with the car or me. You walk to the bus stop and go back to your house. Don't worry at all, don't try to interfere, and let me try to resolve the situation myself. If you get involved, it will be more difficult for me to pull it off. OK?"

"OK," she said with a nod. "Please, don't get arrested in there. Taking a bus in Cuba is worse than going to jail."

I smiled and shook my head. "It's not fair that you should pick me up in a Mercedes and then send me home on a bus!"

I laughed. Even at the worst moments, Chandee could find the humor in a situation.

We were a few blocks away from Lazaro's house. I drove around the block to check the surroundings, slowly enough to observe but not slowly enough to call attention. I was especially careful to observe if there were any cars sitting at a distance to watch any activity around the house. When we passed by the house, we could see two guards sitting in folding chairs by the gate of that magnificent residence. They were both smoking cigarettes and talking to each other. Chandee squeezed my right knee to catch my attention.

"This complicates things more," she said. "Why put guards on an empty house?"

"That actually makes me feel better," I replied. "It tells me that the house really is empty. The thing that worried me more than anything was to find someone inside that house that could take me by surprise."

Chandee shook her head at my stubborn resolution. "I see you've thought of everything, and there's nothing I can say to change your mind."

"Nope."

I saw an empty space near the end of the block on the opposite side of the street. It was a darkened spot, beneath some overgrown trees. I parked there and could see from there the entire front of the house and the movements of the guards. It was perhaps half a short block away. Before I got out, I said, "Remember—one long blast is 'danger.' Two short blasts is 'OK,' in case by accident you touch the klaxon, so that you communicate that it was an unintentional honk."

She looked at me witheringly and shook her head. "I don't make those clumsy mistakes." She got very serious

The Dark Face of Marxism

and pointed her finger at me. "Remember—I want to come back to my house in a Mercedes, not a bus!"

I threw up my hand and waved her off. "Ah, *chinita!*"

I turned to open the door, but she pulled me by the arm and kissed me on the cheek. "Good luck, and please—be careful." This time, she was being serious.

"Don't come to my funeral until you know for sure I'm dead."

She shook her head once more. I got out of the car and crossed the street to the opposite sidewalk. From there, I could see Chandee get out of the car and move around from the back to sit in the driver's seat. I smiled, as it showed that she was well-trained and prepared for any contingency.

I walked along the wall bordering the property. I stooped to pretend I was tying my shoe to let a car pass by me. I jumped and grabbed the top of the wall, scrambled silently up to the top, and cautiously slid down the other side. From the bushes, I looked around and saw no movement. Slowly, I crept from tree to tree and bush to bush to draw near to the kitchen door that opened onto the patio. I tried the door, but it was locked. Over the kitchen door was a balcony that connected with the terrace. I looked up and noticed a slight strip of beige curtain blowing in the door—it had been caught in the door when it had been closed. I started to climb a large orange tree that bordered the terrace.

After I climbed onto the veranda, I jumped inside the terrace and went to the door that had the curtain caught in it. I tried the door—it was locked, but the curtain blocked the tongue of the door latch, so it wasn't completely closed. A gentle push was sufficient to open the door. I thought that this was going to be a great evening for me, since I didn't have to break the door to get in or do anything extraordinary.

It opened into Lazaro's room—I could see pictures of Lazaro and Daniel from happier times. Evidently the last person in here hadn't noticed the curtain. I began to search the room. Everything had been shifted, including the mattress on the bed. The G-2 had already been there. Even nightstands had been shoved away from the wall.

I went through the entire house, from the kitchen to the armory, checking inside the suits of armor. After two hours, I had almost given up but decided to give it one more try. I checked one of the small sofas—nothing.

I thought then that Chandee was right: these people were professionals and had left nothing behind. I felt depressed, because I would have to go back and face her chiding.

Full of frustration, I decided to leave the house. However, I felt the call of nature. I decided to use Daniel's bathroom on my way out. I picked up a Spanish edition of Life from the reading stand where there were new and old magazines. I pulled down my pants to answer the call and opened the magazine. There was a series of advertisements of beautiful resorts around the world. In the midst of all of these was an interview with Fidel and Herbert Matthews. It was an old issue from January 1959. I finished my business and pulled on the toilet paper dispenser. When I did so, the entire assembly flipped out of the wall. The plastic roller rolled underneath the toilet. I picked up the roll of toilet paper, finished cleaning up, and flushed the toilet.

The Dark Face of Marxism

Before washing my hands, I reached under the toilet to put everything back together as it had originally been. As I leaned underneath to get the spring-loaded dowel, I could see a piece of paper underneath the water tank on the toilet. I pulled on it, and a thin paper folder came loose. I placed it on top of the sink. After I replaced the dispenser properly, I closed the toilet seat and placed the folder there. I washed and dried my hands at the sink. I picked up the folder and sat down on the closed toilet.

I grinned from ear to ear. Before my eyes, I had several handwritten notes from Silvano to Lazaro with instructions. One of them mentioned that Che would be very proud of Lazaro if the job was well done, because the Revolution didn't need the weapons of capitalists; it needed the money in order to finance multiple revolutions around the world. Another note reassured Lazaro that he would have no problems in pulling his men out of there, because Silvano gave his word that there would be time enough between the first and second explosions to evacuate everyone from the port. No casualties were expected. One other, of less importance, said that they would recommend that Lazaro be put on the Central Committee "for this tremendous act of altruism" should he achieve success.

I unbuttoned my shirt, concealed the folder inside, and then buttoned my shirt back up. Bingo! This is what I was looking for. Thank you, Daniel! I tapped my belly where the folder was sitting in concealment. In order to protect his father, Daniel hadn't revealed everything to me. But when we had spoken, I could see in his face that he knew more than he was telling me at the time. These hidden documents were very clearly meant to protect the two of them after the plan was carried out.

I felt extremely proud of my judgment and perceptions about my late friend. I got out of the house through the back door and cautiously looked around. Very carefully, I made my way to the wall on the far opposite side from my point of entry. Before jumping up to climb the wall, I looked around to make sure no one was around. I scrambled up to the top. Just then the guards started to check the wall. One headed in my direction. A car drove by, and he saw my silhouette along the top of the wall.

He started to unsling his rifle as he bellowed, "Halt, or I shoot!"

He was about two hundred fifty feet away. Without heeding his words, I jumped to the street and started to run to the sidewalk and across the street. I jumped into the passenger seat, as Chandee already had that door opened for me. "Get us the hell out of here quickly!" I barked.

She kept the lights off and pulled a U-turn to head towards the highway. As we left, we could hear shots being fired but not before we had turned the corner. Fortunately, the street was not very well lit, and the only thing the guard would have seen clearly was the glow of the brake lights as we turned the corner onto 5th Avenue. We were parked near the end of the block, and so the distance for that fast car to cover was very small. We were gone and out of sight, blending in with the rest of the light traffic within seconds.

After we traveled for several blocks, I saw the lights on in a 24-hour pharmacy. I could see an ad in the window for a medication that my grandfather had taken for

The Dark Face of Marxism

rheumatic muscle pain. It had given him severe diarrhea for several days. We had to eventually take him to the doctor, because it looked like he might be developing colitis. When the doctor asked my grandfather if he was a smoker, he said he was. The doctor told him there was an interaction between the active ingredients of the medicine and nicotine, which produced severe abdominal pain and diarrhea. It certainly had the impact of implanting in my memory the name of this medicine.

I instructed Chandee to pull into the parking lot, and I picked up my beret and put it on.

We both got out of the car. Chandee went to the passenger seat while I went to the trunk. "Wait for me here," I told her. "I'll just be a few minutes." I opened the trunk and the box of cigars Che had just given to me. I grabbed a handful of cigars and put them in my side pants pocket. I walked into the pharmacy.

I bought a box of the medication I had seen advertised. I read the warning label which cautioned against smoking for twenty-four hours before or after using this medication.

After I paid, I asked for permission to use the bathroom. I secured the double-locked door and opened the small box. It contained six individually wrapped containers. I ripped one open with my teeth and saw that it contained a dark gray powder. The instructions on the box said to dissolve the powder in a half glass of water or juice.

I closed the cover on the toilet and put some paper towels on top to hold any leftover powder. I took a toothpick out of my shirt pocket and used it to make a small hole in the cigar. I took a few pieces of the compacted tobacco from the center and put them on the towel. Very slowly, I started to fill the tobacco with the powder. After filling a little, I used the toothpick to tamp the powder further into the cigar, and then filled more powder inside, tamped again, and so on, until the powder permeated the entire cigar. I did this with six cigars, using an entire package on each cigar. After finishing each cigar, I picked up the piece of tobacco I had taken out of the cigar and plugged the hole with it. Wetting my finger with saliva, I slightly moistened and reattached the pieces of tobacco of my plug to the whole of the cigar.

I put all six treated cigars in my shirt pocket with the ends sticking out of my shirt pocket as if I were a cigar aficionado. One by one, I ripped up each medicine packet and flushed them down the toilet, making sure nothing was left behind. After flushing, I used a wet paper towel to wipe down the top and bowl of the toilet of any residual powder or tobacco that might leave a trail of what I had been doing. I double-checked my special cigars with the others to make certain that nothing would give away that they had been tampered with, meticulously checking them one at a time. I picked up the empty paper bag and held it as if it still contained my purchase, and I walked out of there.

As I had learned from my uncle, a medication could have different effects on different people, so I knew this was by no means a certainty—but it seemed to be my best shot. I hoped to get rid of my guard dogs with this—both Fausto and the French ambassador.

When I got to the car, Chandee exclaimed, "Oh, my God! You said a few minutes, and it's been over half an hour! What happened to you?"

I patted my stomach. "Nature called."

"Oh, maybe all the stress and that adrenaline rush," she said knowingly. "Did you find what you were looking for at the house?"

"I'll tell you later," I replied mysteriously.

We slowly drove out of the parking lot as we observed several police cars heading towards Lazaro's house. I followed the *Malecón* towards Chinatown as more police cars passed by us in the opposite direction. Apparently they had been put on a high alert.

In a short while, we arrived at Chandee's house. "Well, what did you find?"

"I'll tell you in a bit," I teased again.

"Oh, you didn't find anything!" she accused.

I smiled but didn't answer.

She instructed me to drop her off in front of the store so that she could go around the back to open the gate for me while I drove around the alley. It was closed late at night, and it was now thirty minutes past midnight. I followed as she directed and drove into the alley. She let me in, and we entered the house through the secret hallway. We quietly entered the main house so that we wouldn't awaken the rest of her household. We could tell from the parking area that Mr. Xiang had returned, but we didn't want to disturb him, either.

I followed her to her room and asked her to bring me some eyebrow tweezers, transparent glue if she had any, and long, pointed scissors. After she brought me the requested supplies, I pulled the folder out of my shirt.

"Are you kidding me?" she exclaimed. "Oh, my God—you did find what you were looking for!"

She began to examine the contents of the folder, her eyes growing wide in incredulity. With marked irony, she said, "You already knew about all of this—all these details are in the schematics you had from Che's portfolio."

"Of course," I replied, "but what was not in Che's portfolio were all the names incriminating themselves like we have in there. I don't know if you noticed them, but there are also handwritten notes incriminating Silvano, Che, and the government, promising Lazaro a high position for his help in the sabotage."

Chandee looked at me. "I've got a question for you. Will you please let me know how the hell you knew you would find these papers there? Especially after the G-2 turned that house upside down. Did your friend Daniel tell you something that night when you were at his house?"

I smiled and replied, "I didn't know if I would find anything there or not. No, he never told me anything, but I could read in the distress in Daniel's eyes the night I visited him at the house. I knew that he would try to obtain proof and hide it someplace. All I had to do was look for it and find it. He knew that what his father was doing with Che and Silvano was not exactly holy. He knew that if I got my hands on something like that, I would find a way to expose the truth."

Chandee shook her head and looked at what I was doing with the cigars. "What do you have in mind with those cigars?"

I smiled. "Ruin Fidel and Che's sweet dreams of getting that money in their hands."

She looked at me in puzzlement but stayed silent.

I went through the folder to locate the most compromising notes and rolled them into tiny, thin tubes, small enough to stick into the cigars. After I extracted some of the tobacco from the middle of one of the cigars with the eyebrow tweezers, I inserted the rolled up tube of paper into it. I then slowly filled in the gap with the removed tobacco and put a small amount of glue around the border to secure the filling. After I finished with the first one, I took it in my hands and turned it over before her a couple of times. "Do you see any difference from the others here?"

She shook her head. "None at all. They are identical." She looked at me in admiration. With a smile on her face, she said, "Now I understand better, but my question remains. With Fausto at your side, how are you going to be able to communicate what you intend with this cigar? If they light it, all of your effort will be lost in ashes."

I looked at her gravely. "I'll have to figure that out on the ground. I will do the impossible to make sure that these messages reach their destination and be read not only by the ambassador from Belgium but also the investigator for the insurance company. If I accomplish that, we will be rich in the ecstasy of success. Che and Fidel will be so constipated with frustration, they need one of my cigars."

Chandee looked at me blankly. "What?"

I patted my shirt pocket and repeated, "One of my cigars."

She frowned at me. "Another secret?"

"Don't worry, *mi chinita*, you will know later, I assure you, when I know the results."

"I have a lot to learn from you. I would never have entered that house unless I knew exactly where that folder was to be discovered. You entered it without knowing and found exactly what you were looking for. If I have to be honest with you, I would never be doing all of this work, either, unless I knew for certain the contacts had already been alerted and were waiting to pass this information along the proper channels. Everything could literally go up in smoke in spite of all the work you've been doing. Without a doubt, you are a great optimist, and perhaps this extreme optimism of yours helps you to achieve the things that no one else is capable of. No one else would ever accomplish it because, like me, they lack that optimism."

I smiled and said, "Thank you very much. I consider being an optimist a great virtue in our profession. But I want to give you some advice: never look for help from anybody, especially in this business. Who you ask for help could wind up being your executioner, or at least the traitor who sells you to your enemies. The only exception is the person who has such extraordinary qualities and personality that it's worth asking for help and chancing the consequences. You have to be certain they will never let you down, and you have to be bonded through a measure of human love. Then and only then can you take that chance."

We looked at each other in solemn silence. Then she smiled broadly and blushed a little bit. She took a couple of steps towards me and then shook her finger in my face mischievously. "You are something! You got my color up again!" She hugged me unexpectedly. "Thank you for your confidence, love, and trust."

She kissed me on the cheek. We separated slightly.

"I need to tell you, before I forget," she said, "a very important message about your brother-in-law Canen. Your uncle and the General told me that you can have complete confidence in him. He is one of us, though not a part of the team. He is connected with a group of officers against the communist ideology that have been planning to remove Fidel and Raul from power. They've been trying through different channels to completely support Canen in proceeding with this plan. Even though he's not related to you by blood, he could not be more like you. He has refused to be part of any foreign group or associated with any foreign attachment. His group has nationalist ideas, and they don't want any association with any outside group. They have an old dinosaur mentality that they can, by themselves, turn this situation around. They refuse to see that this is no longer the Cuban Revolution. Even before the success of the Revolution, Fidel, Raul, Che, and those around them had extremely close international bonds with the Soviet Union and the communist bloc in Europe and Asia. This was all through Che—who, as you know, is an agent for the KGB."

I squeezed my right ear and shook my head. "Then I cannot be explicit with Canen in any way, shape, or manner, much less tell him what we're doing. I'm glad he's at least on our side, but his nationalist ideals limit him. He doesn't even realize this is no longer a national fight. It's an international fight, and it's a fight for the security and freedom of the Americas, Europe, Asia, and the rest of the world."

Chandee nodded her head. She replied, "It's sad to see this military lack the ideological education to understand what is really going on. They think that replacing Fidel, Raul, and that group of bandidos is like replacing Batista, and the Revolution can continue forward as if nothing had changed. They don't realize that they're forming an international army—the International Proletariat Union.

In a very short time, we'll have more Russians and other foreign communists in our military, and they will eliminate them slowly. They're dreaming if they think they can still be nationalists. But we should applaud them, not criticize them, and let them believe what they want, because they still stand with us against Castro and his gang. We have to let them fight their own fight, and we can be united later to secure the rest of the world. Time has changed things, and we should all together defend freedom and democracy around the world, no matter our countries' religious and political beliefs."

"Well," I said, "it's good to know at least that he's not an informant or on the side of our enemy. That makes me feel a lot better, believe me, and when I go to visit my sister, I can eat those plantains with a lot more pleasure. By the way, what do you intend to do tomorrow evening?"

She smiled and answered, "Well, I had been hoping my charming knight in armor was going to come and take me to a movie."

I smiled and said, "I will call you after the meeting, and maybe we can meet at the Astral Theater on Infanta. Then I will bring to you the secrets of the Operation: *Tabacos*[4]."

She smiled and replied, "Very well. That is what we will call it—Operation: Tabacos! I wish you all the luck in the world tomorrow, because you will need it."

We embraced and said our goodbyes. "When you leave, just close the doors. It's so late that no one will notice that they're not double-locked."

---

[4] *Cigars.*

The Dark Face of Marxism

Call Things as They Truly Are

When the honest and decent men of this world hesitate while viewing a horrific and indecent act, they are becoming part of it. Though they may look away and bite their tongues to avoid confrontation and offense, these men are corrupting their spirits and integrity. Men who fail to speak out against these heinous acts compromise their decency and become themselves cowards. What irony it is, where a decent man, while trying to be decent and not offend, passes over horrific acts so as not to offend – he no longer is what he claims to be.

Everything in life has a proper name by which it should be called. Whether it is to someone close to you or not, speaking out is the obligation of those who would claim to be good and honest. The extreme murderers, who kill and rape little boys and girls have no heart or principles. Genocidal hatemongering sociopaths and the worst scum of the earth is what they should be called, without hesitation or fear. If we are afraid to say so and offend others, we are afraid of the truth. Those evil ones will not care if you are offended when they kill and destroy what is precious to you, and they do not deserve anything less than condemnation.

Dr. Julio Antonio del Marmol

Dr. Julio Antonio del Marmol

Chapter 3: Operation: Tabacos and the Belgian Connection

The French Embassy to Cuba in Havana

I left Chandee's house to return to Boca Siega. On the trip back, I drove more carefully than I had when I started out, keeping an eye out for anyone else who might happen to be crossing the road with a raft. When I arrived, everyone was asleep save for two guards who greeted me.

I parked the car and took the box of cigars out of the trunk. I said goodnight to the guards and went to my room, where I put the cigars in my travel bag. It was 2:00 a.m.

The Dark Face of Marxism

I woke up late and had brunch. After I ate, I left in one of the black Oldsmobiles for the capitol with Fausto and two soldiers of the escort.

We arrived in Miramar at the private residence of the French ambassador. The ambassador was a dishwater blonde man of medium height with a Hickok mustache and a full beard. He had a very friendly character and greeted us with extreme courtesy, offering us all manner of fruit, expensive chocolates, and a variety of pastries. He offered a cognac to Fausto. The Belgian contingent had not yet arrived.

The ambassador introduced himself in perfect Spanish. "My name is Pierre Andreus."

I replied, "I am Julio Antonio del Marmol, but everyone knows me as the Little Commander."

"Yes," he said. "We all know you to be on TV, always around Fidel. We will call you the Commandantico, like everyone else."

We sat down in a huge, beautiful conference room dominated by a marble table and very comfortable reclining leather chairs on swivel bases.

Shortly after we were settled, he asked his first question. "Do you know the reason Lazaro named you as a witness and stated that should anything adverse occur to him or anyone in his family, you would have the answer for it?"

There was no doubt to me that Che and Pierre ran together, since Che had the previous night asked me the same question.

"No, I haven't the slightest idea," I replied very seriously. "I only had a friendship with his son, and for as long as I did know him, our conversations were always very brief. Che and I were discussing this last night. I came here today because I know this is protocol and you need to take my declaration, but I assure you there is nothing I can add to this puzzle. I don't know myself why he created it, although I'm sure he must have had some reason. Would you like a cigar?"

"No, thank you—wait, are these the ones Che smokes?"

I nodded.

"Yes, I believe I will take one, on second thought. Thank you."

I reached inside my left shirt pocket and handed him one of the cigars there. He smelled it, looked at it appreciatively, and said, "This is a very fine cigar! Are you sure this is one of the ones Che smokes?"

"Yes, it comes from the same harvest. He gave me a box last night."

"Wow, he must like you very much!"

"Probably," I replied.

"Thank you," he said.

"You're very welcome," I said. "Enjoy yourself."

I privately hoped that he would spend the rest of the day in the bathroom.

Fausto looked at me in surprise, as he had never seen me smoke before, but he made no comment. Instead, he asked, "Do you have an extra one for me? I'd really appreciate it."

"Sure," I said with a broad grin. I smelled it myself before I handed it to him. "Here you go."

"You must like cigars," he said as he watched me smell it.

"Yes," I said. "My grandfather was one of the best tobacco growers in Pinar del Rio, and he had one of the

The Dark Face of Marxism

best fields in Guane. Between us, you can call me the Tobacco Kid from now on. I love cigars, especially the ones that are so refined. The leaves are made from the most selected capes."

He smelled the cigar again but put it in the pocket of his shirt. The ambassador bit off the end. Fausto took out a beautiful, solid gold lighter to offer him a light. I recognized it as the one I had seen on Aldames' desk the day of the robbery and shooting, and I frowned.

The Frenchman leaned back in his chair and took a long drag from it.

Fausto smiled and took the cigar out of his pocket. "You've gotten me jealous with that exquisite smell," he said. "I have to light mine, too."

He bit off the end of his cigar and lit it for himself. He also leaned back and took a big puff, followed by a deep inhalation. Very slowly, he began to blow smoke rings, showing the complete pleasure and delight of a professional smoker. He repeated Pierre's observation. "Che must have you in very high personal regard, because he never gave even me such a wonderful present before."

He continued smoking. "My God, this is pure quality!" He raised the cigar in the air. "Look at how beautiful it is in the light—how evenly the layers are burning."

One of the guards knocked on the door. "The gentlemen are here."

Fausto said, "Go ahead—let them in."

Pierre welcomed the two men who walked in through the door. One was tall, with a dark complexion, thin beard, and pointed nose. He had a distinguished look, with deep-set, piercing eyes which scrutinized everything around him. When he looked intently at you, it was difficult to hold his gaze for long. Nevertheless, it was a pleasant, even friendly gaze. He reminded me of Commander Camillo. He was introduced as the Ambassador of Belgium. He said in perfect Spanish, "A great pleasure to meet all of you. My name is Abdul Marcalt."

The other man was short, balding, round-faced, and heavy-set. He wore thick glasses. "Anton Frendic, representative and investigator for the insurance company," he introduced himself.

Frendic put his briefcase on top of the table and began to pull out documents that looked like insurance forms or legal documents. While he did so, Pierre and Fausto enjoyed with sublime pleasure the Habanos cigars I had given them.

The insurance man said, "The reason we are meeting today is because the deceased, Mr. Lazaro Zardiñas, left some testimonial notes before his death naming you as a witness who could expose his assailants, either by name or specifics, as to how they contributed to his death. Our investigation has come to the conclusion that, since Mr. Zardiñas was in charge of the Dockworker's Union, the same assailants who conspired in his death could also be responsible for the extensive damage that almost sank the ship *La Coubre*, along with the casualties for which we are liable. We consider this as extremely strange and have strong belief that the way these explosions originated had malice aforethought."

He then asked me the precise same question that I had already been asked by both Che and Pierre.

I started to think that either all of these men were working together, or I was getting a little paranoid. Thinking clearly, however, I had to admit this was a

The Dark Face of Marxism

rational question to continually ask—it certainly was unusual for a grown man to entrust a youth barely in his teens with such information.

I raised an eyebrow and stroked it with my finger. "I will answer the same way I answered last night to Che and a few minutes ago to Pierre." I swung my right hand through the air to emphasize my denial. "I have no idea why Lazaro did this. He must have had a reason, but I can't imagine what it is. As I told Pierre, I came here out of protocol, but I don't see how I can be of any help to you guys. I guess Che wanted you to hear it from my own mouth."

The investigator took notes of every word I spoke. He looked up. "He never mentioned to you the name of any person who was putting pressure on him or attempting to blackmail him to do something in exchange for some other service or reward?"

I shook my head. "No. We never talked about anything like that at all. I can tell you that the last time I spoke with him, I noticed that he was unusually irritable and worried. I attributed it to the daily pressure he had with the workers in the port and his excessive work schedule. His son corroborated that; he said there had been some friction between the two of them, and his father had been very short tempered lately."

The investigator took notes of that, as well.

Abdul asked, "The son, Daniel, had been your chauffeur in the military corps in your Commandos?"

"Yes, may he rest in peace."

I suppressed the urge to cross myself, though my hand still jerked involuntarily. Abdul noticed and smiled.

Dr. Julio Antonio del Marmol

He glanced out of the corner of his eye to gauge Fausto's reaction. Fausto, however, was wrapped up in enjoying the cigar I had given to him as he sat next to Pierre. Every now and then, the two of them exchanged glances, and once in a while Fausto and Pierre picked up chocolates from the table and popped them in their mouths. Evidently, the flavor of the cigars made a heavenly combination with the chocolate for them. I continued to keep my eye on that pair, waiting impatiently for some symptom from either of them that my medicated cigars were having an effect.

Over an hour later, Anton exhausted all of the questions he had, with Abdul throwing in the odd question meant to take me by surprise. I began to think that my plan had failed. Both Fausto and Pierre were young; perhaps their immune systems were so strong that they could overcome an adverse reaction to the medicine. I was disappointed, as any opportunity to get my messages to these two men was rapidly disappearing with the approaching end of the interview. My mind started to go into overdrive, seeking a way to still achieve that.

Anton closed the folder containing the notes he had been taking, and with an expression of satisfaction, he said, "I've completed my report. It looks like everything will be OK. I don't see any reason for my company to decline the claim. In a few days, at most a week," he said to Fausto, "your government should be receiving a check. I don't know what my superiors will say, but I am completely satisfied."

He leaned over the table and took one of the chocolates. He began to unwrap it.

The Dark Face of Marxism

At that moment, Fausto put his hand on his stomach and said, "Will you guys excuse me? I think I ate more chocolates than I should have." He looked at Pierre. "Where is the restroom?"

I only smiled, but I secretly rejoiced. Pierre leaned back in his chair and pointed. "There's one to the right as you leave the conference room. If that one is occupied, there's another one at the end of the hallway."

Fausto left the conference room in a rush. He even forgot his gold lighter on top of the table.

The Belgian ambassador asked me, "Do you work for Che?"

"No," I replied, "I work for the Revolution."

He smiled and said in a condescending tone, "Well, yes—but you work under the orders of somebody."

I shook my head with a slight smile and squeezed my lips with my left hand in thought. I replied, "Thinking very carefully about it, since you bring up the question, I had been nominated by our Prime Minister and Commander-in-Chief, Fidel Castro, to be the Commander-in-Chief of the Young Commandos of the Rebel Army, a military corps independent of any other military command structure. They delegated to me the formation of the future military forces for the Cuban government, and they instructed me to do whatever I think is necessary. I never received orders from anyone, and in the documents I was given were explicit orders to everyone in any bureaucracy or organization within the government to give me whatever I needed to facilitate this project. That meant that I wasn't under the supervision or command of anyone—aside from the sole discretion and orders of the Prime Minister, I guess. By the same token, since we're talking about this, my military corps will soon be integrated into another political organization. It will be a part of the ideological formation of the next generation. Since no one has told me what my function will be there, the reality is that all of this is in transition. I guess I don't work for anyone; I'm in limbo right now, until all of the reorganization concludes. For the time being, most recently I've joined the team of my friend, Commander Che Guevara. Tomorrow, I don't know—that is another day. I might be doing something completely different. So I don't work for anyone but the Revolution. Wherever the Revolution needs me, there I will be."

Pierre pulled his glasses down his nose and smiled in broad satisfaction at my answer.

Abdul was less than happy with my answer and shook his head, slightly annoyed. He tried to change the subject by directing a question to Pierre. "Where did you buy that fancy cigar? It has an exquisite aroma!"

Pierre smiled and stroked his mustache. "It's a present from our young friend here. This is the kind they grow especially for Fidel and Che."

Abdul smiled in disbelief, though Pierre and I remained absolutely serious. He looked between the two of us and asked, "Really? Truly?"

Pierre said, "Of course." He turned to me and asked, "Do you have any left?"

I nodded my head and wondered which cigar I should give to him—the cigar with information or the one that would give him diarrhea. After a second's doubt, I decided to give him one from my left pocket, with the medication. I didn't want to waste all of that work.

The Dark Face of Marxism

I looked at the table and saw the glint of Fausto's lighter. I was getting very nervous at Pierre's lack of reaction. Abdul took the cigar from me and thanked me. He leaned over the table and asked Pierre for a light. Pierre wordlessly pushed the lighter towards Abdul. The Belgian bit off the end of the cigar and began to light it.

Anton looked at me with a slightly begging expression. Clearly, he wanted one but didn't want to actually ask me. After he watched Abdul light and enjoy his, he finally asked, "Do you have another one?"

I cringed inwardly, but with Pierre still there, I had no choice. I pulled another cigar out of my left pocket, thinking we would need a lot of corks to stop the results of these cigars. Pierre raised his hand and said, "This is the most exquisite cigar I've ever had in my life. In all the time I've been a smoker, I've never had a cigar of such quality. It's superb!"

I smiled and nodded. Pierre asked me, "Aren't you going to smoke one with us, before we smoke all of them?"

I smiled again and touched my left pocket. "These are for my friends. I have a big box in my travel bag—those are for me." I leaned back in my seat and breathed deeply. "With all the nicotine you guys are spreading in here, I can fill up my lungs for a while. Besides, I don't like to smoke when I'm talking. I enjoy the tobacco so much that my saliva sprays over everyone when I speak. I don't want you guys to have to get out the umbrellas to protect yourselves."

They all laughed at that. At that moment, Pierre touched his stomach, but said nothing. He leaned back at the table and carefully put his cigar out. "Excuse me, I have to go to the bathroom for a bit." He left a little rushed as well, and I exulted.

From the table, I was examining the entire room. On either side of the room, I noticed a pair of can lights in the ceiling that were unlit. They may have been surveillance devices, so I had to keep my mouth shut. Outside the room, I could see the patio of this residence with a swimming pool surrounded by lush tropical vegetation. There were two heaters by the entryway to the pool area that were decorated like Roman columns. I thought they might be propane fueled, as the flames were blue. I silently watched Anton and Abdul enjoying their cigars, trying to come up with an excuse to leave the room before they got sick, raising everyone's suspicions.

At one side of the swimming pool, I saw a large cage with green monkeys from Barbados jumping around and playing. I stood up and walked over to the sliding door. I pointed at the cage and said to them, "Oh, look at those beautiful creatures!"

Both men stood up and walked towards me and the sliding door to take a look. Without wasting a moment, I opened the door and stepped outside, the two men following me close behind. As I left, I unbuttoned my right shirt pocket. I walked to the side next to the cage.

We crossed behind some flowering bushes in planters around the pool. Once we were far enough from the house, I looked around to make certain no one was around and that the view from the conference room window was blocked. The planters were blocking the filtration system for the pool.

I took the cigar from the Belgian ambassador's mouth. "I beg your pardon, but I have to stop you from smoking

The Dark Face of Marxism

this anymore, unless you want to get very sick to your stomach." I removed Anton's cigar as well.

They both looked at me in silent surprise. Like lightning, I snatched the two cigars from my right pocket and said quietly and quickly, "Not even a single word of this to anyone—no exceptions. My life depends on you guys. You will find in that tobacco the proof of the conspiracy by the leaders of the Cuban government to obtain multiple benefits from the sabotage of the ship *La Coubre*. We strongly believe that the French ambassador is directly involved as an accomplice with Che in all of this. When you get back to the conference room, quickly light these cigars, so they look like you've been smoking them for a while. But only for a few seconds—if you let them burn too much, you'll destroy the proof inside. Follow my instructions to a T. These people will stop at nothing; if you're discovered, you'll both be killed without consideration. It will look like an accident—car accident, drowning, whatever."

I patted Abdul on the shoulder, since he was closest. "Go—you don't have any time to waste. I will come and rejoin you in a few seconds."

Abdul asked, "Where can I contact you?"

"Nowhere at this moment," I replied. "It's too dangerous. I will contact you as soon as circumstances allow me to do so." He whipped one of his cards out of his pocket. He wrote something on the back and handed it to me.

"I don't need that."

"Please!" he pleaded urgently with me.

I took the card and said, "Go! Now, hurry! You're wasting time. I can find you."

I watched them leave for the conference room, still holding their cigars in my hand. I walked over towards the entryway and tossed both cigars into the flames of the heater. I quickly walked back towards the conference room but stopped for a few seconds by the monkey cage, pretending to observe them. I noticed from that distance that my instructions were being followed—they were lighting the cigars. I walked back to the conference room.

As I opened the sliding door, the opposite door opened to admit Fausto, returning from the bathroom. It looked to all the world like I had left them alone in the conference room and had been on the patio by myself.

Fausto asked me, "What the hell were you doing out there?"

"I love monkeys. I couldn't resist going out there and seeing what kind they are. I confirmed they are green monkeys from Barbados."

"Oh," he said. "You know your monkeys, do you?"

"Yes," I said, "I also wanted to get a breath of fresh air—too much nicotine in this room. Even though I love it, I was getting a little saturated."

Abdul and Anton's cigars both looked burned, but I noticed no smoke coming from either of them. They still had them in their hands. They both looked very nervous, which surprised me. I had expected the Belgian ambassador, at least, to be more used to this sort of thing.

Fausto touched his stomach. "I'm sorry for my delay, but those chocolates are so delicious I overdid it."

A few seconds later, Pierre returned, also looking unhappy. He said, his hand also on his stomach, "I don't know if it was something I ate or if it's those chocolates, but I've been crapping my brains out."

The Dark Face of Marxism

I mentally breathed a sigh of relief—the cigars didn't cross his mind.

Fausto looked at Pierre seriously. "I think it's those chocolates, my friend. We had the same reaction."

Abdul and Anton exchanged serious looks, and I saw Anton had a small amount of perspiration on his forehead. To distract everyone, I asked Pierre, "What kind of monkeys do you have out there? Are those green monkeys from Barbados? They're beautiful."

"Yes," he said, "they were a gift from the Barbados Consul."

I reached into the center bowl of chocolates and grabbed a handful. "Well, I'll find out if this is what made you guys sick, or if it's just because you ate too many."

I put them in the right pocket of my shirt. I opened one and popped it in my mouth. "No wonder you guys got sick in the stomach. This is delicious! And chocolates can be very hard in this tropical weather, especially rich, highly refined chocolate like this." I stood up. "Are you guys finished? If we are, I would like to leave. I have a date later on with a young lady, and I would like to go take a shower and make myself presentable."

The Belgians also stood up and acknowledged that they needed nothing else from me and that they considered the meeting finished. I thought they looked like two of the Three Stooges and wondered how they could be so irresolute. I glanced at Fausto and Pierre, but neither seemed to notice anything outwardly. I relaxed a little when I noticed that Pierre seemed anxious for us to leave, as well.

He stood up and held out his hand. "Thank you for coming over and making your declarations."

Fausto also stood up, and we left the conference room. As we walked into the hallway, Pierre asked if we knew the way out as he touched his stomach again. "Please excuse me, but nature is calling again." He pointed at my shirt pocket. "Be careful how many of those you eat, or you'll be in the same condition."

I took another Habanos cigar out of my left pocket and held it out to him. "Maybe this will help you feel better."

He thanked me hurriedly and rushed towards the bathroom. We entered the parking lot and walked to rejoin our escort by the cars. We said our farewells to the Belgians, and drove along 5th Avenue.

Before we had gone far, Fausto yelled to the driver, "Pull over! By those bushes!" The driver tried to stop immediately, but the traffic was heavy, and he had to look for another place to stop. Fausto yelled in irritation, "*Carajo!* Why don't you stop?"

"A lot of traffic—we'll get killed if we stop here," the driver protested to Fausto.

"Put on the goddamn emergency lights," Fausto snapped, "and stop at the next bushes, please, or I'm going to shit in my pants!"

He sat in the back seat to my left, sweating and pale. He looked at the other bushes. "*Coño, chico!* Right there, chico! Damn, damn, damn! I've already shit in my pants, cojones! Too late!" He put his hand on his pants. "*La puta de la madre que me pario*[5]."

The driver nervously stopped the Oldsmobile. Fausto, cussing and keeping his hand near his rear, jumped out of

---

[5] *The prostitute mother who brought me to this earth*

the still moving car like a rabbit chased by coyotes. He ran into the bushes in a half-limping motion like someone who had a spine injury or was suffering from polio.

The two guards burst out laughing at him, and I couldn't help but join in. Fausto signaled from the bushes to the guards. The one in the front passenger side got out to see what he wanted. A few seconds later, he came back to the car, took a magazine and ripped out several pages, and walked back to where Fausto was hiding. A few minutes later, the pair returned and even though it might have hurt Fausto's feelings, we all held our noses, because the smell was unbearable. The guards and I put our windows down a little. However, as soon as the car started into motion, the smell grew worse. I pulled off my beret and held it over my nose.

Fausto said to the driver, "Put your foot down on that accelerator, and don't take it off until I tell you. If I can't make to Boca Siega, I'll let you know, and you pull over at once!"

The driver said, "OK."

Fausto looked at me in shame. "I'm sorry, man. This has never happened to me before, never in my life. I shit all over my pants and underwear like a baby without any diapers."

"Don't worry about it," I replied. "There's a first time for everything in life. We all go through this. You might be feeling really embarrassed, and your ego's a little bruised, but this will pass. I thought to caution you when I saw you eating so many chocolates, but I didn't want to be rude."

"Don't worry about being rude," he said, "please—next time, tell me!"

I took one of the chocolates out of my pocket and held it up for him. "This," I said, "can kill you, man."

He had already convinced himself about that, and raised his arm in revulsion. "Please, put that thing back in your pocket. Just looking at that is making my ass act like a signal light in the middle of the night."

I smiled and replaced the chocolate. "I told you man, like I said to Pierre—these are delicious, but you only eat one or two at a time. They're like a time bomb and will blow up when you least expect it."

"Yeah," he said, "a bomb of shit. The tremendous gas it produces in me—when I went to the bathroom in the house, I thought I had a symphonic orchestra in my rear end, and the section playing was the wind instruments. I was making all kinds of different sounds, and each time I thought I was done, I had more coming. I have to thank God for all of the time I spent in there, though, because when I went in the car, all I had was water. No more excrement. Just clear, chocolate water."

He put his hands on his stomach once more. We were now on the highway, and he yelled to the driver, "Please, find a corner and stop as soon as possible." He grabbed a magazine and unbuttoned his pants. As soon as the car stopped, he jumped out and ran to the bushes.

The trip back to the beach took us nearly an hour and a half, due to all the extra stops. When we finally arrived, Fausto didn't even wait for the car to park. He got out and ran directly to the bathroom. From my experience with my grandfather, I knew that this was only the beginning. The worst was yet to come in a couple of days for him, and I began to feel guilty about the whole matter. However, it was the best solution I could come up with, as it was crucial for me to be alone with the Belgians. The French ambassador and Fausto would be all right in a few days, which was more than could be said for the innocent victims of the *La Coubre* sabotage, including Daniel and Lazaro. Overall, I decided, this was a small price for them to pay in order to make sure that no one profited from the tragedy.

As I went up to the shower, I couldn't help but laugh out loud as I remembered what Fausto had endured on the trip back. After a long, hot shower in my room, I dressed in fresh clothes, grabbed my travel bag, and went to speak with Fausto. The guards informed me that he was in the bathroom close to his quarters. I knocked on the door and spoke to him through it, telling him I was going into Havana and was going to take the Mercedes.

"Grab whatever car you feel like," he said. "All the keys are in the kitchen by the refrigerator door. Each key has a tab with the make, year, and color of the car."

"Thank you," I replied. "I hope you get to feeling better."

I went downstairs and grabbed the key for the Mercedes. I went down into the garage and saw a beautiful Thunderbird—navy blue and white in color. I hesitated, thinking for a moment to take that one instead, but chose not to abuse my privilege and to stick with the Mercedes.

I shook my head, and a few minutes later, after looking at all the cars there, I got into the Mercedes, started the engine, and drove into the city.

It was about 5:00 p.m. when I arrived in Havana. I pulled over by a line of public telephones near a car wash.

I let them wash the car while I called Chandee, letting her know that I would pick her up at around 6:30.

"That's perfect," she said. "That will give me time to take a shower and get ready."

After I hung up, I called my attorney uncle to let him know I was in town and would be there in a few minutes. I drove along Carlos III towards my uncle's house. They were already waiting for me.

I greeted and hugged my aunt and uncle, and said to him, "I would like to speak with you in private. Something very confidential."

My aunt said, "OK, but you have to have at least a finger sandwich with us, if you're in such a rush."

I agreed to share that with them, and we went in to sit down at the dining room table. I opened my travel bag and pulled the box of cigars out of my bag. They looked at me in surprise. "I didn't think you smoked," my uncle said.

"You're right," I answered, "I don't. I hate the smell of tobacco, but these are extremely special. They have an incalculable value. I want you to please keep this box of cigars in a safe place here until I decide what to do with it."

"Don't worry," my uncle said. "You don't have to give me too much explanation; the less you tell me, the better."

My aunt smiled and said, "You couldn't put it in a safer place, since neither of us smoke. That would be the greatest temptation."

"Thank you both," I said. "I'm only going tell one other person. If I cannot pick it up myself, this other person is authorized to do so, and you will give it to her. She's a young Chinese girl named Chandee. I've left some instructions on the inside of the box and sealed it. If she comes to pick it up, open the box and read the instructions; if not, it will be unnecessary to open it."

"I will do exactly as you instruct," my uncle said.

I smiled. "I know you will." I expressed my gratitude once more.

After chatting with them for a while, we said goodbye, and I drove towards Chinatown. I passed by several stores until I reached the antique store. I stopped in front of the store, where Chandee, punctual as ever, was waiting outside and ready to go. I checked my watch and saw that it was exactly 6:30. She had a beautiful smile on her face.

As I got out of the car to open the door for her, she said, "Thank you for picking me up. My father left town this morning on a business trip to Santiago de Cuba."

"Ooh," I exclaimed, "what a coincidence! Che is there!"

"Ooooh," she said, "you think my father is a double agent or something?" She smiled once more.

"For me," I said, "it is a pleasure to pick you up. I know you don't like to take the bus."

She laughed as she thought about the previous night. I drove from her place towards the Astral Theater. I parked on the opposite side of the street, and we crossed to enter the theater. Chandee asked me, "What's up? How did Operation: *Tabacos* turn out?"

I grinned broadly. "Often when we plan something, we ourselves don't know how things will turn out." I raised my right arm and made an OK sign with my fingers. I closed one eye and said, "This time, they exceeded my expectations. It couldn't have been better, honey." We entered the theater.

We stopped by the concessions stand first. The usher showed us to our seats, and I whispered in her ear all the things that had happened. When I got to Fausto's problems and his accident on 5th Avenue, she spit her popcorn out as she started to quietly laugh.

The movie showing was Alfred Hitchcock's Vertigo, which in Spanish had the additional title *"De entre los muertos"*[6] and starred Kim Novak and James Stewart. Chandee grabbed my arm a couple of times, and exclaimed, "My God! This is a great suspense movie!"

"I love it!" I said.

She smiled and teased, "You're a little morbid, you know?"

"No, I love a great film where you cannot predict how it's going to end or what is going to happen next."

After the movie finished, we walked out into the street, holding hands. We crossed the street towards the Mercedes. A group of young kids and a few adults were gathered around it, and it was the first time I thought to myself that it was not a good car for us. It was so noticeable that it was a bad business card—far too conspicuous for people in our profession. That attention was the last thing we wanted. After I thanked some of the spectators for their compliments, we got in and drove away as fast as we could, heading towards the Rancho Boyeros. This avenue stretched from Havana to José Martí International Airport.

"Are you hungry?" I asked her.

She touched her stomach. "Yes, I only ate a light lunch of fruit and a few croquettes before you came to pick me up."

---

[6] *"In Between the Deaths"*

The Dark Face of Marxism

I looked at my watch. "Oh, my God! It's nine-thirty! I'm pretty hungry, too, since I only ate some hors d'oeuvres at my uncle's house. I'm going to take you for the best *media noches*[7] in all of Havana."

She laughed. "How in the hell do you know what the best in Havana is when you're from Pinar del Rio?"

"*Chinita, chinita,* if I tell you they're the best in Havana, they're the best in Havana. Remember who I am—I have fresh info from the secret sources."

"No," she disagreed, "the best *media noches* is in Casa Potin."

I nodded and said, "Yes, *habanera*[8], even though you don't believe it, this man from Pinar del Rio is going to show you something new. You never will go back to Potin. I tell you this with authority, because I've eaten at this place once, and I've eaten at Potin. It's like you're having sex with one single person—how can you know if the sex is better with another person or not?"

"Oh, you!" She shook her head. "OK, but why did you have to compare it with sex?"

"It's just a comparison," I said innocently.

"OK, I'll hold judgment until I have what you say is the best *media noches* in Havana. What is this place called, anyway?"

"It's called El Parador[9]."

---

[7] *Midnight sandwich*

[8] *Lady born and raised in Havana*

[9] *The Place to Stop*

She looked skeptical. "Well, at least the name is original. I don't know about the *media noches* yet. I'll let you know when I eat it."

"Boy!" I replied. "You are challenging."

We drove along the multilane avenue, passing by a circular fountain in the middle of the street. We continued towards the airport. I took a note out of the pocket of my shirt and handed it to her.

She took the note and opened it. "What is this?"

"This is the address of my attorney uncle on Carlos III. They have a package of extreme value in their possession. If something happens to me or if I call you and give you the instruction to pick it up, be sure that this package reaches the hands of the General or my other uncle. Memorize the address and then burn that note. I don't want them to get hurt or implicated at all. It is of extreme importance, not only politically but also for you and your family. We cannot predict the future, but this can ensure the future of anyone. I want you to listen to me very carefully. It has ten pieces inside. Before you give it to my uncle or the General, you will take one piece as insurance for yourself and your family."

"Yes, yes," she replied uncertainly, not understanding what I was talking about.

"Inside you will find a note explaining everything in great detail. I don't want to tell you too much more, but consider everything I just told you to be classified and sealed, between you and me only. Don't even reveal this conversation with your own father, unless I tell you differently or if something happens to me. Do you understand?"

She looked at me gravely. "Nothing is going to happen to you, and please don't scare me more than I already am. This is another one of your mysteries?"

"Yes," I answered. "Eventually it will all make sense."

"OK, I will do as you tell me."

"Thank you very much."

"No, thank you for your confidence. I will never betray you, I assure you. I would die first." She said the last with such strong determination in her voice.

I smiled and replied, "I know. I know for sure when I see someone I can completely trust without losing a single minute of sleep, and that person is you. Let's consider it between you and me an extension of Operation: Tabacos."

She looked at me and smiled. "What? Is it a double tobacco?"

I nodded mysteriously. "Something like that. Multiple tobaccos."

We were only a few miles away from the coffee shop. A loud noise suddenly erupted over our heads, the sound of a motor like a helicopter's rotor, and a strong light shone down on us. It sounded like it was right above the roof of our Mercedes. I instinctively took my foot off the accelerator.

"Wow!" I said. A propeller commuter passenger airplane tried to land right in front of us in the middle of the highway.

"What is that?" Chandee exclaimed.

Smoke rose from the pavement as the wheels touched down. The craft slowed down as several cars pulled over to avoid the plane. Several workers along the right side of the road abandoned their jobs and walked along to watch the whole scene unfolding. The plane stopped, and we slowly drove closer, looking for the logos.

Chapter 4: Codename GPFLOOR, the Main Piece on the Chessboard

It was a plane from the USA, and I realized that the plans for espionage and terrorism I had recently read about in Che's schematic were functional and completely in motion. This was one of the first points in their plans: to hijack planes and bring them to Cuba. There were several objectives to this plan, including psychological and economic goals. It was the beginning of the way they would export terrorism around the world later on. The plan right now was to reroute two to three passenger plans per week from North American airports to the Cuban capitol of Havana.

The engines had been shut off, and several cars were stopped on both sides a short distance from us. People were getting out of the cars and walking over to examine the sight curiously. I opened my door and said to Chandee, "Let's find out what's going on here."

Once outside the car, Chandee asked, "Do you know what this signifies?"

My eyes were glued to the door of the plane. My peace bond was already off, and my hand was on the hilt of my pistol. "I will explain later, but I can tell you this is part of this government's plan to create disruption on a major scale. First in the U.S. and then later in the Americas and around the world. Disruption and confusion create division."

"What do you mean?" she asked.

"Very simple—when you disrupt the people and the governments do nothing to keep them safe, you create division and strife."

The door of the plane opened. If my surprise had been great when I saw the plane landing in front of us, it grew even greater when I saw the man standing in the door. He looked exactly like Yuri, Marko, and Marcelino. With two Cuban flags in each hand, he yelled in very poor Spanish, "*Cuba, si, Yankees no! Abajo el imperialismo Yankee*[10]!"

Two men joined him on either side, also bearing Cuban flags. All three repeated the same expression like broken records. We stood there in the middle of the road, looking at these three fools.

"The fourth leg of the table." I hadn't meant to speak aloud.

Chandee turned to me and said, "What did you say?"

"I'll tell you right now, this isn't good at all. Apparently Che's plan has been working."

She looked at me in concern but still not understanding to what I was referring.

The first police cars and fire trucks arrived at the scene. More patrols and emergency vehicles started to arrive, and they began to deplane the passengers. They brought small minibuses and loaded the passengers inside, including the three men with the Cuban flags. They,

---

[10] *Down with the Yankee imperialists!*

however, didn't remain on the bus for very long. Soon, the G-2 arrived, and with extreme courtesy removed the three men from the bus, offering them mineral water, cigarettes, and Habanos cigars. I could see the men speaking with the authorities, but I was too far away to hear anything.

Because of my uniform, we weren't stopped, and I walked closer to the patrol cars. I came within three or four feet of the man who looked like the other three, drinking from a bottle of mineral water. I nodded my head in greeting, and he returned my nod. The three men were loaded into the back of one of the G-2 cars and were driven off in a different direction from the other passengers.

The resemblance of this man to Yuri, Marko, and Marcelino was so extraordinary that if someone were trying to identify any of these men, they would be utterly indistinguishable. I knew this as I had seen all four up close myself. I walked over to a lieutenant by his patrol car.

We saluted, and I asked, "Do you know, lieutenant, where they're taking these men?"

The lieutenant was short and dark-skinned, with a very short mustache. He replied in a friendly fashion, "I believe they are taking them to the headquarters of the G-2."

"They don't speak too much Spanish, eh?" I asked.

"No, almost none. But one of them speaks fluent Russian. I understand it very well, having studied it for the past two years in night school."

"That is very good, comrade," I replied. "Russian is the language of the future."

"I told the G-2 agents that he told me he wanted them to take him and his two friends to Commander Ernesto

Guevara. He was very cocky; I think he has a chip on his shoulder."

I nodded and smiled. "Actually, I'm on Commander Ernesto Guevara's team. He is not in the city. He left very early this morning." I wanted to impress the lieutenant to get more information from him.

"Oh!" the lieutenant exclaimed with increased admiration and respect. Chandee stood near me, and he suddenly took notice of her, assuming she was part of Che's team as well. He smiled and greeted her politely. "Hello, how are you doing, *compañera*."

Chandee looked at him. "Hello, comrade," she replied.

"How did you get here so quickly?" I asked him. "I know there's not a police station between here and the next town, and it's probably about fifteen to twenty minutes back to Havana. You got here right away."

"They called us almost two hours ago," he answered. "They told us to be prepared for a plane that could land anywhere at any minute."

"Oh, that long?"

"Yes. Evidently, something's been going on for a while."

"Hm," I said, "then someone knew this plane was coming."

"Yes, actually, we could see this plane circling around for a while from the station."

I raised my right arm. "Well, lieutenant, we're going in that direction, but it's going to be difficult to get through all this traffic and congestion. I'll turn around and get that *media noches* in El Parador some other time."

He raised his arm in protest. "No, no—Commander, don't worry." He patted the hood of his patrol car. "With this baby, we'll get you through here no problem. Just follow me."

"OK," I answered, "thank you."

He turned on his lights and siren, and we followed him through the congestion. As we passed by him at the end, I waved to him from the window and called out once more, "Thank you!" We continued on towards our destination.

After we reached the coffee shop, we sat in a comfortable booth, and ordered our *media noches* and *guarapo*[11]. As we ate, I explained to Chandee some of the details related to the incident we had just witnessed.

I learned later on through my sources that the flight engineers in the air traffic control tower had had no idea what to do with the plane when they asked permission to land. They had to put the plane in a holding pattern until someone in the bureaucracy could tell them what to do with the hijacked aircraft. It took so long to get the green light that the plane ran out of fuel. No one dared to give the final approval for the landing until someone at the top could be reached to give it. The pilot had no choice but to land on the highway at that point.

Originating in Dallas, Texas, it was the first of many hijacked planes headed to Havana.

As the government made it more and more difficult to leave Cuba, people would steal planes and boats to leave the island. Castro and Che used their network of spies in the United States to hijack planes to Cuba as a way to blackmail the U.S. government to return the stolen planes and ships in exchange for the return of the hijacked

---

[11] *Sugar cane juice*

vessels. At the same time, it created a pipeline to transport spies from the U.S. into Cuba without leaving any kind of record.

    Meanwhile, the G-2 broke down the door of Marcel and Fraya's house in Pinar del Rio and arrested them. The good people, who had saved my life after injuries I sustained during the theft of Che's portfolio from the regiment, were held in an underground facility and subjected to torture and interrogation. The only thing found in the search of their house were two bottles of contraband guayabita del pinar, which Marcel claimed to have bought from someone in the street. They were accused of manufacturing the liquor, and it was excuse enough to detain them.

    After many hours of interrogation without any success in breaking either of them down and nothing else to hold them for, the man in charge of the inquiry lost his temper. In his frustration, he began to beat Marcel in front of Fraya. Both Marcel's eyes were swollen completely shut. Fraya screamed insults at the torturers and begged them to leave Marcel alone, insisting he had done nothing wrong.

    The agent in charge moved Fraya to a different room with a large window through which she could see them continue to torture Marcel. They felt the isolation would make it easier to break them down psychologically. Marcel lost consciousness, and remained so for a while in spite of repeated attempts of the interrogators to revive him.

    Finally, they were able to rouse him. They continued the beating, asking questions; Marcel continued to maintain his innocence. They stopped asking him about the liquor and began interrogating him about being involved in counterrevolutionary activity and espionage. As this was going on, the man guarding Fraya held her face against the glass partition so that she was compelled to watch her husband's torture.

"We know you gave a couple of bottles of the liquor to the Commandantico to give to his father," one of the interrogators said. "What kind of relationship do you have with this kid? You have any connection with spies outside of the country? Are you his contact? He told us you gave him those bottles for his father, and he also told us that you hid Che's portfolio for him."

Fraya's eyes bulged, and she screamed, "That is not true! The portfolio is empty, and the Little Commander took its contents!"

All the interrogators stopped beating Marcel and went into Fraya's room. They looked at her in surprise. She was bound by hands and feet to her chair. Marcel stared at her in recrimination. Fraya realized the vast indiscretion she had made and tried to rectify it. "Yes, the plates of food he brought to us from his sister's wedding! He picked them up and took them back to his family."

The leader of the G-2 team grabbed her by the lower jaw and twisted her around to look him in the face. Fraya looked panicked.

The fat balding man screamed in her face so closely that his saliva sprayed over her face and into her mouth. "You stupid nigger! You think we're morons? That is not what you just said to us. I don't care if that portfolio is full, empty, in three thousand pieces, whatever—I want it! If you tell me another lie, I'll pull your teeth out!" He put on a set of brass knuckles on his right hand.

She looked at him with an expression blended of anger, terror, and defiance. She said, "You don't have a mother, boy? What a great warrior you are, hitting a woman tied by her hands and feet."

The leader screamed at her, "Yes, I got a mother, but she is a decent woman, not a nigger counterrevolutionary bitch who deals in contraband!" He didn't release her face, and punched her in the mouth with his right arm. Fraya screamed in pain and spat out a few bloody teeth. Her upper lip was burst and bleeding, and the blow stunned her into semi-consciousness.

Marcel was watching this from the other side. In a voice filled with pain and frustration, he yelled, "No, no! Not her, please! Tell me what you want to know, and I will tell you. If I don't know, I will invent it. Just don't touch her anymore, please. Tell me what you want me to testify to, but don't hurt her anymore! For God's sake, she's a nurse!"

A few men went back to question him. A tall, dark-skinned agent asked him, "Where is Che's portfolio?"

Marcel put his head down and murmured something.

"What? What did you say? Louder!"

"Burned," Marcel said a little louder. "Burned in one of the charcoal ovens."

The leader heard that and left Fraya to join the group. He kicked Marcel in the knee with one of his boots. He screamed, "If that is true, we will go back to your house, and you will dig in those ovens until you find at least a piece of that portfolio! We have to have proof that what you're saying is the truth. I need evidence to show to my boss."

"You're not going to find anything," Marcel said. "Only ashes. It's been too long, and too much time has passed." He was about to continue, but the leader stopped him.

"You'd better pray to whatever you believe in, nigger, that we find something we can show to Piñeiro or your wife will not only lose the rest of her teeth—she will lose her life! Where are the documents from inside the briefcase?"

"He took them with him," he murmured, once more barely audibly.

"*Carajo!*" the leader exclaimed. "You'd better say things louder—we can't hear what you're saying."

Marcel raised his head up. "The Little Commander took all the contents with him."

The leader screamed to his assistant, "Porfirio, go to my office and call Commander Piñeiro and tell him we need authorization to search the Little Commander's home. Tell him that the charcoal man has confessed."

They brought some papers for Marcel to sign. The assistant went into an office, picked up the phone, and dialed a number.

A muted conversation ensued, and a few minutes later, he said to the leader, "Commander Piñeiro wants to speak to you, boss."

"Hold on," the leader said. He said to Marcel, "Sign here." Marcel signed the document.

The leader gathered up the papers and went into the office, leaving the door open. He picked up the receiver and said, "Yes, Commander? Yes, it's me, Lieutenant del Balle. Yes, sir, I'm sure. I have his signed confession in my hand." He paused for a while. "Believe me, Commander, this won't be an embarrassment to anyone, but it will be an achievement for you. I'm pretty sure I'll find the proof I need." He looked apprehensive and touched his neck. "Yes, sir, I understand. I'll put my head on the plate for you, because I'm certain I'll find what you're looking for. But we have to move very fast. The black man assured me that he burned the leather attaché case. He also assured me that the Commandantico took with him the contents. The only place he could hide all this documentation is in his house."

He made a victorious pump with his arm. "OK, then! Don't worry, Commander. We will find it, no matter where he's hidden it. We'll have the evidence to put that little son of a bitch behind bars or in front of a firing squad. OK, Commander, I will order the search right now. Good-bye."

He hung up the phone and returned to the torture chamber. "Porfirio, get all the cars ready. We'll need the tools to break doors and furniture. We have the green light, and we have to find this, or my head will roll. We'll even dig up the noses of these people until we find what we're looking for!"

In the coffee shop, Chandee and I were finishing our dinner with a dessert of flan topped with shredded coconut. After we finished and paid, we drove back onto the highway to return to Havana. We were passing by the place where the plane had landed, and the traffic had started to slow down. Only one lane was open in both directions, as the police were still controlling traffic because the emergency workers had not yet figured out how they were going to tow that large craft back to the airport. We finally crept through the congestion and found ourselves in more normal traffic the rest of the way.

Chandee said, "You know, I sometimes try to imagine for myself what life might be like outside of Cuba. When I see my friends leaving the country, I just don't know if I could ever accustom myself to living in another country." She shook her head. She continued sadly, "I don't think I could ever leave Cuba. When I think how I could never come back here, I get a pain right here, over my heart."

I smiled and said, "Don't ever say 'never.' I read in a book that 'never' doesn't even exist. When we use that word, without even knowing it, our subconscious considers the possibility of doing the exact opposite of what we say we will never do."

Chandee smiled and waved her hand over her head. "Whoa, that's too deep. It shot right over my head!" She reached out with her left hand and squeezed mine. "You know, I like you very much, but you're prohibited to me. Your heart is in the hands of one of my best friends, Yaneba." She reached inside her shirt and started fluttering it over her heart. "When you talk like that, my heart goes like this, and you give me goose bumps."

She released my hand and started to flutter it like it was shivering. "You conquer my soul, and I want to say with all my heart, 'Goodbye, Yaneba, my great friend'. As the old saying goes, between good friends, what is mine is mine, and what is yours is mine. Now, your irresistible Julio Antonio is mine, and I'm not sharing him with anyone!" She giggled mischievously.

I pointed at her with my right hand and said, "*Chinita, chinita*—keep playing with me, and one of these days I will believe it. Then you'll be in big trouble."

She pointed her finger back at me. "In trouble with you? Noooo, if you are anything, you are a complete gentleman."

I smiled and shook my head. "*Chinita, chinita cubanita*—you are like a little sardine with olive oil, constantly slipping out of my fingers. OK, if I don't go back tomorrow to Pinar del Rio, I will pick you up for a fancy dinner at the Hilton—or, as the new leaders call it today, the Havana Libre." I added that last part with a touch of sarcasm.

We arrived at her house. I stopped the car in front of the store, got out, and opened her door. She got out, embraced me, and gave me a long, strong kiss on my cheek. "You take care of yourself, OK?" she said. "This is very serious now." She touched her chest with her left hand. "I have a very deep love for you."

I brushed her cheek with my hand. "Me, too—I have the same love for you."

I drove back to the house in Boca Siega. The soldiers informed me that they had to take Fausto to the hospital, as the diarrhea had turned into severe colitis. He couldn't even leave the toilet. They gave him a couple of shots, which made him feel better, and he was able to return to the house. He was sleeping under sedation at present.

I went to bed, but I couldn't sleep that night. I was afflicted with horrible nightmares, like someone was persecuting me, and no matter how far or fast I ran, I couldn't get away. By the same token, even though the man following me was very near, he could never seem to quite catch me.

I rose in the afternoon very tired. I took a hot shower, dressed, and went to Fausto's room. He told me that he

The Dark Face of Marxism

had instructions from Che that unless the investigator or one of the ambassadors wanted to speak to me again, I could return to Pinar del Rio today if I wanted to. He still wasn't feeling well, and asked, if I didn't mind, to wait until Che returned from Santiago del Cuba either tonight or tomorrow morning. I let him know that I had no problems waiting. He gave me some vouchers for food when I told him that I wanted to take my friend to dinner. After I ate some fruit and a few pieces of cheese and orange juice, I left around 6:00 p.m. towards Havana.

When I arrived, I called Chandee and let her know I would be there in a little while. She let me know that she was already waiting for me. Shortly after, I reached her house and picked her up. As we left her house, something caught my attention. A car started to follow us a few blocks later and tailed us until we arrived at the Hilton.

Chandee saw me continually checking the rear-view mirror. "We have a tail?" she asked.

"I believe so," I replied, "but it doesn't look like it's any danger. It looks like it's a passive civilian. Evidently, someone wants to know our movements. If this continues, I want you to tell your father immediately, so that he's prepared and not caught by surprise. I don't want him to be compromised for any reason."

"Very well," she said.

They treated us like royalty when we arrived at the hotel in that car. We had an exquisite dinner—quiche Lorraine, lobster bisque, shrimp in a Béarnaise sauce for Chandee, and filet mignon with a rosemary and mushroom wine sauce for me. After we finished, I ordered crème brûlée and some napoleons as well as Cuban guava and coconut pies for Chandee to take home to her family. Even though we were having a great time, something wasn't letting me relax and enjoy this.

"If you don't mind waiting for a few minutes," I told Chandee, "I want to use a phone to call my mother in Pinar de Rio. I had a bad dream last night, and until I hear from my family, I won't be at peace."

She smiled. "For God's sake, go and make that call! I'll wait for you here and enjoy these lovely pastries."

"Don't eat too many, or you'll put on some weight and start to get plump."

She smiled and puffed out her cheeks.

I smiled and went to the telephones. I felt a release, eager to get this off my chest once and for all. There was a long line of phones next to the elevators. I picked up a phone and gave my number to the operator. She made the connection and let me know that I could talk now. My youngest sister, who was still single and living at home, answered.

"It's your brother, Julio Antonio. How are you doing? Is everything OK?"

My sister answered in a very unusual tone, "No, no—let me pass you to Mima, so she can explain to you."

A few seconds later, Mima came to the phone. She was sobbing.

"What happened, Mima?" I asked.

In between sobs, she replied, "Some very rude imbeciles from the G-2 woke us up before dawn. They made the house a disaster! They even ripped the mattresses in the bedrooms. The door to your closet is broken. These cretins have turned this house into a calamity!" A knot formed in my throat as I heard that, and my stomach began to tremble, just at the thought of the documents I had in my closet under the shoe rack.

"Calm down, Mima. If anything has been broken, it can be replaced, but your health cannot. Don't let this upset you. What did they tell you was the reason they did this?"

I was trying to give strength to my poor mother, even though I was beginning to lose my own calm. I was impatient to find out what had happened. I had to control myself, however, because I wouldn't accomplish anything rushing her.

I breathed deeply several times as she continued her litany of what the G-2 had broken in the house.

"Mima, what happened? What did they tell you? Mima, stop—stop, please! Did they find anything? Did they arrest anybody?"

She understood my anxiety and regained control. "No, my son. Relax. As I told those morons when they came in, they would be leaving with empty hands the same way they came in. This is a decent house, I told them, and they would find no contraband here, which is what they said they were here to find. They left with empty hands, exactly as I told them they would. They left with their tails between their legs." This last she said with pride.

She started to sob again. "Those animals even broke open the cover on the piano keyboard! They couldn't wait for me to get the key for them!"

"It's OK, Mima, calm down. Don't get upset. It's not good for your health."

"How can I not be upset, my son?" she demanded. "You should see what they've done. It's a disaster. They came here with their Captain Leiva, not even dressed in military uniforms but looking like hobos. He told me

Marcel, the charcoal man, accused you of buying contraband liquor from him to give to your father and friends. Ha! I knew that was not true! It was all lies—inventions for these abusers to find whatever the hell they had in their heads to look for." She started to sob again, "I've already called your father. He's coming home from Guane, and I've called Canen and your sister, and they're also on their way over here. When do you plan to come back home?"

"Probably either tonight or tomorrow. Stay calm. These sons of bitches will pay a high price for doing what they did to you and our family."

"Don't say bad words, my son," she interrupted me. "You only bring yourself down to their level. Come back home quickly. You have to return to your studies, your music, and the things you like to do. Your education is the only valid thing you will have in your future."

"Yes, Mima, I know," I said lovingly. "But I cannot cut the commitments I have with these people all at once. It has to be done slowly. I don't want to create problems for myself, nor more problems for you guys."

"I know, my son. I know you're smart and know what needs to be done and how. Take care and come home. I love you very much."

"I love you, too, Mima. I will be there as soon as possible."

I hung up the phone, heartbroken at the thought of my mother dealing with this humiliation. I knew their methods and how they would conduct a search of those they thought were against the revolution. I knew these were Piñeiro's dogs, and I knew how much they loved to scream at and insult people, trying to find evidence that might not even exist—sometimes even fabricating evidence to prove that the person they are investigating is a counterrevolutionary. I thanked God and Jesus Christ that apparently they hadn't found the documents. I had brought the diamonds with me and concealed them with the Habanos cigars, safely lodged in the security box at my uncle's house. What I couldn't fathom was how, if they had broken into my closet, these professionals did not find the plastic bag beneath my shoe rack.

Of course, they might actually have found it and were just pretending not to. They might have taken it to show to Piñeiro, who by then would have shown it to Fidel. They would have only to proceed with my arrest once they got the green light from him.

I was completely lost in this train of thoughts and remained there, standing with the receiver still in my hand. The phone rang, snapping me out of my reverie. Thinking it might be Mima calling back, I answered the phone. "Hello, who is this?"

A feminine voice said, "Yes, sir. I'm sorry, this is the operator for the telephone company. You need to deposit an extra three quarters, one dime, and one nickel. You owe an extra 75 *centavos*[12] for the long-distance overtime."

"No problem," I answered. I deposited the coins.

The operator said, "Thank you. Have a great evening, and thank you for using our service."

"You're welcome," I replied and hung up the phone. Still worried and frustrated, I directed my steps back to our

---

[12] *The Cuban quarter was worth 20 centavos*

table where Chandee was grinning from ear to ear when she saw me.

She took my left arm and squeezed it with some strength. "Look to your right," she whispered. "See who is sitting there."

Ava Gardner

Marcello Mastroianni

I turned and saw the Cuban actors Rosita Fornés and Armando Bianchi. With them sat the American movie star Ava Gardner and the famous Italian actor Marcelo Mastronianni. They noticed that we recognized them, and Ava Gardner raised a hand and wiggled her fingers to us in greeting. We bowed our heads to return the greeting. Chandee was smiling broadly; I courteously tried to smile, but my worries made it a trifle wan.

I wasn't thinking about the actors. What crossed my mind was that Che's promise to make some phone calls might have merely been a hook to bring me in and make me do what they wanted me to do. Behind my back, instead of calling off Piñeiro's dogs, he may have unleashed the entire pack. As I linked all of these things together in my brain, I thought this all might be a very complicated trap to catch me and bring me before a firing squad, exactly as Canen had tried to warn me. His words kept returning to me in the midst of my mental anguish.

My disturbed state was evident. When I looked at Chandee smiling and so happy in that magnificent restaurant, sitting in the same room as her favorite movie and television actors, she could perceive my turmoil. She stopped and asked, "What happened to you? You're the color of my napkin."

I held my linen napkin to my mouth and coughed in an attempt to clear out the knot in my throat. I took a sip of water and replied, "I have multiple reasons to be worried. My mother just informed me that the G-2 came to our house very early this morning and conducted a meticulous search of the house—particularly my bedroom."

Chandee paled. She put her right hand to her mouth. "Do you have anything compromising there?" Her eyes were filled with panic, and she held out her other hand to my arm as she waited for my answer.

I looked at her gravely. "What do you think?" was all I said. She raised both hands and covered her face in anxiety. She shook her head.

I hurriedly try to reassure her. "Calm down. My mother said they didn't find anything. Act very calm and natural, because those two people at the table to your right who came in after us haven't taken their eyes off of us. They might be the same people who followed us from your house. I think it's time to quietly get out of here and leave the building."

"Yes, I think that is the most prudent thing to do, under the circumstances."

I raised my right arm to signal my need for service to the waiter. He saw me and approached our table. "Could you please bring our bill?" I asked. I took my wallet out of my uniform pants.

The waiter held up his hand. "I'm sorry, Commandante, but your bill is already paid. Rosita Fornés and Armando Bianchi already picked up the tab."

Bianchi saw us speaking to the waiter and saw him gesture in the direction of the table. He smiled and gave us a reverence with his left hand. I smiled and returned the gesture with my right. I wanted to give a tip to the waiter, who was still standing by our table.

With a great deal of class he smiled broadly. "No, no—what are those people going to think if I accept a tip from you when they paid your bill and provided me with a generous tip? I would look like a greedy and dishonest person. I don't think you would want me to look like that, would you?"

I put my wallet away and smiled. "No, I don't. My intention was to reward you because you are an A class waiter and provided excellent service. I wanted to compensate you, not punish you." He smiled in satisfaction, brushed the table with a small brush, picket up our plates, and walked away.

I said to Chandee, "Wait for me for a few seconds. I want to go over there and express my gratitude to your idols."

She smiled and nodded. "Yes, they are my idols, especially Bianchi."

I walked slowly over to their table. Before I could even extend my hand to anyone, I said, "Good evening, my name is Julio Antonio del Marmol. I just came over here to thank you for your extreme kindness and gentility. When it comes from people as famous as you are, the courtesy is multiplied by a thousand." I shook hands with Armando and Marcello and kissed Rosita's and Ava's hands.

While I had Ava's hand in mine, she smiled from ear to ear and said in very good Spanish, "Oh, my God, there are still gentlemen on this earth! And such a young gentleman, too! You are the youngest Commander in this revolution, and it is a pleasure to have you with us. I believe you are the closest friend Fidel Castro has. Rosita and Armando have been telling me that you are by his side at almost every single speech. Is that pistol real?"

"It is," I answered. I unsnapped the holster. "Do you want to see it?"

"No, no," she said. "That's OK."

Rosita asked me, "How old are you?"

"Thirteen," I answered. "I will be fourteen in May."

She smiled knowingly. Ava asked me, "What day in May were you born?"

"The twenty-first," I replied.

"Ah," she said, "you are a Taurus!"

"Half and half," I said. "I'm on the cusp line between Gemini and Taurus."

Ava grabbed my hand and said, "Why don't you come with us? Do you like music?"

"I love music—I study it and play the drums."

"Really? Oh, you're going to love this! We're going to a soiree with classical music."

"I love all kinds of music," I answered.

Bianchi said to me, "It's very nearby. It's in the penthouse of the Focsa Building, a few blocks from here. Maestro Carlos Anzas, the director of the Symphonic Orchestra of CMQ television, will be playing piano for all of us."

I thought for a moment about that. Even though I was completely devoted to music and would love to listen to Maestro Carlos Anzas, I hesitated because my frame of mind and demeanor weren't conducive to mingling with these people. Before I decided this selfishly, I gestured to Chandee to involve her in the conversation.

Ava had not let go of my hand, but she did now as soon as she saw me motion to Chandee. Rosita noticed I was calling my companion over and said, "You can bring your girlfriend with you."

"No," I said, "she is not my girlfriend. She is only my good friend."

Chandee came over, and I introduced her to everyone. Marcelo said with a wink to me, "If she is not your girlfriend, you shouldn't waste any time and hurry up before someone else gets her. She is a very beautiful and exotic *chinita*." I smiled at his use of my term for her when she was bugging me too much.

Chandee curtsied and said, "Thank you very much, sir, for your compliments."

Marcelo said, "It's not a compliment, sweetie, it's the truth. You are a taker."

Ava nudged Marcelo. "Knock it off—she's too young for you!"

I smiled and asked Chandee, "Do you want to go to a soiree with Maestro Carlos Anzas? They've invited us and told me it's only a few blocks away in the Focsa Building."

"I love it!" she said. "But I don't know if you have the time."

I knew Chandee was dying to go and mingle with all those people, but she was intelligent and leaving the door open for me to bow out, knowing the turmoil I was in. Thinking of the great sacrifice she was offering to make, I decided that I could enjoy it as well and so replied, "We can go. I'm not in any rush."

"Very well," Bianchi replied. He took an invitation from the beautiful white coat he was wearing and handed to me. "Give this to the valet, and they'll key you up into the private penthouse elevator. We'll see each other in a little while."

We thanked all of them, said goodbye, and left for the lobby of the hotel. I noticed the two men who had been observing us while we ate rushed to pay and almost ran behind us. They hadn't even ordered food, just drinks. I thought they were clumsy agents and could at least be more discreet. As we passed the phones in the lobby, I asked Chandee, "Do you mind waiting for me here? I want to call Fausto in Boca Siega and see if Che has returned yet or not."

"No, go ahead," she said.

I left her sitting in the lobby and turned suddenly, catching the men by surprise. They ducked into the gift shop in the lobby to look through some magazines. I passed by them and looked to make sure I could recognize them if I ever saw them again. I went to the phone and called the safe house. One of the guards answered.

"How is Fausto doing?"

"He's doing better," he answered. He then put Fausto on the line.

"Fausto," I asked him, "you're getting better, eh?"

"Well, at least I don't have to go every five minutes," he replied, "but the diarrhea hasn't stopped completely. Che called me to find out how everything went today in your deposition. When I told him everything went better than we had planned, practically to perfection, he was very, very happy. He told me he will be back tonight for sure. He doesn't know how late, though."

I said, "I will probably be late, myself. I'm going with some friends to a soiree in Vedado, in the penthouse of the FOCSA with Maestro Carlos Anzas."

"Go ahead and enjoy, man, you deserve it."

"I need it. I had a very bad day and some distressing news from my family in Pinar del Rio."

"What happened?"

"Well, my mother told me the G-2 searched the house and destroyed everything they found in their way." I didn't know if Fausto was really surprised, or just pretending, but his reaction sounded sincere.

"What sons of bitches!" he exclaimed. "Let me tell you something—I used to work for Piñeiro, before I joined Che's team. I was one of his most trustworthy men. The reason I left him and will never work with him again, even if he's the last person on Earth, is because he is a poisonous snake with multiple heads. I can assure you that whatever happened with your family, he had something to do with it. That whole thing has his signature on it!" He sounded very resentful—or it could have been extremely good acting.

"Can you imagine it?" I said. "My mother has a heart condition, and these sons of bitches break in at dawn. My father was the main backer of the Revolution, and his cousin, Menelao Mora Morales, was one of the engineers of the attack on Batista's palace and died in the attack! He was the one who took the *Radio Reloj*[13] to call the Cuban people to arms and rebel against the Dictator."

"Take it easy, man," he said. "Che will put him in his place. If Piñeiro is afraid of anyone, it's Che. When I tell Che about this, all hell is going to break loose. I can guarantee you that. Che doesn't like him at all! Go and enjoy, relax—we'll take care of this later."

We said goodbye and hung up. I went back to the lobby, got Chandee, and retrieved the Mercedes from the valet parking. We drove to the FOCSA Building.

When I arrived at the underground parking structure, I realized they had to be some of Piñeiro's dogs from the G-2. The car following us was a different one, and the men inside it were not the same men as before. In a

---

[13] *The radio station*

government like this one, the only agency that would have that kind of manpower was the G-2.

When we arrived at the valet parking, two attendants simultaneously opened both doors for us. One gave me a ticket, and I handed him the invitation. He motioned to the captain attendant, who was dressed in the full uniform with large boots, epauletted jacket, and top hat. He walked us to one of the elevators, opened a side compartment, and inserted a key in the revealed keyhole. He pushed the button for the penthouse as he held the elevator door open.

The FOCSA building in Havana

He bobbed to us politely and asked, "Do you want me to escort you to the penthouse?"

"No," I answered, "that's not necessary."

The man was tall, light-skinned with a neatly trimmed mustache. He spoke with a British accent. "You two have a pleasant and delightful evening."

We both thanked him at the same time. He stepped off the elevator and removed his hand. The door closed. Chandee smiled broadly as she observed the luxury of the elevator, with its gold trim, small lights, and ceiling mirror accents.

She took my arm and asked, "Can you imagine what my friends will say, when I tell them about going to a soiree with Rosita Fornés, Armando, and all these other famous people?"

"Don't get too excited," I cautioned her. "You might see even bigger celebrities."

"No, these four are enough for me," she replied. She touched my shoulder. "It's unbelievable what you can accomplish with this uniform."

"You know," I said, "I've gotten accustomed to it, but in the beginning, it made me feel uncomfortable. Even guilty."

"Guilty? Never! Utilize to the maximum what you have to use against them. What they're giving to you and spending is the money from your family, my family, and all the families all over. They're just giving it back to you. Enjoy what is legitimately yours. Very soon nothing will be in private hands here in Cuba. All the wealth will be in the hands of the government and we all will lose what our ancestors worked for all their lives. Do whatever you can to disrupt this system, especially when you can use their own weapons against them. You're better than any of them, and none of them deserve it as much as you do."

Dr. Julio Antonio del Marmol

The bell of the elevator indicated we had just arrived at the penthouse. The doors opened, and we were taken by the surprise of the moment. The elevator was in the middle of a vast room. The immense living room was filled with people dressed in full evening attire, making both Chandee and I feeling very under dressed. Even the wait staff were dressed in tuxedos and black tie. Ten waiters constantly circulating among the guests, serving drinks and food. The penthouse had beautiful marble floors, with sweeping staircases leading to an upper level, where a small symphonic orchestra was seated and playing Richard Strauss' *Also sprach Zarathustra*, one of my favorites.

It felt like some kind of introduction as we entered. It filled me with mixed emotions, as I remembered my father's love of classical music. It took me back in time to a more nostalgic period in life, as I remembered my childhood, walking in my grandfather's tobacco fields, and I could almost see before my eyes the beautiful countryside. We went to the fountain with the punch. We didn't know how much liquor was in it, but no one stopped us. An attendant offered us each an exquisite Baccarat glass of the punch. We walked over to a dais on the other side, where stood a beautiful white baby grand piano. We stayed there and listened to the lovely music.

It was a mix of the aristocracy: what was left of the old rich and famous movie stars with the new class, as I could see the Minister of Culture, the Minister of Education, and other high officials from different departments of the government. Soon after, Rosita and Armando appeared with Marcelo and Ava. They saw us and waved, and the four of them made their way over, politely avoiding most of the people who were trying to speak to them. With them was a balding, heavyset man of medium height. We knew him on sight, but they introduced the Maestro to us as part of the customary courtesies.

"In a while," Rosita said, "the Maestro will delight us with his music."

Maestro Anzas was a very down-to-earth man and very cordial. He handed me one of his cards, and it identified him as a composer and director as well. "The youngest Commander of the Revolution," he said. "I've seen you many times on TV. You're probably very famous even around the world."

"Not as famous as you," I said, "because your fame is solid and based on talent. That is the fame that endures for hundreds of years. Political fame is like a wave in the ocean—it changes constantly according to the cycles of the moon."

He smiled and looked around. "Ah, ha! Very profound and very deep! The youngest Commander of the Revolution will one day be a great leader."

Everybody smiled, and Chandee could no longer hold back. "You don't even know yet. When you have a chance to have a more extended conversation with him, then you will realize how much truth is in what you just said!"

The Composer smiled and nodded. "And, of course, you would know that better than anyone, because I assume you are his girlfriend."

Chandee smiled and shook her head. "No," she replied, "not that. We are best friends." She affectionately took my arm.

Anzas asked me, "If you like music so much, why don't you study it?"

I smiled and replied, "I play the drums. The Revolution has taken me away from it, but I studied *solfeo y teoria*[14] and took piano lessons. I want to be a composer, like you."

Anzas looked at me companionably. He put his arm around my shoulder and said, "Good, good! I see talent in you, and I haven't even heard you play yet. It gives me great pleasure to hear you say that."

He clapped his hands together in a strangely effeminate way. It appeared that he was so taken by what I had said that he unwittingly stepped out of the closet for a second, because as soon as he realized what he had done, he quickly regained his composure. He said seriously, "By the way, on my card, you have my phone number there, as well as my address. If you need any advice, call me or come over. Bring your friend with you, as well. She's a pleasant and adorable girl. I would be more than glad to teach you everything I know about music." We both thanked him. "You're welcome any time. Call me."

The master of ceremonies stepped up to a microphone. "In a moment, put your hands together for the great maestro, composer, and director of our great CMQ Television, Carlos Anzas. He will produce with his golden fingers the most exquisite music you will ever hear."

Everyone stood up and started applauding respectfully. He stepped up to the dais and thanked everyone. He sat down at the piano, and said, "The first piece I will offer you is by Ludwig van Beethoven. 'Moonlight Sonata.'"

He turned to give some instructions to the musicians around him, and they began playing. When he was

---

[14] *Musical reading and theory*

finished, he said, "Now, I will play 'Rhapsody in Blue' by the great virtuoso, George Gershwin." After conducting this one, he went on to Beethoven's Symphony Number 5 in C minor.

We stood there in rapt attention. Something touched my leg, and I looked down. Chandee was pointing to the elevator. Exiting the elevator were Piñeiro, followed by Che, and after them were the three men we saw exiting the plane. Four guards also came in behind them, but Fausto was missing. My hands started to sweat, as thousands of possibilities crossed my mind, none of them precisely good. My joy abruptly vanished, and I could no longer hear the music; I only heard the drums in my ears and the voices behind them reciting the words, "Ready, Aim, Fire!" followed by the shots reflected by the drums in my ear and my heart.

I thought nothing good could come of this. Piñeiro and Che were looking so friendly together, like they were on a honeymoon. In the most cordial way, Piñeiro bent over to say something to Che in his ear, and they both smiled. The entire group stayed close to the elevators to avoid interrupting, but every eye went to them. Even Carlos Anzas glanced at them curiously as they stole his audience from him.

My legs started to tremble slightly. I tried to nonchalantly massage one leg and then the other, in a discrete attempt to stop them. *What the hell are these two doing together?* I thought. *Che wasn't supposed to return until much later.* I leaned over and whispered in Chandee's ear, "Let's look for a place to sit down. I don't know how much longer I can stand up."

The music started back up, but I didn't notice it. I had to control my nerves and focus my thoughts so that I would be able to answer intelligently any possible questions that might get put to me. Those two manipulative men were probably here for my head, so I had to appear to them calm, like I had nothing to hide.

Using my training, I began to breathe deeply and regularly through my nose and mouth. I mentally repeated to myself over and over that I knew nothing would happen, I was loyal to the Revolution, and if anyone had anything against me, I wanted to see proof before my eyes.

These thoughts went through my head in the time we walked over to one of the corners of the vast room until we found a few empty armchairs and a loveseat. We decided to sit in the loveseat so that we would appear to be a couple of teenagers in love. I briefly wished that I could be an ostrich. I wanted to be imperceptible. However, such luck was not to be mine.

As soon as I looked up to see what Che and his crowd were doing, Che saw me and raised his arm. He mimed to me that as soon as the music stopped, he would come over to me. I realized that he spotted me so quickly because we had been the only people to move at that particular moment and so had drawn attention to ourselves rather than blending in unobtrusively. I acknowledged his signal with my hand, and I gulped.

"Shit, shit, shit," I muttered as I saw Piñeiro gave me an oily smile and a nod. His smile gave me goose bumps. I wondered why he should be so happy. He was famous for having a serious face everywhere he went: we called it his funeral face. Seeing his teeth like that gave me the chills, especially as I thought about Marcel and the tortures he must have endured. I had to wonder what he might have revealed. I worried that I might leave this soiree in handcuffs and straight to the firing squad. I continued my breathing exercises: inhale deeply through the nose, exhale slowly through the mouth.

Chandee noticed this and looked at me compassionately. She reached out and took my hand. "I know you're going through a very bad moment," she said, "but try to relax and control your nerves."

I leaned in and whispered, "Is it that obvious?"

"No, no," she lied. "It's my feminine intuition. I saw you when you watched them come in. You changed colors, and I understand that, after what happened at your house in Pinar del Rio."

I replied, "Yes, especially after Che confessed to me his antipathy towards Piñeiro. I have to ask myself what they're doing together, unless they both are trying to find me. In that case, that means nothing good at all."

"Calm down," she repeated in a voice filled with empathy, "calm down! Remember, you are always in control. Don't lose your nerve. Maybe it's all a coincidence."

I looked dubious. "Well, we'll found out very soon. Whatever happens here tonight, you are just my friend, and you've only known me a very short period of time from visiting your friends and family in Pinar del Rio. I don't want you to be in any trouble. I'll not only have to worry about getting myself out of the situation, I'll have to worry about you as well. Believe it or not, my main regret in the whole thing is that if I have to end this beautiful night in handcuffs, you'll have to return home in a bus. I know how much that's going to bother you."

"OK," she smiled, "I have my Julio Antonio back. I know you will handle it; you're my hero!"

I shook my head. "*Chinita, chinita cubanita*—even heroes get killed in the movies. You know what? I have to leave you for a little while. I have to go to the restroom for a few minutes. Are you going to be OK?"

"Sure, sure—go."

"Don't take your eyes off of these guys. I want to know what you can read at a distance from their demeanor."

"Don't worry," she assured me, "I won't take my eyes off of them." She released my hand.

I excused myself as I moved through the crowd and headed towards the bathrooms. The luxury of the bath was unbelievable. Any normal family with three or four children could have lived comfortably in the bathroom alone. A tall, skinny black man wearing a black tie greeted me with extremely courteous manners. My business at the urinal took only a few seconds, since I didn't really need to go. I just needed to get away and refresh myself a little. I went to the sink and rubbed my face with soap and cold water several times. As I reached for the paper towels, the man handed me a beautiful cloth towel bearing the crest and monogram of the penthouse's previous owners.

"Thank you very much," I said.

He smiled affectionately and asked, "You haven't had a very good day today, eh?"

I half-smiled and asked, "How do you know?"

"Because you just did what I normally do when I'm under a lot of pressure. It works for me and always make me feel better. Did it work for you in the same way?"

This time my smile was fully genuine, and I nodded. "Yes, sir."

He returned my smiled. "I'm very glad, and I hope you have a better evening."

I reached into my pocket to give him some money, and I deposited a few pesos in the tip container. He looked at me gratefully and said, "Thank you. Thank you very much."

I handed him the towel and said, "Thanks to you, my friend."

He held out his hand and said by way of introduction, "Chopin."

I took his hand and shook it. "I'm Julio Antonio del Marmol."

"I know who you are," he said. "You are the Commandantico. I see you by Fidel on all the television programs for the past year."

"Yes, sir," I replied, "that's me. I cannot deny it."

At that moment, Piñeiro and Che entered the bathroom with their escort behind them.

Dr. Julio Antonio del Marmol

The Man and His God

When I was growing up, I remember clearly that men embraced more than one country; sometimes they embraced more than one flag. On occasion, they even loved more than one woman and had more than one son by them. Always, however, when you tried to convince those same men to turn and embrace a different god by force or take away the god they already have, you will discover and be surprised how angry they can become when you touch that subject. They are unwilling to accept or compromise on that particular issue in their lives.

Dr. Julio Antonio del Marmol

Chapter 5: Double Games

I started in surprise.

"Oh, my God!" Chopin exclaimed. "This is my night. I not only have the Commandantico in here, but I also have Che and Piñeiro. All I need is Fidel to walk in, and my night is complete!"

Che smiled, and Piñeiro nodded abruptly. "Thank you," he said with some harshness. "Could you excuse us for a little bit?"

"Sure, Commandante—what do you need?"

"Could you please step outside? We need to have a private conversation."

Chopin picked up the sign that read "Closed for 20 Minutes for Cleaning" and held it up. "No problem! I will see to it that no one comes in and disturbs you."

"That's not necessary," Piñeiro said sourly, "just go and take a break or something. Our men here will see to it that no one comes in."

"Hey," Chopin said in his friendly manner, "it can't hurt. People will see the sign and not even attempt to come in."

Piñeiro shook his head in disgust. "Whatever," he said dismissively.

All four men of the escort left the bathroom behind Chopin. I leaned against the sink, expecting the worst. My hand slid down to rest close to my pistol, in case I needed to draw it to defend myself. Che took the initiative.

"Piñeiro has something he wants to tell you." He looked at the G-2 chief. "Go ahead," he said meaningfully.

My heart seemed to slow for a few seconds, as Piñeiro's voice seemed to slow down like an LP record played at 45 rpm, and his lips moved slowly. Still moving in slow motion, he removed his uniform cap. Finally, he said, "I want to give you my deepest apologies for what my men did to your family and house in Pinar del Rio."

My heart suddenly started to beat a Perez Prado mambo.

"I had no idea what was going on until Che communicated it to me a little while ago."

I remained serious, but I knew better.

He massaged his forehead in embarrassment. "I've already given an order to the man who led that search to replace anything that was damaged. The dubious confessions that originated all of this had been extracted from the charcoal man after being beaten almost to death in front of his wife, who also lost several teeth. Information obtained this way is inherently unreliable. Of course, people will sign anything in the hope of stopping the torture. I want you to know I've had people following you here in Havana under orders to protect you following the attempt on your life in Pinar del Rio. Che has asked me to cease this immediately, however. But my people never were following you to harm you."

Who would actually believe any of that? I thought.

He dramatically swept his left hand to his chest. "I, in particular, have always looked at you with admiration, like you were my son. I would never doubt your loyalty to Fidel or the Revolution. You believe me, don't you?"

The Dark Face of Marxism

I didn't answer but merely nodded. I was skeptical; I couldn't understand why he was apologizing to me like this. I also could not figure out what business Che had there. The answer had to be in the details, but I didn't have any.

Che stepped forward and gently but firmly pushed Piñeiro aside to embrace me. "Thank you very much for your excellent work at the deposition yesterday with the ambassadors and that insurance company investigator. Everything went so well that the investigator assured us that we will receive a check in two weeks, if not before. The French ambassador, Pierre, is so fond of you that he has asked if I will allow him to take you to Paris with him. He wants to show you off. You are a character from a movie."

Piñeiro listened to Che's praise with a sour expression, his mouth working like it was dry, or perhaps he was feeling a little nauseous.

"I called Pierre," Che continued, "and asked him to join us here, but he's very sick, apparently some kind of stomach flu. But he said he would love to see you again. You made a great impression on him! Also, he told me as a good communist, you like to share and that you're a very good kid. You weren't selfish and offered them the excellent cigars that I gave to you as a present."

I had to control myself to keep from bursting out in laughter.

I smiled and said, "The next time you talk to him, thank him from me for all these great compliments. I have to tell you, though, that the Belgian ambassador didn't want to believe that those cigars came from you."

Dr. Julio Antonio del Marmol

Che shook his head. "These capitalists are so distrustful, they never believe anything you say. What can you expect? He's probably a CIA agent!" He put one of his arms around my shoulder. "You go and call your mom and tell her I said that first thing in the morning tomorrow, people from the Department of Illegal Property Seizure will bring a brand-new piano to replace the one that was damaged during the search."

I looked at Piñeiro in recrimination and then nodded to Che. "Thank you," I said.

We walked out of the bathroom. The G-2 head looked like he wanted to run out of there. I saw Chopin outside and said, "Thank you very much, my friend." I winked at him. "You are a good man."

"Thank you, Commandantico," he said. "Thank you!"

Che said in a low voice, "Come with me. I want to introduce you to the fourth leg of the table. This is a very special leg. I want you to take a good look at him and give me your opinion later on when we see each other in Boca Siega. I want to talk to you about a few other things."

We made our way through the crowd. Piñeiro walked behind us unhappily, speaking to his bodyguards. The music stopped, and I could see Carlos, Rosita, and the others could not take their eyes off of us as we walked around the room. As we walked by Chandee, I said, "I want to introduce you to a friend. Che, this is Chandee, one of my best friends."

"You are his best friend?" Che said to her jovially. "He is my best friend, too! You take good care of him, OK?"

"Of course," Chandee said as she raised her left hand in a salute to him. She smiled and asked me, "Is everything OK?"

The Dark Face of Marxism

I made an OK sign and replied, "Excellent."

"I will let him come back to you in a minute," Che said. As we walked away, he asked me, "Is she just a friend?"

I smiled and nodded ambiguously. "Well, you know...." I let him take me to the group by the elevator. The three men were drinking champagne out of the Baccarat glasses. Even up close, it was difficult to distinguish the man from either Yuri, Marko, or Marcelino. As we drew close to them, Che said something in Russian to that man. He introduced me, and the man held out his hand to me.

"I'm Lee Oswald," he said. "*Mucho gusto.*"

The real Lee Harvey Oswald

I smiled and replied with a nod, "I'm Julio Antonio del Marmol, el Commandantico." He looked at me in bewilderment, like he didn't quite catch what I had last said.

He asked Che something in Russian, who replied in the same language. He then smiled like an idiot—or pretending he was an idiot. He said, "*Mucho gusto. Mis amigos*," he continued in broken Spanish, pointing to his two associates. He pointed to the first one and said, "Kresken."

He was a tall, blonde man, who stepped forward and held out his hand to me. "*Mucho gusto*."

Lee pointed to the second man and said, "And this one is Malkov."

Malkov also nodded his head and held out his hand. He repeated the same words, as if they had all learned them by rote before coming to Cuba: "*Mucho gusto*." His skin was white, almost albino, with straight dark hair. Both were of very muscular build, like they were bodyguards or specially trained agents from the KGB.

Piñeiro could apparently no longer take the cold shoulder, as we had been utterly ignoring him. He said politely, "Well, I will leave now." He looked at Che. "I will attend to those things you told me to do right now."

We said goodbye to him, and he left with two of the guards behind him. The other two remained with Che. I knew them, and we nodded to each other.

Che spoke to Lee and his associates in Russian. He gestured towards me with his hand and they nodded to me. His body language seemed to indicate he was telling them he needed to say something to me. He held my shoulder and moved me away from them. Once we were a little separated from their group, he asked, "What do you think of our fourth leg?"

I shook my head in amazement. "Unbelievable!" I exclaimed. "You can't tell any difference between those four men—they might be quadruplets."

Che smiled and stroked his beard. "I'm glad you think like that. I think so, too. But this one is completely

The Dark Face of Marxism

different from the others. He thinks he's smart, and he has in his mind that he will be pinning the donkey's tail on our ass, but it doesn't even cross his mind that I will pin the tail on his ass. By the time he realizes that, it will be too late."

I didn't understand completely. I only had pieces of this plan. He saw my puzzled expression and said, "Don't worry—I will explain in detail later."

"OK," I said.

"What do you think of the apology from Piñeiro?" he asked. "I made him come over here to do it."

"You want me to tell you the truth?" I asked him.

"Of course. Always."

"False and very unconvincing. In my opinion, those men in Pinar del Rio would never dare to act like that and go to my house without the consent of someone extremely high up in the G-2, and that somebody had to be him. None of them would want their heads to roll. You know that."

He smiled and shook his head. "You're too smart. Of course I know that. And that is why I forced him to come with me. He said he would apologize to you later, and I told him no. I wanted him to give you that apology in my presence, and not some half-assed apology later on with no one around. Did you see the shame in his face? That is the reason he left so quickly, like a dog with its tail between its legs."

I nodded to him. "Thank you—thank you very much."

"You're welcome. It's nothing—that is the reason we are friends, why we're working together now, and why we'll work together in the future. By the way, Piñeiro assured me that he will call the G-2 in Pinar del Rio and make sure that your friends, the charcoal man and his wife, will sleep in their house tonight. That is why he had to get out of here."

"I hope you're right and that son of a bitch lets those poor people go home. I cannot understand why those who get a little power in their hands like to abuse those who are defenseless and helpless." I shook my head and said sourly, "I don't know if this will ever end."

Che looked at me solemnly. "That, chico, is the reason we are fighting and trying to destroy all the religions that divide men and the capitalist system that has enslaved everyone around the world."

I nodded but thought, You've forgotten that all of this is the product of your socialist ideas.

I cleared my throat to contain what I really wanted to scream aloud. Instead, I said, "Well, we will meet later in Boca Siega. I'm going to take my friend back to her house and call my mother before it's too late and they go to sleep."

"I will have a conference with these men," he replied, "and we will put them on a plane to Russia. It probably won't take me more than an hour or two. I'll see you back at the house."

We said goodbye and I went back to Chandee, who was waiting impatiently in the group with Rosita. As I walked up, the first thing out of her mouth was, "Is everything OK?"

I smiled and said, "Yes, excellent. I'll explain later."

Ava Gardner burst out immodestly, "I came to Cuba with the intention of sleeping with Fidel, but I've been here for a couple of weeks, completely frustrated. Maybe, if you introduce me to Che, he could put an end to my frustration." She looked at me coquettishly.

Everyone burst out laughing. Rosita blushed and clapped her hand to her mouth. "Ava!" she exclaimed. "These are minors! For God's sake, have you no shame?"

I elbowed Chandee and said, "Ava, if that is really what you want, I can introduce you to Fidel at our next gathering."

She raised her hand to her cheek. "Really?"

"Yes," I replied, "it's not a problem at all."

Marcelo clearly didn't like the shameless way Ava was behaving. A little uncomfortable by her display of sexual frustration, he said to Armando, "My friend Bianchi—I think we have to let our beards grow and throw our deodorant into the trash. We'll then have no worries about the opposite sex anymore. They'll run into our arms."

Chandee raised her arms in revulsion. "Wait a minute, that doesn't apply to me at all! Stinky and unhygienic men are like getting up in the middle of the night hungry, and all you can find is a raw liver a la vinaigrette in the refrigerator!"

Rosita smiled and said, "You're right, honey. Who wants to eat that?"

Everyone laughed at the comparison. The composer had just rejoined our group and suggested, "Why don't we go and sit down more comfortably? Now we're at the intermission. Let me rest my feet."

During the intermission, the small orchestra was playing more contemporary music, starting with "Smoke Gets in Your Eyes" and "Summer of Love," then transitioning to some modern mambo music.

Che had already left, and I said discreetly to Chandee, "I think we should leave now. I want to call my mother before they go to bed."

We said goodbye after Chandee exchanged phone numbers with everyone. As we walked to the elevator, I told Chandee about what had transpired in the bathroom. She shook her head unhappily. We got the Mercedes from the valet and drove off into the night.

She said, "Don't have even half of a small doubt that Che might have sent him to search your house in order to pretend now to be your benefactor. Since they didn't find anything incriminating, it's a perfect excuse. You saved his life, and he's paying you back by getting you out of this mess without even compromising himself. The only ones who suffered in this are that poor, miserable woman who lost her teeth and the man with swelling that will take weeks to go down. Maybe you think I'm off."

I shook my head. "No, not at all. You're a lot smarter than I thought—that's a very strong possibility that I will contemplate. Thank you."

In a frustrated voice, she said, "These people are all of the same ilk. You should walk with lead feet on a glass roof with Che. I think he is the worst of the whole bunch. Even Castro, with all his conniving, only touches the surface of the vindictive, cold-blooded murderer Che can be. This man is godless with only one mission: to bring the world under the control of Satan. That is what I believe in my heart."

"You love him very much, don't you?" I asked teasingly.

"If you can kill somebody with your eyes, he's already got my darts in his heart. If you see him start to shake in

The Dark Face of Marxism

his legs and collapse before your eyes, that is my poison working in him. Please don't save him!"

"Don't worry, honey," I assured her, "I know who he is. I've been trained to deal with people like him. Piñeiro, too." We drove by the University of Havana, and turned off the street into a parking structure. I parked the car, and said, "I'm going to make a phone call to my family."

The University of Havana

"Go," she said. "Don't worry about it."

I left her in the car and walked to the row of phone cabinets. I got inside, dialed the operator, and was put through to my house in Pinar del Rio.

My father answered the phone. "Hello? Hello?"

"It's me, Julio Antonio."

"How are you doing, my son?"

"I'm very well, Papi. How are you guys doing there, after all of this convulsion?"

"Oh, everything is fine. A little while ago, Captain Leiva and his men left the house. They gave us all kinds of apologies and excuses for what happened. They said a truck will come early tomorrow morning with a new mattress, and a carpenter will repair your closet door. Everything that was even scratched during the search will be fixed. Don't worry about it. Everything is in the clear, and according to Captain Leiva, it was all a tremendous error that will never happen again."

I shook my head in disgust. I had to carefully control myself, as my father still sympathized with the Revolution. He wasn't just drinking a glass of the Castro Kool-Aid—he was drinking from a fifty-five-gallon tank of that rhetoric. He was purposefully blinding himself to the humiliation and trauma that Mima, my brothers, and my sister had been exposed to. It was perhaps easier for him, as he had not been present during the G-2 search. He knew nothing of the kinds of games I'd had to play in order for this to be rectified.

"You know how your mother is," he continued. "Emotional. And the worst thing to her was what they did with the piano. That is what affected her the most."

"You tell her, Dad, that this is the reason I called tonight. Che guaranteed me that a new piano will arrive in the morning. Well, not a new piano—you know, Dad, one taken from the home of someone who has already left the country."

I heard him chuckle lightly. "Well, it doesn't have to be new, my son," he said, "so long as it gives happiness to your mother and replaces the other one. What is the big deal about a piano?"

The Dark Face of Marxism

I couldn't hold it back any longer. "Dad, it's not just the piano. Think about it. These people arrived in the early hours of the morning, wake Mima and the others up, make a mess of the house, cut up the mattresses, and all the rest. It's not the piano—it's the humiliation. That humiliation is why, a little while ago, Che forced Piñeiro to apologize to me!"

"Oh!" he exclaimed. "He did?"

"This is an abuse comparable to the kind that the dictator Batista did, Dad. This is the kind of thing that so many people died in this Revolution to end! I'm extremely distressed over all of this, and it's not just because Mima is being emotional. It's because this should never have happened! You don't know what was behind all of it. It's just a bullshit excuse because I bought a couple of stupid bottles of guayabita to give to you!"

"OK, OK, my son. I understand. Calm down. Everything is already taken care of, and Mima will be very happy when I tell her in the morning what you just told me. She's already gone to bed, and she wasn't really happy because of the piano situation. She told me the carpenter would not be able to repair the piano. 'What does a regular carpenter know about musical instruments?'"

I laughed. "That's my Mima."

"Yes, yes, as always," he laughed.

Almost always, Mima was right in everything she fought for. On that, we could both agree.

"OK, my son," he said. "Thank you for your call and worrying about us. When are you coming back?"

"Possibly tomorrow."

"Very well, your mother will be waiting for you. I will have to leave early for Guane tomorrow morning. But it will be doubly good news for your mother."

We said our goodbyes, and I hung up. I walked back to the Mercedes and noticed two men inside another car parked not too far away from us. I shook my head and muttered, "What a liar that 'Redbeard' Piñeiro is. With one hand he apologizes, and with the other he stabs a knife into your back." When I got in, the first thing Chandee did was ask me, "Did you notice our new tail?" She subtly indicated the car with a gesture and her head.

"Yes, I noticed. It's great that they're so stupid. Anyone with a microscopic piece of common sense would realize they're being followed."

Chandee said, "I've been thinking while you were on the phone that we should change our MO. Whenever we go to any place, we should tell everyone that we are romantically involved." She raised her arm and turned on the vanity light in her visor. "If you think about it, the only logic that justifies the two of us going around together to the movies and restaurants, especially the luxury ones like tonight, is that we have a romantic relationship. Eventually, if this isn't that way, it will look suspicious. It could attract attention, as you said before, to my father and the others working around us."

"Yes," I agreed, "you're right. We do a lot of stuff like that already, holding hands and all that."

"Yes, but we never make any displays of affection. Even tonight, we deny to all these people that we have a relationship. Some won't believe it, because we're so young. But we should make it obvious, not hidden."

I nodded. "Yeah, if we're playing this game, we should play it seriously. From now on, we will make a point of it. Please remind me to always act as if we're a couple. Whenever somebody asks us, whatever we say isn't really that important. It's what we show to them. I think it's a good idea."

She grinned broadly. "Well, then, since we've come to an agreement, we should start right now. Let's give a demonstration to the guys following us." She opened her arms and brought me beneath the glow of the vanity light. "Get a little closer to me and give me a passionate kiss on the mouth, under the light. They'll see us clearly, and if they want to take a picture, they'll have a picture of us kissing each other."

I edged close to her, leaned over her seat, and put my lips to hers, giving her a gentle stage kiss.

She had other ideas, however. She wrapped her arms around my neck and caught me completely by surprise by giving me a deep French kiss. She was shockingly strong. I started to get aroused. I thought that this was a very dangerous game for two young people to play. But I said nothing, because I didn't want to sound too prudish.

After making out for a little while, she pulled back a little and unbuttoned a couple of buttons on her blouse. She took my hand and placed it directly on one of her breasts. She leaned over me this time and began to once more passionately kiss her. That contact of my hand on her firm breast was like an electrical charge for me. I started to get very excited. In response to that excitement, I began to explore her other breast with my other hand.

She continued kissing me and made no objection to my explorations. A few minutes later, I followed my sexual instincts. It caught me completely by surprise, and I certainly hadn't planned it, but I began to undo the rest of her blouse. She offered no resistance or any objection. I grew more stimulated, and I pulled one of her breasts out as my other hand slightly raised her skirt as it reached in between her legs. This time, Chandee halted my hand from going any further in my quests for discovery. Very gently, she pushed me away and began to reorder herself. She began to fix her hair in the mirror and button her blouse back up. She smiled in satisfaction and said, "Look—apparently we gave them a great display, because they're leaving."

I hadn't noticed in my distraction. I looked in the rear-view mirror and saw the car leaving the structure and wending its way back into the traffic. I took off my beret and scratched through my hair. I put my beret back on and looked through the interior rear view. I was very embarrassed, because in my excitement I had allowed my sexual instincts to go farther than I should have. I worried that I might have crossed the line with her.

"Well, I can take you back home now, since we got rid of that tail." I started the engine, reversed, and drove out of the structure.

I felt better when Chandee drew close to me, took one of my arms around her, and said, "You were perfect! I'm sure those G-2 agents left convinced that we're not just boyfriend and girlfriend, but are also passionate lovers."

I smiled and nodded. I replied, still slightly embarrassed, "Well, that's what the whole thing is about, no? You did a great job, too."

The Dark Face of Marxism

We drove towards her house in an awkward silence. When we arrived at her house, I told her, "I might go back to Pinar del Rio tomorrow. But before I leave, I would like to see you, because I believe Che wants to talk to me tonight. He wants to reveal some new confidence to me. I believe that what I did with the ambassadors yesterday has caused him to bring me closer to him. Evidently he has had too many compliments about my performance, and he wants to keep me around. He told me before he left that he would give me more details about Lee and what is going on with his plans. I believe what he's going to tell me is in reference to the things we already have partial information on regarding his plans for world domination."

"Yeah, maybe we can have lunch tomorrow at the Hilton."

I smiled. "You like it, eh?"

She looked at me patiently. "Who's not going to like it—that exquisite food?"

"By the way," I said, "speaking of exquisite food, you never told me about the *media noches* in El Parador."

She laughed. "I've been waiting to see if you would forget! I thought that if I didn't bring it up, you wouldn't follow up."

I shook my head. "You are something—you don't like to admit you were wrong and tell me that I was right."

She hugged me and said, "You are right. Definitely. That *media noches* was the best in Havana!" She paused and nodded. "I don't know what they put in it, but it must be some spice or something. The flavor lingers in your mouth for a long time!"

I gave her a reverence.

She continued, "No doubt about it, you are a great spy—a master. I've been living here in Havana, and I didn't even know that the place existed, much less that they had the best *media noches* in Havana."

I got out and went around to open her door. When she got out, she added, "By the way, you are a very good professional kisser."

"You're not too bad yourself," I said. "You really caught me by surprise. But you're not saying that because you want lunch tomorrow at the Hilton, eh?"

She smiled and put her hand under her blouse and fluttered it over her heart. She raised her right hand and said, "I swear it's true, so help me God. Now I understand why you have all these girls flying behind you like bees after the honeycomb."

I shook my head and smiled. "*Chinita, chinita*, you are something difficult to digest. You surprise me every minute. You have a good evening, OK, and take care of yourself."

She waved to me as I walked to the car and left.

I checked in the rear-view mirror to see if I was being followed, but the tail had disappeared. I smiled as I thought to myself that the guys at the university weren't even G-2. But Chandee had assumed they were, and as the General and my uncle would say, when one assumes, ninety-nine percent of the time one will be wrong. It was also possible that they weren't Piñeiro's dogs; they could be someone else's. They might even be my own dogs watching my back. Whatever the breed, however, they apparently didn't care for the display of affection we had given them.

The Dark Face of Marxism

I drove on to Boca Siega at a decent pace so that I could avoid any more late-night aspiring fishermen. When I arrived, the escort told me that Che was on the terrace and had told them to let me know where I could find him when I arrived.

I parked the car and walked up the stairs to join Che on the terrace. He said hello to me with a great deal of affection. I thought to myself that, given a week or perhaps days, when the insurance company declines his claim, he probably will be somewhat deflated.

He said, "Come on, sit down, sit down! You made a great impression at that interview. The Belgian ambassador, Abdul Marcalt, just called Pierre a little while ago with an invitation to a party he will have tomorrow night at his embassy. He told Pierre that you are an extraordinary kid, and he wanted to extend the invitation to you as well. He would like to get to know you better."

Che raised his right hand with its cigar and gestured towards me with an expression blended of humor and resentment. "The invitation is to you only and to no one else. Even I am not invited."

He pouted. I couldn't tell whether he was still in jest or if his ego was genuinely bruised. I started to think that these guys might criticize each other, but they were all the same. If Fidel's ego was the size of the Eiffel Tower, then Che's must be the size of the Empire State Building.

I wondered how stupid the Belgian ambassador could be, since I had told him explicitly not to contact me, especially as I had put that information in his hands so recently. Evidently, this man didn't know the meaning of the Spanish word for danger.

If he really was a spy, he had learned very little about the first thing any spy has to know: protect under all circumstances the identity of your contact. You have to respect what he tells you, because he knows better the circles in which he moves. Under no circumstance put at risk the source, or you will lose him—either at the hands of your enemy or through his own decision to withdraw from your side. He will consider you unreliable and reckless.

These thoughts prompted me to reply at once to Che, "I'm not going to be here tomorrow. I'm not going to any party with these guys."

Che stroked his beard. "You may have to reconsider. It could be a great opportunity for you to get close to this guy. You might be able to penetrate them and get some valuable information out of them."

"I'm sorry to disagree with you, but I don't think these people will ever be able to trust me, since I'm too close to you and Fidel. He might be trying to convert me to their side. I don't have time for that game. I've got better things to do. Besides, I just spoke to my father and I promised him that I would be having dinner with them tomorrow. I won't be in the capital."

"Well, you should think about this. Perhaps the next time you have an opportunity, you can get close to them. You never know what you can learn from them."

"I will, but I should leave in the morning. I want to have lunch with my friend Chandee."

He smiled and said, "Your friend? Or your girlfriend?"

"I'll be honest with you. You know—since we're both still so young, if we tell people we are lovers or romantically involved, they could look down on us. I think it's better out of respect to our families and the adults around us to be discreet and call her my friend."

He nodded and said, "You are a very smart kid, and that is what I call in my book being cautious." He raised his hand and circled it around. "It's a very high level of diplomacy. It's very good that you have respect and consideration for your elders, because you will learn very much from them if you earn their trust and admiration, as you've earned mine."

"Thank you."

He waved that off. "What I'm telling you aren't compliments. It's what I really feel about you. In our work, it's very difficult to completely trust anyone. That is why it's very refreshing to be able to sit down with somebody you know has no envy or resentment towards you, and doesn't want to take away your merits or position. With that person, you have the freedom to speak openly, which is something you can't do with the others out of fear of betrayal. For example, let me ask you: what do you think about Lee and the other two—Kresken and Markov?"

I looked at him and wondered what Che wanted to tell me. Despite what he said about trusting in me, he was still hesitating. It was like he was pushing to see how I jumped, asking me this question to see if I had a good judgment of character regarding those individuals. What he couldn't know was that I had been reading and studying many times the details of his plans that were in his briefcase. Little by little, I had been putting the puzzle together.

I leaned back in the armchair and said, "Lee Oswald looks like a common geek. Maybe that's what he wants us to think, to take us by surprise. From my point of view, this man could be extremely dangerous. The other two look like muscles without brains. My impression of them is that they are only a pair of bodyguards, like the men of your escort: loyal and valuable, and extremely brave. They are around to defend you against all physical harm. But I don't think, intellectually, they are very reliable, because they don't have the capacity to see a psychological attack disguised as a friend against you—or anybody else, for that matter. They simply don't have the mental or ideological facility to see it in order to stop it."

Che laughed and shook his head. He raised his right hand. I thought for a few seconds I might have gone too far. After he brought the hand down and took a long puff on his cigar, I was relieved of my doubts as he said, "No wonder Fidel had you as one of his favorites. If you talked like this the first time he met you, only a year younger, you probably blew his mind completely. Kid, honestly," he asked, "who taught you all of this? Every time I open my mind and talk to you, you shock me."

"Thank you. If I have to be honest with you, maybe it's a combination of the reading from books, the examples of my uncles and father, and something my mother says you cannot learn in any university. It's something you're born with: intuition and common sense."

He nodded appreciatively. "Your mother has an extremely good reason to say that. I know a lot of doctors and attorneys who have no common sense at all. But let me tell you something you might consider extraordinary. You hit the nail on the head." He took his beret off and raked his fingers through his hair. "Lee Oswald is a professional spy for the North American Naval Intelligence. He is an expert in military telecommunications and radar. The CIA, in conjunction with Navy Intelligence, have polished and prepared him to make him more sophisticated. He is to be sent to the Soviet Union to penetrate us and to give us bogus intelligence, with the plan of confusing and derailing our great satellite and radio programs. They've instructed him thoroughly to give us information that has no real value, not capable of damaging anything, so that he can earn our trust and confidence. But he's made vital mistakes: I won't list all of them, but one of them is to go to the extreme of wanting to renounce his North American citizenship and become a Russian citizen." He paused, and then asked, "You don't think this is over the top and strange?"

I nodded. I observed him attentively and watched every movement he made, scrutinizing his demeanor as he spoke. Che didn't even realize that he had been telling me that the North American intelligence had sent Lee Oswald as a spy to the Soviet Union to penetrate "us," rather than using the word "them." Since when did he, Che, consider himself Russian or consider himself a member of the Union of Soviet Socialist Republics? Of course, in my mind, it was very clearly an admission from his own mouth that corroborated what I had discovered in his briefcase: Che was actually an agent for the Soviet KGB.

I said, "How can you be so sure that this man is a double agent and not a legitimate defector? If he's really a defector, he could be invaluable for our future plans."

Che waved both hands in the air in negation. "No, no, no. This is the part you don't know yet. We have spies inside the American Central Intelligence as well as intelligence networks around the world."

I noted once more the use of the word "we." This was only a year after the Revolution had won, and Cuban

Intelligence was still in its infancy. That "we" could only indicate that he had already been a member of an intelligence network for many years, long before he met Fidel in Mexico and introduced him to the Marxist idea of global control and the destruction of all forms of democracy in other nations.

Even though I knew about his real affiliation, there were still missing pieces in the puzzle. But they were slowly coming together and fitting to perfection as I grew to know Che's plans better through our conversations.

I remained silent, and he pointed in the air with his right index finger. "This is what I will teach you, slowly, day by day, because all the great plans require a lot of time to put together. As the masters in this game, we will use their own spy as a patsy to destroy the leader of the most capitalist country in the world. This can result in one of two things. One is an internal civil war, if we succeed in using the confusion to destroy the North Americans' respect for their government. If the masses are convinced their own government had something to do with killing their own president, or even better, if we implicate their intelligence networks as accomplices through our propaganda machinery, the effect will be magnificent and the results beyond calculation.

"There is also the possibility that instead, the country's discontent will cause everyone, with our unions' help, to call a national strike, which would paralyze the entire country. It would be a peaceful response to their sense of outrage, and it would completely collapse their economy."

He clapped his hands and exclaimed, "La! That will be the birth of the North American Socialist Revolution. If we accomplish this, the capitalist system will collapse, starting with the North Americans and then spreading by a chain reaction to the rest of the world. The worst-case scenario is that neither of these things happen. However, even then, the act of killing the American president will create such confusion and destabilization in the social establishment, a lack of trust in the government, and the loss of faith in the morality through the failure of their preventing it. Then it will only be a question of time before we can manufacture an individual with the proper Marxist ideology within the United States, which we can put in power through a good propaganda machinery, because people will be looking for hope and change. When that happens, that nation will finally belong to us, along with the rest of the world. We won't have to fire a shot or lose a single one of our comrades."

I reclined in my seat and said as I stroked my chin, "I don't want to be a pessimist, but if all you say doesn't happen and the last option is the only one left, it will take many years for that to come about, and I don't think either you or I will be around."

He waved his hands in the air to stop me. "Oh, no, no, no! You're wrong. Everything I've told you is already in motion. This will take only two or three years, and both of us will see the result and enjoy it."

"Ah, ha!" I said. "Then we will have the first privilege to get those brand-new cars for each year coming out of the North American factories without paying a cent for them. We'll be the builders of the entire structure."

He looked at me with a straight face and said, "Exactly!" in a tone that carried his strong conviction.

I wondered to myself what he knew that I didn't. This looked to me like a Utopian dream. I said nothing, however, and kept probing his nerves. I asked again, "What about Kresken and Markov? Are they with Lee, or are they with us?"

He smiled and looked me directly in the eyes. "What do you think?"

I nodded thoughtfully. "As I told you before, they are bodyguards. I assume they are your guard dogs, taking care that the rabbit doesn't run away."

He grinned broadly. "You will be a great grand spy in the future, extremely valuable for us and our international plans. Let me tell you, in order to mastermind and implement this huge plan to change the world, you must also have a master's patience. When you rush, you make mistakes. In order to avoid making those mistakes, everything has to be done very precisely, meticulously, step by step. The first and most important step is disinformation. Our counterintelligence will be in charge of that.

"This spy, Lee Oswald, will be the keystone of this plan. That is why we need to keep him close to us. We will keep him very busy and distracted, make him believe that his plans and the misinformation that he brings to us has been working to perfection. It's very important that both he and his superiors believe everything is working fine, so that this is what he reports to them, and they report the same to the others. In the meantime, we will use him to spread disinformation to them, which will give us time to complete our plans. We'll always be three steps ahead of him and his intelligence network. By the time they realize what is going on, it will be too late. The serpent will be decapitated. Even then, they won't completely realize how we pulled that rabbit out of the hat. They will have already removed the rabbit from the hat minutes before the magician comes on stage for the final act and the curtain exposes him to the audience.

"This act of defeat will obligate their own intelligence to hide the truth, even if they have some pieces of what really went on. This will be a tremendous embarrassment and source of shame for the CIA and the rest of the U.S. intelligence community."

He paused for a moment and took a long puff on his cigar. I asked again, "What if some of these individuals you have in place to enact this master plan have last minute remorse, like Lazaro did?"

He shifted violently in his seat. "What?"

"Yes," I bored in, "it can happen. One of these individuals could decide at the final moment they don't want to partake in this plan."

He moved like he had been hit by lightning as he was reminded of what happened with the ship *La Coubre*. He stroked his nose and blinked several times. "Because of these sad, half-assed accomplishments in the past, we're not going to use one, we're not going to use two, we're going to use three agents, as well as one ghost rider. That one is the deadliest, most trustworthy, and efficient one. That way, if one or even two of the subjects change their minds, we'll still have one to do the job plus another in the shadows." He got a satisfied smirk on his face. "Now that the plan is entering its final stage, the last step will be the exact determination as to the place and time this will occur. A plan like this requires exactitude. We'll have to determine the time to the very minute of the hour, so that there is no way for this prey to escape from the hunters. I can assure you that nothing will fail. We won't determine when, however, until our spies learn the exact itinerary of the prey. That final step cannot happen until we have that information." He looked at me then. "Who do you think sent Lee Oswald to us?"

I shook my head. "I have no idea."

"Do you remember Mr. Rubenstein—Jack Ruby? He's one of us. That is the way we work," he said assuredly.

I leaned back again in my chair. I nodded thoughtfully. "Well, if there's something I can help you with," I raised my right arm accommodatingly, "I am at your service and in the service of the International Proletariat Revolution."

He smiled at me. "You already did, because the vast fortune we inherited from the capitalist system is running out. All of these great plans cost us billions of dollars each day. The money that comes in from the insurance company, that you helped to secure, will be a tremendous injection to our finances for our future plans."

I looked at him and nodded. I thought that if he didn't get the money from someplace else, he was going to have a rude awakening, and that dream of his was going to become a pipe dream with as much substance as a poet in love with a fictional girl. I smiled at that thought and replied, "It made me very happy to know that I have been able to contribute a small grain of sand to that huge mountain pyramid that is your master plan."

He was the one who smiled this time. "Yes, you have indeed contributed, but a lot more than a grain of sand, *compañerito*."

I smiled again, as he had never addressed me that way before. I removed my beret. As I ran my fingers through my hair, I asked, "Who will take me back to Pinar del Rio tomorrow? The guards told me when I came in that Fausto is still sick, and they didn't think he'll be well for a few days."

"Actually, I will be leaving early in the morning to Santiago de Cuba, because there are still some things left undone there. We can take you in the helicopter, but you said you wanted to see your lov—I mean, your friend, and take her to lunch. By then, we'll already be in Santiago de Cuba." He took another puff on his cigar. "If it's not a problem for you, why don't you take one of my cars? When Fausto gets better, he can bring it back."

I nodded and said, "That's not a problem for me at all. After I have lunch with Chandee, then I will be on my way back to Pinar del Rio." He smiled, raised his left arm, and stood up. "Thank you very much," I said.

"You're welcome," he replied. "I'm going to sleep now. I have a long day ahead of me tomorrow. You have a good night and day tomorrow."

"You, too," I said.

He turned to walk away. He was a few steps from the stairs when he turned around. He lifted his right hand and gestured toward me with his cigar. "Good job with that deposition," he said. "You completely complied with what we agreed for you to say."

"It was nothing—it was only what I was supposed to do."

"That's why I thank you. No matter how carefully you tell people what to do, they seem to fail at actually doing it. Good night." With a wave, he entered the house.

I remained there, sitting in the dim light of the terrace, thinking about everything we had discussed. I was very worried. The General and my uncle had both told me that the intelligence community hadn't taken any of these plans seriously. To them, they were just more pipe dreams from the communists, because they didn't have the kind of manpower it would take to kill the President of the United States. The Cuban government was simply too weak in these, their first steps. They didn't have the kind of power or public support to accomplish a plan of this magnitude. According to them, something on this scale would need more than a few million dollars and willing men. It would require contacts in global intelligence to execute successfully, which the Cubans—they thought—didn't have. The plans were considered romantic dreams of the Cuban communists to create buzz and recruit new members in their plan to conquer the continent and then the world.

On the contrary, I was daily observing each step forward their plans were taking and seeing how meticulously the pieces on the chessboard were being set in place. The consequences would be catastrophic, and ignoring these warnings only made success seem that much more likely. On the surface, of course, it looked unrealistic, but Marxists were usually so fanatic that they were capable of convincing others to join them in their unreasonable dreams. I was fairly certain that Che had not yet told me all of the details, but I knew that there had to be something more behind all of it. Che certainly had no doubts that he would achieve something great with his plan.

I thought that both the North American and global intelligence had no idea that these new players born in 1959 with the Cuban Revolution would change the espionage game on a worldwide level. These people didn't just intend to change a regime or a country. They had the

The Dark Face of Marxism

KGB—one of the world's most sophisticated intelligence networks—and one of its agents infiltrating a key country in the Americas with their only goal being to convert the other leaders to the Marxist ideology, even if in the process they had to kill half of them. This now was a completely different game, seeking to gain control internationally at the political and economic levels—something the normal intelligence network was unaccustomed to doing.

I shook my head and whispered inaudibly, "This son of a bitch will catch everyone with their pants down."

I stood up and walked towards the house, still buried in my worries. I knew I had to speak to someone immediately, before it was too late. I went to my room and tried to pacify my thoughts. I tried to remember that I could not take everything Che told me at face value. In the same way he was using Lee Oswald to sow misinformation with intelligence, there was the possibility that he was doing the same thing with me. If they had any suspicions that I was the spy they were seeking for in vain, then logically, he would fill my head with false information to see what I would do with it. All these thoughts filled my mind as I crawled into bed and tried to compose myself to sleep. When I got up in the morning, I would be more refreshed and better able to assimilate all the fresh information Che had given me.

I woke late in the morning and took a hot shower. Che was already gone, and I said goodbye to everyone else in the house. I left Boca Siega around 11:30. When I reached Havana, another driver hesitated in indecision whether to run a yellow light or not. I slammed on the brakes. My travel bag in the back seat flew forward, and several items fell out and rolled around on the floor.

I drove through the Vedado. I saw a musical instrument store, and decided to stop there. Mima had asked me to pick her up some blank sheet music when I had the chance. I entered the parking structure and took a few minutes to look for my wallet, which had been my travel bag, and to neatly replace the items that had fallen out.

I exited the car and walked towards the music store. A black 1960 Buick with a couple in it drove past me. They looked very wealthy and quite well-dressed, and as I opened the door to the store I noticed that they had parked near my car. I entered the store, thinking that it wasn't going to be too long before that poor couple left Cuba, and Heaven only knew which leader in the government would wind up with that beautiful Buick in his private collection.

I entered the store, and a wrinkled man looked me up and down with a sour expression. It could have been because of my uniform, or perhaps it was his natural personality. Regardless, his eyes fixed on my gun and then he stared at my long hair. He had a goatee sprinkled generously with white hairs.

"Can I help you?"

"I need some blank sheet music," I replied. "Do you carry it?"

"Do you want it in a binder or single sheets?"

"Maybe both—if you have both, give me two binders and about fifty single sheets."

"The package comes in a hundred sheets. If you order by sheet, it costs you more, almost double. If you buy by package, it's less expensive."

"Very well," I replied. "Give me two packages. Thank you."

"You're welcome," he replied.

He went to fill my order. As he did so, the couple, who had entered shortly after I did, used the opportunity to come over to me while the man was distracted.

The gentleman asked me with a broad smile, "Are you a composer? Do you write music?" He appeared to have been listening to our conversation.

"Yes," I answered, "but I'm not very good yet. I'm still a student. This is for my mom."

"Oh, I see," he replied. He pulled out his wallet with his G-2 identification. In red, smaller letters it read, "Special Unit, Office of the Prime Minister." He held his hand out to me. "Nice to meet you. My name is Efrain Cordovales." He pointed to the lady next to him and said, "She is Tatiana."

She was a very beautiful, blonde woman with caramel eyes who had a very aristocratic deportment and exquisitely feminine manners held out to me a hand with long, well-manicured nails. "Tatiana Almendares. Nice to meet you."

I kissed her hand, which smelled of very expensive perfume. I asked, "How can I help you, *compañeros*?" I had already seen that ID for state security before, and I knew they were legitimate agents. For this reason, I was extremely cordial and let them do the talking.

"The Commander-in-Chief sent us to pick you up, if you would please be so kind to come with us," Efrain said. "Our office is very close by. We'll bring you back here as soon as you finish speaking with him."

"Of course," I replied, "it's not the slightest problem. But there's no need for you guys to take me. I already know the place, but I can follow you wherever you want to go, and then I can leave on my own. That will be less inconvenience for both of us."

The two looked at each other in concern and indecision. They didn't want to create any friction with me, and my reputation clearly preceded me. Efrain said, "That's OK—you can follow us in your car. I don't see any problem with that."

After I paid for the paper, we got in our cars and I followed them closely to the Prime Minister's office, even though I already knew where it was. I wanted them to feel comfortable that I was indeed behind them. We passed the guard post, and I returned the guards' salutes. We drove down the street inside the compound, houses on both sides that had once been private residences but were now converted by the Castro brothers into general quarters draped with long Cuban flag banners, pictures of Revolutionary martyrs, and slogans. I was surprised to see a picture of my late friend, Camilo Cienfuegos, hanging there. We parked our cars in the middle of the block and walked into one of the residences. We saluted the door guards as we entered.

We waited a short while in the lobby and then were escorted to a conference room. Two very cute young ladies dressed in *miliciana* uniforms asked us if we wanted anything to drink. Even though all three of us politely declined, they brought in a tray of ice water and glasses and placed them on the thick pane of the glass-topped table. The containers must have belonged to a very wealthy person, as they were frosted and rimmed with gold. They laid out napkins of fine linen embroidered with exquisite patterns.

About half an hour later, we had been sitting in silence, idly flipping through various European magazines of different titles. Efrain and Tatiana would occasionally smile and ask me a question of no particular importance, attempting to make small talk. My answers were very short, and they eventually lapsed into silence.

I realized it was likely these were the agents who had been tailing me the night before or that they were on the same team. They might even have been the ones parked in the university lot when I called my father. I wondered as I waited patiently what new drama Fidel had in mind. I couldn't understand what motive this interview would have or how the hell they knew I would stop in that particular store. If they had been following me, they were so sophisticated that I never noticed them on my tail.

I tried to relax. I understood that nothing bad could come out of this or these two wouldn't have been treating me with such courtesy. I breathed deeply and thought to myself, Patience, Julio Antonio. Patience is a virtue that not everyone has. You do. Relax.

Finally, after nearly an hour had passed, Efrain and Tatiana started to yawn, probably in boredom after the long wait. Fidel appeared in the door with two bodyguards, a large smile on his face and a big cigar in his hand. We all stood up.

"How are you guys doing today?"

We all said we were fine.

"How have Efrain and Tatiana been treating you?"

"No complaints, very well." I added, "So well, in fact, that I began to think they wanted to adopt me."

Fidel laughed and shook his head. He held out his hand and took mine in it. He said, "I like your sense of humor!" He turned to them. "Is this kid not something special?"

Efrain and Tatiana remained standing. They said no word but nodded and smiled. Still holding my hand, he asked, "You want anything to drink, a Coca-Cola or something?"

I said, "Thank you, if you have some Jupiña, I'll take one."

"If we don't have it," he said as he released my hand, "we'll get it for you." He looked at one of the guards. "See if we have any. Tell the guys outside that if we don't have any, go and get a couple of cases. We should have everything on hand, especially for our Revolutionary guests. We can't say we don't have something." He looked very happy, even ecstatic. He said to Efrain and Tatiana, "You guys can wait for us outside?" He gestured to the conference room door. "That way, when we finish, you guys can take the Commandantico back to wherever it was that you picked him up."

Efrain held up a hand. "That won't be necessary, Commandante. He followed us in his car."

Fidel pointed at me. "Good for you! You can't go around trusting everyone that shows you a badge."

"Let me clarify, Commandante," I said. "It's not my car; it's Che's. He's just lending it to me."

Fidel sat down. "I cannot blame you for not wanting to get in these guys' car after what happened to you in Pinar del Rio. I've been informed. If something like that happened to me, I wouldn't get in the car with Efrain and Tatiana." He paused and placed his index finger on his temple in thought. "Well, maybe Tatiana." She smiled. He

The Dark Face of Marxism

shook his finger. "Even with a beautiful girl like this, though, you have to watch out. You never know who she's working for. The prettier she is, the more dangerous." He pointed and shook his finger at me. "You're very smart. By the way, that car doesn't belong to Che—it belongs to the Revolution. That means it belongs to you, to me, to Efrain, to Tatiana, and to everyone in the country."

I smiled, thinking that the sentiment sounded very beautiful. But by the time the people in the city took those terrible buses from the public service, cars like the one I drove would go to these guys' garages. Could Fidel really believe what he was saying, or did he think he was the only smart man in town and the rest of us idiots? I couldn't comprehend for even a moment that this intelligent man could believe a word of that. I remembered my mother telling me once that the liar repeated his lie often to ensure that the people would believe it.

He raised his right index finger high. "By the way, when you get out of here, go and see Captain Omar Fernandez, the Minister of Transportation. He will be waiting for you to pick whatever car you want." I wonder what I had done this time to deserve that.

I smiled and said, "Thank you, Commandante."

"They already told me that the Volga Che let you use is completely wrecked after the incident in Pinar del Rio, when those counterrevolutionaries tried to hurt you. But they didn't count on you being smarter than them! You slipped out of their fingers like butter on a breadstick!"

I nodded although I knew the people who had done that weren't counterrevolutionaries, as he called them. In the end, though, no one would argue with him. I thought for a minute of a famous saying in Cuba about those from

Jalisco, Mexico. When they argue, they always win, because even if they lose, they pull out a revolver and kill their opponents. This saying was why Fidel's secret nickname in military circles was Jalisco; if you argued with him, you would either lose the argument or go to jail and perhaps the firing squad. I certainly wasn't about to argue the point.

Efrain and Tatiana remained standing stiffly at attention, even after Fidel and I had sat down and started to talk. Fidel looked at them and raised his left hand to gesture his dismissal. "OK, you guys go and get lunch. It's getting late, and you brought him here. Now I want to talk to him in private."

After they said goodbye and left the room followed by the guard, the two girls returned with a tray containing several bottles of Jupiña, glasses of ice, and a high-ball for Fidel. One of them emptied most of a bottle of the soda into a glass and handed it to me with a napkin, while her associate handed Fidel his drink. We thanked them, and they started to leave. Fidel said to one of them, "Tell everyone out there not to bother us."

"Very well, Commandante," she said and left.

I took a long sip from the glass and emptied the rest of the bottle into it. I looked at Fidel to see him take a swig of his high ball. He smiled at me and said, "Che told me how well you handled the deposition before the Belgian ambassador and the insurance company investigator. He told me how you impressed everyone at that meeting. Your handling was absolutely stupendous! Che also updated me on what happened at your house in Pinar del Rio. I know, unfortunately, the egos and personalities of those around me are not easy to control."

The Dark Face of Marxism

I couldn't tell if he was being truthful or not.

He continued in frustration, "I told Piñeiro that this will be the last time that I ever hear that any of them bother you at all—your family included! I don't care if they come with goddamn gossip or creating bullshit, telling me things that have no foundation that you're going around with little worms, teenagers, or people disaffected with the Revolution, I told him *quien carajo*[15] doesn't have some relative or friend that hasn't left for Miami or doesn't like our political ideas?"

He tapped his chest with a forefinger. "Even I! The mother of my only son left with the gringos to the USA!" His expression showed his disappointment. "*Que coño*[16] can I do about that?"

He took another sip from his glass. He shook his finger in my face. "Don't think for a minute I'm not checking up on you, as I said to Piñeiro a little while ago."

I thought to myself, Oh, shit.

"Your first girlfriend is a *miliciana*, the daughter of one of our ministers. She's also studying in the Naval Intelligence Academy. The other girlfriend you're hanging around with now, just this morning enlisted with the *milicianas*. That means you are a good influence on these people! That's not counting the fact that her father is a good Revolutionary and a member of the CDR."

I scratched my cheek with my left hand in confusion. I was taken completely by surprise. I had no idea about any of this. If what he was saying was true, Chandee couldn't

---

[15] *Who the hell*

[16] *What the hell*

have picked a better time to join the civil militia. I admired the smart move by Chandee and thought of what we did the night before. For a while, I had started to think that all the show had been unnecessary. But now I realized that, based on these results, Fidel must have sent his own dogs to corroborate whatever negative, malicious information Piñeiro had told him. Between his own observations and Che's information, he had become completely convinced that I was clean as a whistle. He probably unloaded on Piñeiro at that point. I breathed a gentle sigh of relief and continued to listen attentively.

"A little bird recently told me how the Belgian ambassador tried to humiliate you by asking you who you work for," he went on. "You expressed the great satisfaction and pride in working not only for me, but for the Revolution. I told this to Piñeiro, and I also told him that I couldn't say the same of all the Commanders in the Revolution. They all have the presumption of replacing me as the Maximum Leader of this Revolution, and they all want to be emperors, not legionnaires. I tell them, 'Some of you, I know, are saying a lot of shit about me behind my back, just to feed your egos in front of the people. If somebody tells you how big a gossip somebody else is, it's because that guy is the biggest gossip in the whole town. That's why he criticizes the other—because he doesn't like the competition. And you guys are the ones who say my ego is the size of the Eiffel Tower!" He raised his arm.

I smiled at hearing Fidel repeat what Che had said about his ego.

"You've heard him say that, eh?" Fidel asked.

I said nothing, but I continued to smile.

"I know you're a big man, and I won't push it, because I respect that," he said. "All I ask is that you remember who your loyalty is to and that you not deprive yourself of your honor. You don't have to say anything. Just take your beret off if you ever you heard him say that." I continued smiling, but didn't move. "I promise you, I will never repeat what you say. Everything in this conversation is strictly confidential between you and me."

I took off my beret and said, "In that case, Commandante, I have to take off my beret because I have to scratch my head."

Fidel looked at me seriously as I put my beret back on. "Thank you. I want to tell you something." He gestured to me with his cigar. "Speaking of ego, I have to say something on that subject. Che is a great guy and a good Revolutionary. However, his ego," he nodded his head emphatically, "is too large for the entire land area of Argentina to measure!" He shook his head. "It's a great pity. Nobody wants to work with him. He only has a small group of people, and he's always trying to get people from other departments to join his team. But nobody stays with him for long, because he's always taking all the credit for himself. No one likes to work with somebody who takes all the credit and glory away from the individual accomplishments within the team. No, no, no—that is not fair. I've told him that hundreds of times, but this Argentinian never learns!"

Fidel smiled and added, "It's true what the Cubans here say: the best business in this whole world is to buy an Argentinian for whatever he's really worth and then sell him for what he believes he's worth." He laughed then.

"Of course, that's if you can find an idiot that wants to buy that valueless package and gives you that much money!"

He picked up the glass of liquor and took another sip. He stroked his beard and said, "Don't forget to keep your eyes and ears open. We have a lot of traitors among us, and those around you, especially the ones close to you, are the only ones really capable of inflicting major damage to you and whatever you're doing. That is why the counterrevolution within our forces are the most dangerous—they are the ones who can be the most effective. So, again—keep your eyes and ears open, and anything you see or hear from any high-ranked officers, you bring it to me immediately."

I nodded and replied, "Of course, Commandante. That is the way I always think. My loyalty is only with you—for you and the Revolution."

He nodded in satisfaction. "Atta boy!" he exclaimed. "That is the reason you have all my trust."

"Thank you," I replied.

He raised his right hand and pointed it as he shook it at me. "You earned that trust. By the way, when the intelligence courses begin in the Soviet Union, I want you to be the first one there. You will be a great intelligence officer, maybe in charge of one of our international forces. Maybe you could even replace Piñeiro, because we all get old eventually."

I smiled at that and thought that if the G-2 chief heard that, he would need an antidiarrheal. He was already paranoid enough, having to deal with Fidel. The thought of having me replace him would probably drive him to jump out of an upper story window of the G-2 building.

The Dark Face of Marxism

Fidel stood up, and I did likewise. We walked towards the conference room door together. As we met by the door, he put his hand on my shoulder, and we walked through the door. "Remember what I've been telling you about Che. Don't take anything he tells you too seriously."

I nodded. "Yes, I understand."

After we said goodbye, I left the building and walked towards the Mercedes. I looked at my watch and saw that it was nearly 2:00 p.m. My stomach started to rumble, as I hadn't eaten yet, and I thought of Chandee waiting for me to have lunch. Before much longer, it would no longer be lunch but dinner. After I left the compound, saluting the guards as they opened the gate for me, I looked for a public phone. I found one at a coffee shop, and I pulled over, got out, and dialed Chandee's number. She answered and I said, "Hello, it's me."

"Oh, thank God!" she exclaimed. "I thought something bad had happened. You're always so punctual, and this is so out of character for you."

"I'm sorry," I said, "I was caught up in something I couldn't say no to. But let me correct you: I never gave you a specific hour I would pick you up. I know I said lunch, but we can call it 'linner,' since it's between lunch and dinner."

"Don't worry about it," she replied. "I ate something light, so that I wouldn't behave improperly at the table and eat like a pig when I'm out with you."

I smiled and said, "Even if you tried very hard, you could never behave like that. If there's anything you have in abundance that I like a lot, it's class."

"Thank you," she replied. We said goodbye, and I drove to her house.

A holding cell at Villa Marista

Chapter 6: The Sorrow of Losing My Friends

When I reached the store, she was waiting on the sidewalk in front, as usual. I got out and opened the door for her. We hugged, and she got inside.

"You're not going to believe what just happened," I told her. "It's going to absolutely astound you."

While we drove to the hotel, I gave her a brief summary of my meeting with Fidel.

When we arrived, I gave the keys to the valet. During the meal, I explained my delay and related to her my conversation with Che the night before. I confessed my worry about Che's accomplishments with his plan so far, and she assured me that she would communicate these things with her father, who would then relay them to the General and my uncle. After we finished our meal, we had some napoleons with a strawberry sauce and almond ice cream. I said with a smile, "It's really great that you went today to register with the militia."

She looked at me in shocked surprise. "How on earth did you know that I did that? Don't tell me you have people following me now!"

I pointed at my temple and said, "ESP."

She was frustrated at my jest. "No—how did you know? I wanted to give you a surprise today, being dressed in a militia uniform, but the stupid lady in the recruiting office was incapable of doing even a simple thing right. She gave me a blouse three sizes too large for me! How can you look at a card that says I'm a size three and then give me a size six? Now I have to wait until tomorrow to bring in the uniform and exchange it. Please, tell me—how did you know?"

"As I said before, you're not going to believe it. Fidel told me today during my meeting with him." I shook my head. "You don't even know how opportune your action was this morning. Registering with the militia was probably the best thing you could have done to help me."

She looked at me in wonder. "What difference could this make for you?"

I smiled and replied with a question. "You remember those individuals we thought were watching us last night at the university?"

"Of course, *claro* I remember."

"They were from the state security—but a special unit from the Prime Minister's Office. They were Fidel's agents. He was the one who sent them to check us out and verify the accuracy of Piñeiro's accusation against me. Fidel wanted to see if they had any foundation at all. When they saw our lovely, romantic display last night, they went back and reported to him that we are together. Then this morning, you go to register with the militia—"

"Oh," she interrupted, "I get it now!" She raised her hand to her face in surprise. "There's no doubt now that God is on our side. Even though my father told me a thousand times I should go and register, every time I thought to do it, my stomach grew queasy at the mere thought of being dressed as a *miliciana*, something I completely despise. I would always tell myself to do it tomorrow. I've been postponing that until tomorrow for a long time now! I never considered it important until last night. But I see now the importance this can have for both your security and mine. I didn't realize it until I saw you so close to Che and Piñeiro. While I was waiting for you in the car, I decided to give those jerks watching us such a wonderful little view—I had no doubt they were government agents. Who else could it have been?"

I said, "Yes, there's no doubt that God is on our side. Every single thing you've done in the last twenty-four hours corroborates my story and removes any doubt in Fidel's mind about the credibility of Piñeiro's accusations about my loyalty."

Chandee smiled and said, "Did you ever hear the old saying that God works in mysterious ways?"

"Yes," I answered with a nod, "I have. I also heard that God protects the innocent. We've confirmed both in the past few hours."

She held my hand over the table and asked, "Is there something bothering you? Everything seems to be going so well, you should be very happy and relaxed after all these events, but you seem nervous or impatient for something."

I grew very serious at that. "Well," I replied, "I'll tell you that you're learning a very valuable lesson in our work: to study the demeanor of someone and determine how they feel. I believed my demeanor had been pleasant and normal, but you correctly perceived that I'm nervous and impatient." I pointed at her. "That is very good. Before I say anything, though, I want to ask you to keep this completely confidential."

"Of course. It's not the first time you've asked to keep something between us."

"Remember when you asked me if I had something that could compromise me in my house when the G-2 searched? I have something extremely compromising under my shoe rack in my closet, and my closet was exactly what Piñeiro's men went straight for, evidently looking for precisely that. Under that rack, I have duplicates of documents I found in Che's portfolio, along with notes in my handwriting attempting to decipher this scheming man's schematics and an enormous amount of currency from North America and all around the world. According to Mima, they didn't find anything." I paused and massaged my forehead. "That is what keeps bugging me. I cannot understand, if what Mima said is true, where the hell everything went. Do you understand my worry now? There was no way I could ask Mima about it over the phone. Until I get back there and can talk to her in person, thousands of assumptions continue to crowd my brain. That is why I'm so nervous and impatient, as you detected so well. I need to get that water out of my ear."

She smiled and squeezed my hand. "Calm down—take it easy. Your Mima probably searched your room, found what you have in there, and moved it to a place she felt would be more secure. What other logical explanation can we give for that? Do you think, if they found all those documents, that Fidel would talk to you like he did today?"

I nodded. "Yeah, that's why it's been driving me crazy. So many assumptions cross my mind, and I kept thinking, what if one of Piñerio's men found it with the intention of keeping the money, and using the documents against me in blackmail?" I looked at her in confusion.

The Dark Face of Marxism

"I don't know. I don't know," I repeated with a shake of my head. "Millions of things have crossed my mind every minute in these last hours. Even when those people approached me in the music store today and told me Fidel needed to speak with me, the first thing that shot into my head was that this was it. I assumed the worst, but I was wrong again. That's why I don't want to think any more about this, because the possibilities of whatever happened to that plastic bag are too many. I don't want to torture myself anymore with it. Eventually I will have a logical explanation, and that probably is in the heart and head of Mima."

Chandee squeezed my hand again and gave it a gentle shake. "Take it easy—take it easy. There's no point in worrying about something that's out of your control. You'll just drive yourself crazy. In a few hours you'll be home and rid of those doubts, once and for all."

I nodded and called the waiter over. I paid for the lunch, and we left the hotel to drive to Chandee's house.

As we drove down past the *Malecón*, she said, "Thank you for the meal. This is something anyone could easily get accustomed to: good food, being treated with courtesy and respect, and so on. Sometimes I ask myself if it would not be a lot better for you, instead of being filled with all these worries and uncertainties, to ignore everything that's been going on in our country, about socialists and Castro, and to simply lie back and live la dolce vita? This government, actually, has been offering it to you. If you think about it, the comfort and privilege they constantly drop at your feet is something everyone else wishes to have." She lay her head back against the headrest. "This life you're living right now could be the envy of many—

even me, if it weren't for my rebel spirit and the convictions my father instilled in me. I have to tell you the honest truth: if I had everything you have, I really would have to think twice about just ignoring everything, closing my eyes, and enjoying the ride and all that comes with it—food, cars, privilege, everything. Just let the train go until it takes us wherever. Like everyone says, life is too short, and we have to enjoy it for however long we're here."

I looked at her in surprise, my expression a little skeptical.

"No, no—don't look at me like that," she added, looking at me very seriously. "If you analyze this very coldly, like I was just telling you, what you have in your hand right now is what most people spend their entire lives working for, more often than not only achieving a middling success compared to you. That's why I had to ask myself back at the hotel what the reason was that you would risk your life and what really motivates you to jeopardize yourself and your family. My father hates this, but your father likes it and supports this government completely."

I returned her grave look and asked, "Are you questioning me out of curiosity, or are you questioning my legitimate integrity as a freedom fighter?"

"Both," she replied curtly.

I smiled. "Very well. If you continue along this route, you will graduate very soon to be a professional spy."

She looked at me in surprise. "You want to tell me that you're not upset that I distrust you and put your loyalty in doubt?"

I smiled once more. "Nope. Why should that bother me? That is precisely one of the first things they taught me: don't trust anyone completely. Your best ally today could be your worst enemy tomorrow."

Her look transitioned to a blend of surprise and confusion. She placed her hand on her chest and said, "That including me?"

I nodded. "Yes, my friend. That is the way it is. Of course, I trust you a lot more than I trust Piñeiro, but—"

A punch in the shoulder interrupted me.

"You!" she exclaimed. "How dare you put me on the same level as Piñeiro? Are you just kidding me?"

"Nope." My look remained serious, but she looked so upset that I couldn't hold a straight face any longer, and I burst out laughing. She hit me again in the shoulder—this time, quite hard. The car swerved wildly on the road. "Ouch! That one hurt!"

"It was meant to."

"Just a few minutes ago," I chided her, "you doubted my loyalty, and I find it normal. Why are you getting so upset because I doubt yours?"

"I'm sorry," she apologized again, "I shouldn't have hit you so hard. You almost lost control of the car because of it, and that's not cool."

"You just caught me by surprise," I said. "If it makes you feel any better, my comparison between you and Piñeiro was just a joke. I wanted to test your reaction. I didn't expect it to be so violent. But in everything else was true. In our work we have to constantly use our common sense and not blindly trust in anyone. You always have to hold the pot by the handle, and if you cannot grab it by the handle, you had better have a spare one—an insurance policy. It doesn't guarantee much, but at least it gives you the tranquility of having an emergency exit that only you know about."

Chandee said, "You really follow everything you've learned to a T."

I shook my head. "Not always. Sometimes we have to improvise. That is the secret—knowing how to improvise when it's absolutely necessary."

She nodded in agreement.

We arrived at her house, and she said, "If any emergencies come up in the near future, you'll have to communicate directly with my father. I will be leaving the city for several weeks. They're finally sending me on an intensive training course. They want me to be more prepared so I can be more efficient by your side."

I smiled. "Congratulations! That's what you wanted, isn't it?"

She smiled and nodded. I stopped the Mercedes in front of the store, but as I was about to get out, she grabbed me by my right arm. With a sad face, she said, "I'm sorry, but I have to tell you something really unpleasant."

I wondered why, after so many hours together, she was only now choosing to tell me whatever her news was.

She looked at me and understood my questioning expression. "I'm sorry, I know I should have told you this sooner while we were having lunch. All day long this has been going through my head in circles, but I have to be brave and tell you, even though it crossed my mind to go away and let someone else be the bearer of bad news—but that is the coward's way."

"If you don't get to the point and tell me, you're going to kill me with anxiety," I teased. "Look at my hand, I'm sweating. Let me tell you, honey, the way hasn't been invented that will turn bad news into good. It's best to do it quickly, like having a tooth pulled or getting a shot. The quicker the better." I made a quick slashing motion. "Just like that! The pain is only felt for a moment, and the person you have to tell doesn't go through the calamity and suspense, which can often be worse than the news itself."

She replied tartly, "I'm glad you're taking this so lightly, but here goes."

She took a deep breath, and tears welled up in her eyes. "Yaneba and her family have been killed. A MiG shot them in international waters. No survivors. Marlina called this morning to tell me." She shook her head, the tears becoming more pronounced. "I'm sorry, but I don't have the courage to tell you in any other way."

I sat in silence for a few seconds in shock. I shook my head in stunned disbelief. "No, no, no—it cannot be. What proof do they have that it was them—that everyone was killed? It cannot be right."

Chandee looked at me compassionately, understanding that I didn't want to accept that reality. She caressed my cheek with her hand, two tears rolling down her cheeks. She looked at me with her reddened eyes. "A fisherman, a friend of Josue, gave the testimony. He saw the whole thing through his binoculars. He said he saw the plane come down and strafe something that he couldn't quite see, so he investigated. He saw a North American Coast Guard ship approach the crime scene after the MiG left, but it was too late. They didn't take any survivors. When he reached the wreckage, the Coast Guard had already left. There was blood all over the place, pieces of wood floating on the surface, and the entire area saturated with sharks in a feeding frenzy, eating what was left of the victims. The fisherman found a piece of wood with the name of the boat and home port on it: Elena, Las Canas."

I dried my tears on the back of my hand after listening to her recitation. A vivid image arose in my mind of that night of Josue backing the boat in towards the shore so that it would be easier for everyone to board. I saw the name of the boat at that moment and could clearly see the sad face of Yaneba waving goodbye to me.

"Do you know who that fisherman was? What is his name, where does he live? I'd like to know more, and I want to see what's left of the boat."

"Hector Garcias. He lives only two or three houses from where Yaneba's family lived. They knew each other very well. It's been a terrible shock to those against the government in Las Canas, and they've been in a very quiet mourning over the news."

I pulled my hand away and got out of the car, a knot in my throat. I was almost overwhelmed by my grief, but I didn't want to weep openly in front of Chandee. I took a handkerchief out of my pants, dried my face, and blew my nose. I went around to the other side of the Mercedes and opened the door for her.

She looked at me in affectionate compassion and asked, "Are you going to be all right? Are you sure you can drive all the way to your house after this?"

I nodded. "Of course, of course. Don't worry about it." I put my hand on her cheek. "Thank you for your compassion and being straightforward with me. I really appreciate that."

She could only nod.

The Dark Face of Marxism

"Changing the subject," I said, clearing my throat, "I want you to put a lot of attention on your training. It will be very important to your survivability in the future."

She nodded half-heartedly and gave me a big hug.

After we said our farewells, I left that place, my heart rent with sorrow and grief. Ever the optimist, I thought that that man, Garcias, might provide some hope that somebody had survived that terrible attack. Perhaps the United States Coast Guard had rescued someone from the wreckage after all.

I turned onto the main highway. Before I left the city, I stopped at a bakery to purchase some pastries for Mima and my family. A couple of hours later, I arrived back at my house. I said hello to everyone, and my neighbors came out to admire my latest acquisition, complimenting me on the car.

I walked to my bedroom. After I slung my travel bag over the bed, I rushed to the closet. I removed the shoe rack and opened up the compartment. It was empty. I stood before the mirror in the bathroom next to the closet, rubbing my forehead in anxiety. I wondered where in the world that bag could be. In the mirror, I saw the image of my mother and I started violently.

"Mima," I said, "you scared me."

"You're too jumpy, my son," she said. "What is going on? Why are you so worried?"

"I have a lot of reason to be jumpy, Mima, but you scared me because I wasn't expecting you."

She smiled and looked at the open compartment behind my shoe rack. She pointed at it and said, "Thank God that whatever you had in there I took the day after you left for the capital with Fausto and the rest of Che's gang. The next morning, when I started to clean your room, I found that bag with all that strange money and those documents inside. When I saw the American dollars and I read some of the notes you had in there, my legs started to tremble so uncontrollably that I didn't think I would be able to go downstairs without falling. I realized the major trouble we all would be in if this wound up in the wrong hands—like those of the government, whose hands came looking for it not much later."

She closed the toilet seat and sat down on it. She held on to the vanity with her right hand while her left massaged her forehead in frustration and worry.

She looked at me very seriously and said in recrimination, "Julio Antonio Marmol! How could you bring this here, to your own house? It would sentence not just you but all of us to death!"

I replied in sincere repentance, "I'm sorry, Mima. At that moment, I didn't think that it would be more secure anywhere else."

Mima shook her head. "The people you're working for—adults, I assume—didn't ever tell you not to bring anything close to the place you live? Your home would be the first place they would search if the government developed any suspicions about you."

I gulped. It had indeed been one of the first things I had been told.

"Yes, yes—they told me that several times, exactly what you just said. But this was an emergency, and I had to improvise. The night Fausto came to pick me up, I'd been planning to relocate this package and remove it. Everything happened so fast, though, with what happened to Mr. Aldames at the jewelry store, and everything got complicated."

"Well," she said, "thank God and His Son, Jesus Christ, and the Virgin Mary, that I found your hidden treasure instead of those dogs from the G-2, or we would all have been arrested and put in front of the firing squad. Even your father, who sympathizes with these hypocritical socialists."

She stood up, came over to me, and hugged me. She whispered in my ear, "I'm very proud of you, but you have to be careful. Even though they didn't find anything on you this time, the next time I might not be there to help protect you."

She put both hands to her head. "These socialists are a hundred thousand times worse than that dictator Batista. That poor charcoal family, Marcel and Fraya. Their faces were almost deformed from the beatings they took. They both came over here to apologize, because they might have said something incriminating during the beatings. They were really worried about you and wanted to know if you were OK. You should go visit them at their house right now, let them know that you're all right, and that you forgive them, even if they were indiscreet. Make them understand that you know any other person would do the same under the circumstances. It's very important to let them know that you forgive them and you care for them. Thank God we're all OK!"

She raised her hand to her eyebrows and said incredulously, "I don't know how you managed to get out of that situation without a single scratch or bruise on your skin." She shook her head in amazement. "There's no doubt in my head or my heart that you have Jesus Christ at your back all the time."

She stepped towards me and hugged me once more. "I have to be completely honest with you. In the middle of this whole ordeal, while the search was going on, even though I was crapping in my pants at the thought of these people uncovering the spot where I'd hidden those things, my greatest remorse was that I couldn't even tell your father. For more than twenty years, I've shared all of my secrets with him, and now I could not tell him absolutely anything at all for fear of a violent reaction from him. Nothing this government does is negative to him, and everything that is terrible he says will be better later on. I cannot understand how these people got him to the point that he started to believe that Fidel Castro is a resurrected prophet. It's more appropriate for this murderer to think of himself as a reincarnation of Satan."

She hugged me hard. "Thank you for the pastries. You're such a great son, remembering your Mima all the time. I'm very proud of you. But don't make the same mistake again. Don't ever bring anything compromising here to the house again. If it's compromising," she pointed to the ground in emphasis, "you bury it, and you don't even tell your Mima where. Do you understand?"

"Yes, Mima, I understand."

She leaned in to whisper in my ear, "The plastic bag is on the patio under the tank of *sarcocho*."

I raised my eyebrows in surprise, and said happily, "I must tell you the tremendous irony that is. That was precisely the way I hid it after I took it. The only difference is that you put it under, while I hid it inside!"

She looked repulsed. "Phew! Believe it or not, my son, that was also my first idea,"

"As the Bible says, from dust we come, and to dust we return."

She smiled, crossed herself, and said, "Amen. That's right, my son."

I grinned from ear to ear. This time it was I who hugged her. "I'm not only very proud of you, Mima, but I don't think if I were born a thousand times again I would ever have a better mom than you."

"Aww," she said delightedly and returned my hug. She gave me a couple of emotional kisses on the cheek. Before releasing me, she warned once more, "Be very careful. There's no doubt that there's someone in the circles you're moving in that is not looking at you with friendly eyes. It may be due to envy, but it's dangerous for you. We have to stop and fight this atheist government, or one day they will destroy the most basic freedoms we have. To do this, however, we have to be astute, so that we don't leave open an opportunity for them to hurt us."

I replied proudly, "That is precisely what I've been doing for a while, Mima. Somebody has to stop them, before it's too late."

"Yes," she agreed, "but be very careful, please, my son."

"OK, Mima."

"Who are you working for?"

I looked at her gravely. "I cannot tell you, Mima. I'm sorry."

"You don't have to break your secret or tell me any names. I just want to know if that person is a member of our family. That will make me feel a lot better; if he's part of the family, he'll never betray you and will take care of you a lot better than a stranger. If it's one of the family, close your right eye. If it's a stranger, close your left eye to indicate that he's part of the left wing."

I looked at her gravely. To tease her, and since it was partially true, I closed both eyes. She made a frustrated noise, and I thought that it wouldn't really compromise anyone, so I winked my right eye at her. She smiled in pleasure. She tapped her temple with her left index finger and smiled mischievously. "I can imagine who it is."

I held up both hands. "Oop!" I said. "That is all we're talking about today, Mima. I need to go in a while to Marcel and Fraya, so that I can find out what really happened. Probably by tomorrow I will remove that package from the house."

"OK," she said. "I will make your absolute favorite dish tonight: cow liver steak in wine sauce with pimentos and mushrooms."

I rubbed my stomach. "Oooh, *que rico*[17]! What is the occasion of this special treatment? What did I do to deserve it?"

"You think it's too little, to send me a brand new spinet piano—almost new, at any rate? They brought it to me, and I knew that even though I liked the one they broke better, that you would have something to do with this. If you hadn't interfered, Che would probably have given us a kick in the rear end. My son, I'm going downstairs to start things in the kitchen. Say hello to Marcel and Fraya for me, OK?"

---

[17] *That is delicious!*

The Dark Face of Marxism

"OK, Mima."

As she left, she said, "It gives me great happiness to have you back here with us."

"Thank you, Mima. Me, too. There's nothing better than being home."

I watched her disappear down the stairs. I started empty my dirty clothes out of my travel bag into the hamper. Something struck me at that moment—even though I had told Mima that I would remove that package the next day, I decided to take it tonight. I could see no reason to leave it any longer there. Mima was right. If something went wrong, I would not only compromise myself but my entire family. I took the now-empty travel bag and went downstairs to the patio. I walked to the small hallway under the stairs where my parents had put the *sarcocho* tank. There wasn't much in it yet, and I was able to raise the tank up. I saw that everything was there, and I carefully wiped the plastic free of the dirt from beneath the tank and put it inside my travel bag. As I passed the kitchen, I saw that Mima had already served up some plantains.

"Are you going on another trip already?" she asked.

"No, Mima—I'm just changing one of my plans we discussed and taking care of that chore now."

"OK, my son. Be careful."

As I walked through the living room, I looked at the spinet. I went over to it and looked it over. It wasn't the same quality as the baby grand we previously had. Heaven knew what family it had belonged to previously, but I thought a little remorsefully that at least it would give a little satisfaction to Mima. If left in the large warehouse where the government stored furniture, it would probably wind up being eaten by termites. At least Mima would get better use out of it.

I left the house and drove towards Leocadio's ranch. I planned to hide all of this stuff there. As I drove, I made sure to go through different neighborhoods to ensure that I wasn't being followed. I even stopped the car in one neighborhood and turned the lights off. I waited for at least fifteen minutes to make doubly certain I didn't have a tail.

I drove past the turnoff for the ranch as if I were leaving town towards the Jupiña factory. I abruptly made a U-turn before leaving town and drove back to the road I should have turned down. After convincing myself that I was truly alone, I felt more relaxed and drove on towards the ranch. "Well," I said to myself, "evidently Fidel and Che's word for once is truthful. Doesn't look like anyone is on my tail."

When I got to the ranch, the large gates were closed. It was only 7:45 p.m., and that was unusual at this time of day. Leocadio only closed those gates very late at night. I stopped the car, opened the gates, and proceeded inside the ranch. When I got to the house, I was received as usual by canine music. The entire pack had come to say hello to me, especially Kimbo.

He growled at the other dogs, demanding more exclusive attention from me. It was like he was telling them to get away from me. After I petted all of them a little, I embraced Kimbo as my special friend. I realized after a while that Leocadio wasn't at the house. I looked around but didn't see him anywhere. The front door of the house was closed, and there was no sign that he was there. I took my flashlight and travel bag out of the Mercedes. I walked towards the stables, followed by Kimbo. The other dogs lazily lay down on the front porch beneath the hammock.

I looked at the barn in the distance. I could see a light moving around that might have been from a lantern. No sooner had I seen it, however, than it disappeared again. Even though it was dark, the area was brightly lit by the full moon. The glow of the moonlight and the stars reminded me of the crazy night on the highway to Las Canas when Yaneba came up with outrageous idea of making love in the middle of the road—the last night I spent with her. Distracted by those thoughts, I walked towards the barn in Kimbo's company.

I opened the heavy doors to the barn. I entered and scanned the surroundings with my flashlight. I walked to my left in the building where the sawhorses and tack were stored along with some tools. I looked at all the things hanging on the wall.

I pulled out my commando knife and started to probe at the wood close to the floor. I worked it between two planks of wood. Two nails came out easily, as if they had already been removed before. I pulled the loose nails out with my fingers and put them in my shirt pocket. Using the knife as a crowbar, I managed to remove one plank. I laid it by my feet and felt around inside the resulting hole.

A few seconds later, I pulled out a shoe box. I put that on the floor by my feet, opened it, and removed a piece of black velvet cloth from the jewelry store. I unwrapped the cloth and examined that beautiful stone by the light of my flashlight, observing how it cast sparkling miniature stars across my pants leg. I wrapped it back up and put it back inside the shoebox.

I unzipped the travel bag and removed the plastic bag. I opened it and began to unload the wrapped dollars, meticulously putting them in order on top of the cloth in the shoebox until it was filled up. There were only two bundles left before I could fit nothing more in the box. I decided to leave them with the other foreign currencies. I put the shoebox back inside the wall and then carefully put the plastic bag with all of the documents inside.

Kimbo began to growl. "What's up, boy?" I asked him. "What's going on?" I shone the flashlight around but saw nothing. I picked up the piece of wood to cover the hole back up. As I did, someone directed a powerful box light at me. I whirled around.

A voice said, "I'll take it from here. Put your hands up and don't make any stupid moves. I'm pointing a .45 pistol at you. You know better than anybody what that bullet can do. If you don't want to die here tonight, do what I tell you."

I raised both of my hands. Kimbo started barking aggressively.

"You better calm that dog down before I shoot him."

"It's OK, Kimbo," I said, "calm down. Calm down."

Kimbo lay on the floor, but continued to growl.

The voice said, "Take your pistol out of the holster and slowly toss it to your right."

I did as directed.

"Now take your commando knife and do exactly what you did with your pistol. . . . Now move to your left." He used the light to gesture. "Sit down over there on that bench, where the saddles are. Sit facing the wall, your back to me. I'm going to handcuff you until my partner comes in."

I thought to myself that these must be G-2 or other government agents. I wondered how the hell I hadn't noticed these people after all the precautions I had already taken. I should have seen someone behind me, even in a civilian car.

As I walked over to the bench the man had lit for me, I thought how devastating this was going to be. Not only would he have my handwritten notes, but the most valuable diamond in the entire haul was going to be in his hands.

Kimbo was getting agitated again. "Calm that damn dog down before I shoot him."

"Kimbo, come here, calm down." I wondered what recourse I had. I was a little upset with myself, having felt rushed to get these things out of the house. I probably should have waited a few days, as I might have managed to shake any watchers. They had already searched the house, so that would have been actually safer, at least for a while.

I had to force myself accept that it was too late for regrets.

I heard some noise behind my back. Kimbo jumped and attacked the man. I heard a shot and Kimbo's yelp of pain. The light rolled along the floor, pointing away from me. I turned and saw in the dim light of both flashlights two silhouettes rolling on the floor. I ran over to where I had dropped my flashlight. I looked by the saddles and found it. I pointed the beam towards the silhouettes and saw a young kid with dishwater blonde hair wrestling with a large, fat man. I had no idea who they were, but I knew that kid would not be able to control such a large man. I searched for my pistol with my beam, knowing that this kid, whoever he was, would soon need my help.

I stepped on something hard in the hay that was strewn around the floor. I pointed the light down towards the floor and saw that it was the man's .45 pistol. Apparently, as they wrestled, the weapon had skittered away only a few feet from them. I picked it up and pointed the flashlight at them. The man was already on top of the kid and back in control of the situation.

I was about to say something to the man when I felt something cold on my neck.

"Drop the pistol slowly."

I slid it down by my leg and let it drop into the hay.

"Move it in front of you." A hand reached around and snatched my flashlight out of my left hand.

As I felt him lean forward to take my flashlight, I heard a grunt of pain as I was nearly deafened by the blast of a shot right next to my ear. To my surprise, the fat man before me fell to the ground on his knees. The man behind me likewise fell down, brushing against me as he collapsed. I pointed my flashlight as I spun around.

Chapter 7: The Innocent Fugitive

The first thing I saw was the badly beaten face of Marcel, armed with a blood-smeared sickle. The man who had been behind me was on the floor, and I shone the beam of light on him. He was clutching at a hole at the left juncture of his neck and shoulder, and with both hands he was trying to staunch a gusher of blood. Beside him lay two pistols—the one I had just dropped to the floor and the one he had been holding to my head. I bent over and picked up both weapons, putting one under my belt, and keeping the .45 in my right hand. I pointed the flashlight as I turned slightly to the young kid who had been wrestling with the fat man. He had a black eye and was bleeding slightly at the mouth from a broken lip. He was still on his knees, trying to recover from his fight.

"Are you OK?" I asked him.

He nodded. "I believe so." He struggled to rise to his feet. The fat man was still on his knees, leaning slightly to his right against the stall wall of one of the stables. There was a bullet hole in his left breast, his head slumped forward. I took a couple of steps to him, took his wrist, and checked his pulse.

I turned to the others and said, "This man is dead." I turned to Marcel and asked him, "Are you OK?"

He nodded but said nothing.

I saw the large mag light they had used and picked it up from the floor. I walked over to the mortally wounded man. I took the pistol from my belt and handed it and the large light to Marcel. "If he tries anything funny," I instructed him, "shoot him in the head."

I took my handkerchiefs out of my pockets and folded them into a bandage. I lifted his hand and placed the pad over the wound. "Put pressure on it," I told the man, "until we decide what to do with you."

He looked at me with glassy eyes, death reflected in his face. There was a flicker of guilt in his expression as he looked at me, and he tried to smile. Perhaps he was thinking that only a few minutes before, he had been trying to get rid of me, and here I was, trying to save him from bleeding to death. I searched his shirt and found a small wallet.

Before I opened it, Marcel said to me, "This son of a bitch is Lieutenant del Balle. This is one of the bastards that almost beat me to death and removed some of Fraya's teeth. What heroes! They spent the entire day today digging through the charcoal ovens at my house, tearing them apart to the point they're barely usable, looking for evidence to send us all to prison or the firing squad. They couldn't accept the idea they had abused their power and that their bosses had suspended them from duty for ninety days without pay. Of course," he added, "I know you probably had a lot to do with this."

His expression grew discontented. "But this is not enough for me, and it won't return my Fraya's teeth. It also won't make up for all the humiliation and abuse we received from them. However, that is the way their superiors excused the wrongdoing and washed their hands of these disobedient imbeciles. Believe me, this punishment was given to them only as a justification, and is just a slap on the wrist."

He looked at del Balle's half-dead form and took a couple of steps to him and pointed at the fat man. "Come on, you bastard—go ahead and tell Porfirio to call Piñeiro to ask permission to return to you the life that is escaping through your fingers right now." Marcel spat on him and turned back to me. "You should not even have given him those handkerchiefs. This bastard doesn't deserve it." He raised his right arm. "Ask him how much he enjoyed all the tortures he subjected us to, trying to incriminate you, practically coercing me to say that I had taken Che's briefcase."

I put my left hand on Marcel's shoulder as he held the light. "Calm down," I said. "I only gave him my handkerchiefs as a humanitarian gesture, one that he never gave to you guys. Look at him—he's dying, and if he has a piece of decency left in him, he's dying ashamed of his actions. He used to believe he was omnipotent, on top of the world—he never saw himself like this. But we're not like them; even though they are our enemies, and we're killing each other, it doesn't mean we shouldn't display common humanity to each other when one side is stricken and unable to cause any more harm to the other."

I shone the beam of my flashlight around the barn. In one of the stalls on the opposite side of Porfilio, I saw the bloody body of Kimbo. I walked over to him and checked him for life. He seemed very still, so I moved him slightly to be sure he was still breathing. He was, with difficulty. He was unconscious, and his injury was critical. I found a small bullet hole in his back and a large wound by his left front leg. I removed my shirt and wrapped him in it.

I looked at Marcel. "Look at what these bastards did to my dog."

The young, dishwater blonde boy said, "I'm really, really sorry." His freckled face was very sincere.

I looked at him mournfully, and two tears escaped my control and rolled down my cheeks. Maybe my friend Kimbo had given his life defending me. The youth held out his hand to me as he still crouched on the floor. "Leonel Rodriguez," he introduced himself. "Thank you very much."

I looked at him in surprise as I tried to dry my tears on the back of my hand. I replied, "My name is Julio Antonio del Marmol. The thanks must be from me to you, for your attempt to defend me from this huge man." I pointed at Porfirio's body.

Leonel smiled and said, "In that case, we both have to thank each other. You don't remember me, do you?"

I looked at him more carefully. He wore the uniform of the regular army. He looked familiar to me somehow, but I couldn't place his face in my memory as to where I had seen him before.

Leonel unbuttoned his shirt and exposed a bullet wound scar on his right shoulder. "The day they were transporting me to the regiment, to the firing squad on the charge of being a counterrevolutionary, you distracted the lieutenant and the soldiers with Jupiñas. The only reason I was able to escape with my life was you. That's why when I saw you in trouble a little while ago, I tried to help you." He picked up an iron bar from the floor. "Unfortunately, when I jumped on that big man to hit him on the head with this, he moved forward. Instead of his head, I got him on the back and lost the element of surprise. In consequence, he almost killed me. My plan backfired."

I replied, "Thank you very much. You were very brave, considering your physical size and constitution compared to this immense man's. You really were David to his Goliath, and it's a miracle that you brought him down to the floor and were able to wrestle with him as long as you did."

Marcel interjected, "Yes, there's no doubt that every single saint and virgin was on the side of you guys today. I had nothing to do with what happened here, either, until midnight. That is the time we were supposed to pick up Leonel. Leocadio and I were to take him in my wagon to the mouth of the river where a fishing boat should be waiting tonight to get him out of Cuba. Leocadio's been sheltering him all this time since his escape. Fraya, Leocadio, and I took care of his wounds, the same way we did with you." He shook his head. "Is it not ironic how history is repeating itself once more tonight?"

I looked at my wristwatch and asked curiously, "If you weren't supposed to be here until midnight, why are you here this early?"

Marcel nodded and pointed towards the sky. "As I said, all the saints and virgins were with you guys today." He pointed at the men on the floor. "When these bastards left my house, I followed them close to see where they were going. I had a bad feeling in my gut about them. Sure enough, they stopped here at Leocadio's farm and evidently decided to check this area. I said to myself, 'Thank God for this premonition,' and I found that sickle.

When I saw what was happening, I did what seemed appropriate."

"Amen," I said.

At that moment, we heard a squeaking hinge and all whirled. The gleam of a kerosene lamp lit the barn.

Leocadio stood there in the light. "Leonel!" he called. "Are you OK? I heard a shot."

"Yes, yes," the youth replied, "I'm back here. Marcel and Julio Antonio are here with me."

Leocadio shouldered an old shotgun as he walked in. He saw Marcel and me and asked in surprise, "What are you guys doing here?"

We explained to him what had happened, and Leocadio tried to apologize to me for not telling me before about Leonel. He hadn't considered it necessary and hadn't wanted to bring me anymore worries or complications. He felt he would be able to handle it with Marcel.

"When Marcel got arrested," he said, "we decided to rush up the situation before the G-2 took it into their heads to search the ranch. They know Marcel and I know each other, you see."

Suddenly, we heard a horrific scream behind us, and we whirled around in surprise. We walked to Lieutenant del Balle with our flashlights in hand. His eyes bulged out of their sockets, and with his free hand he held a hand up. He looked at us in terror, and screamed again, "No! No! Aaaahhh!" He held up his bloodied hand off of the bandage. He seemed to be fending off someone threatening to take him. He was dying in terrible agony and fear.

The Dark Face of Marxism

"I've seen men die like this before." Marcel crossed himself and mumbled a prayer. "No doubt about it—Satan is taking him to Hell."

He crouched over the body of Lieutenant del Balle and checked his pulse. "Maybe Satan is taking him someplace even worse—for this guy, Hell is too nice. But he no longer exists here with us. He's dead."

"What do we do with the bodies?" Leocadio asked.

"I'll need your help," Marcel replied. "The most prudent and smart thing to do, given the circumstances, would be to bury them Trojan style."

"What is that?" Leonel asked. "Why don't we drop them in the river and be done with it?"

"No, no," Marcel said, "that could be very dangerous. Remember that these are the ones who were recently interrogating us while we were in jail. If the authorities find the bodies, they could say that we did this in retaliation. The best way is a Trojan burial. We'll put them in one of the charcoal ovens that they broke themselves, and we'll make sure that no evidence is left behind. They will disappear. The charcoal might turn out to be a little sour, not the best quality. I'll take the chance of a few complaints from my customers that the charcoal won't light properly, though. But I need help to get enough wood quickly enough to make both ovens functional so that both of them can run all night long. If we do this by morning, there will be no trace left of these bastards—only ashes."

"Don't worry," I replied. "I'll take care of that. I'll bring you some help. How many people do you need?"

He spread his arms and shrugged. "The more the better. Three or four people—more, if possible. But the most important thing now is to get these bodies out of here. As soon as I get home, I will place them inside the ovens, cover them with the wood as best as I can with whatever I have handy. Then the people you bring to help us won't have to know what is inside the oven, and we don't have to share with anyone what we're doing."

I smiled. "You're learning, eh? The fewer people who know, the better. I'll tell them that, as a result of your arrest, you're behind in your work, and you're very worried about not being in compliance with meeting your customer's orders."

"Good thinking," he said.

Leonel said, "I can help."

Marcel shook his head. "No, you stay here. You need to be ready when we come back to get you. But I don't want you anywhere near our house, and I don't want the authorities to see you there. We've already been through hell to make your exit ready. You just be ready to go at midnight."

Leocadio said, "OK, I'll go with you and help with the bodies."

"OK," Marcel said. "I'll go and get the wagon."

He left the barn, and returned a few minutes later. He opened the barn doors, and the three of us wrapped the bodies in grain sacks and tied them off. After we put the bodies in the wagon, we covered them with bales of hay. Marcel and Leocadio left in the wagon towards Marcel's house.

Leonel helped me to remove the documents and shoe box from the barn and carry them to the Mercedes. After I put them in the trunk, I asked him to bring me a shovel. We wrapped Kimbo in a couple of sacks to keep him warm, and carefully put him in the car's back seat. I got in, and drove away from the ranch.

As I drove, I looked for a strategic place to follow my mother's suggestion and bury all of the dangerous materials that were in the trunk. I noticed off to the side of the road about half a block away a large Poinciana tree. I had seen it many times as I rode Diamante around the area, and determined that this was my best spot.

I dug a hole about fifty feet from the tree, and buried my treasure there after first wrapping all of it in a large plastic bag. After I covered the hole, I rolled a small boulder to mark the spot. It was large enough that I could not pick it up but could still roll it. I cleaned my hands as best I could on one of the sacks in the car.

I drove to the only veterinarian in town, a man named Raimundo. He had a clinic on one side of his house. He examined Kimbo and told me that the bullet had not damaged any vital organs. He assured me that he would do everything humanly possible to save Kimbo's life but that I would have to leave my dog there for a while. He gave Kimbo some shots, and assured me that he would be OK. I left the small clinic in the hope that my good friend would survive this ordeal.

From there, I drove to the house of my huge mulatto friend Pablo's house. The straight-haired youth was always ready to help me whenever I needed him. He lived in La Jia, the poorest neighborhood in town—so poor that the houses were virtually built of cardboard and leftover aluminum sheets. He received me with a big hug. After I explained to him that I needed his help, he said, "Let's go—no more talking."

A little while later, we had picked up other friends—the friendly black boy Abel Cisneros (or as we always called him, Cisneros) and the crazy joke expert Roberto Quintero (or Kinqui). Kinqui had earned his nickname because he had once told us that during a weekend visit to his grandfather's ranch, he noticed that his grandmother sticking her finger in the rear end of one of the chickens. This was how they used to make sure that the chickens were ready to lay eggs on the farms. But after he had seen his grandmother do that and it started to lay eggs, he decided to explore his sexuality and checked the chicken, but not precisely with his finger. Our friend Arturo gave him the nickname 'Kinqui' due to the English connotation of the homophone he had heard in an American movie.

Kinqui lived not far from Sandra's house. I nearly ran over Sandra's brother, Julian. He had seen us getting into the Mercedes and ran towards us, forcing me to slam on the brakes.

"Are you crazy or what?" I yelled. "I nearly ran over you!"

Julian was a little scared and replied, "I'm sorry, I'm sorry! I thought you saw me waving to you. I saw you guys leaving Kinqui's house." He paused to catch his breath. He looked at the Mercedes. "My God, this is a beautiful car. Does this belong to your father?"

"No, no—it's Che's, but it's on loan to me until they fix my Volga."

"Ooh, a Volga!" he exclaimed, wiggling his eyebrows. "Sandra and I are on a weekend's vacation. She told me that if I saw you, I was to let you know to stop by, because she wants to talk to you."

"OK, I'll stop by tomorrow. I'm very busy right now, and we'll probably be working very late."

Julian asked me, "Where are you guys going?" It was clear he wanted to be invited along.

However, I had little trust in him and even less in his sister now, so I deflected him by saying, "We're going to the Regiment. I'm in a rush, but we'll talk later, OK?"

He could see he wasn't welcome, and so backed off and said goodbye.

We drove by the ranch and on to the house of Marcel and Fraya. When we arrived there, I could see that all was in readiness, and they were working at covering the bodies with even more wood. I pulled in towards the house so that the headlights wouldn't illuminate the ovens and reveal to my passengers what lay in the ovens.

Marcel saw my car and came over to us at once. I got out with my friends. Marcel smiled and said, "Are these the voluntaries you're bringing to me, Julio Antonio?"

"Yes, *compañero*," I replied. "We're all ready and in the disposition to win the battle."

I introduced my friends to Marcel, and he said, "Leocadio will take them on a couple of trips, and later I will take them on a couple of trips."

"Very well," I said.

"OK, muchachos," Marcel said, "get in the wagon."

I was about to climb into the wagon, but Marcel stopped me. "Hold it, you'll go in the next trip. I want to talk to you, and Fraya wants to say hello before she goes to bed. It's getting late, and I don't want you to miss her because she's gone to sleep."

"OK," I said. My friends disappeared with flashlights in hand as Leocadio drove them in the wagon on the hunt for wood to fill the ovens.

We went inside the house, where Fraya welcomed me with a joyful hug, though slightly embarrassed. "You don't know what joy you've given me to know that you're OK. We both thought you had been arrested, and Heaven alone knows what those bastards would do to you." She looked at me, and I saw the mixture of joy and guilt in her eyes. She asked me, "You want a hot chocolate? I've just made some."

"No, no," I said, "don't bother."

"It's no bother at all," she protested. "I've made it for all of us, as well as your friends. It's very nice and noble of you to help us so."

"OK," I acquiesced. "Since you've already made it any way, I accept your invitation. I remember you make excellent chocolate."

As she walked into the kitchen, Marcel said, "Sit down, please." He motioned for silence putting his finger to his mouth. He whispered, "Don't tell Fraya even a single word about what happened tonight, please. She's had enough with what's been going on these past few days. I don't want to worry her anymore."

I nodded in agreement. I held my hand up and whispered, "Don't worry—I won't say a word."

Marcel nodded and smiled without speaking. Fraya returned with a small wooden tray and three steaming mugs of hot chocolate. There was also a plate of *churros*[18].

---

[18] *A Cuban string of doughnut dough covered in sugar.*

The Dark Face of Marxism

After she put the tray down on the table, she handed mugs to Marcel and me and took one for herself. She moved the tray in the middle of the three of us, and we dipped churros in the chocolate.

As we started to eat, she said, "I'm sorry I created problems for you. When these bastards started to interrogate and torture us, I heard one of them say that you told them about the bottles of guayabita, and it crossed my mind that you had been arrested, probably tortured, and so had told them that."

Two tears rolled down her cheeks, and her eyes were moist with more. "Please, forgive me," she said remorsefully. "I know you told us that you would never talk, even if your life was on the line, but when they mentioned the empty portfolio that you had left for Marcel to burn, I freaked out and said something I should not have said." She reached out, took my hand, and kissed it. "Please, my boy—forgive me." By this time, she was weeping openly and no longer was able to speak through her sobs.

I placed my other hand on top of hers. I gently removed the hand she had grasped and caressed her face. "I have nothing to forgive you for, because, thanks to God, I had no bad experience from it. We learned from this, and I repeat to you now: don't ever believe anything these people from the government say, because I don't know anything about you. Nothing happened here, which means I have nothing to say about it. Nothing exists—do you understand? But, if anyone has to ask for forgiveness, it's me, for bringing all of this to you guys and getting you involved."

Marcel replied, "You don't have anything to ask forgiveness for, either. When you came to our home and we helped you, we were already involved. We could not keep letting these people continue to commit these abuses like they had been doing. But remember—all of this happened for a reason, and they were probably looking for an excuse to harm us. There's no doubt in my mind that whoever told them about the guayabita bottles also provided them the reason to do what they did." He raised both his arms and exclaimed, "Thank God I was there! I used my eyes to warn Fraya, because I knew they were fishing, and she shut her mouth in time."

I caressed my mouth with my left hand. "Neither one of you guys ever mentioned the two bottles you gave me that day, and the only other person who knew was Tite, who is now in Miami. I know for a fact that I never told anyone. Not even my father knew, because he never received them—I gave them to Leocadio as a gift. The only witness that day," I said with sadness, "is Sandra. I remember now that she recriminated me for interceding for you with the sergeant and the guards when they wanted to search your wagon." I shook my head. "Even though we didn't part on very good terms, it never crossed my mind that she would turn government informant. I have to talk to her as soon as possible, but I have to be very careful and diplomatic so I can uncover the dark hand behind the chain of events that led to you guys getting arrested. We have to be careful in the future."

Marcel and Fraya looked at me compassionately. Fraya shook her head and said, "My boy, remember always that a communist is like a thief. You never can trust them, because they have no loyalty to anyone. Sooner or later they will disappoint you."

I shook my head in disappointment and bit my lower lip in frustration. "Well, after all, the good thing is that we aren't communists and so understand loyalty better than anyone. Maybe this will be a bittersweet experience in the future."

Marcel nodded and said with a half-frustrated smile, "We are absolutely in agreement. On the one hand, we can learn who we can trust, but on the other hand, we've had a close shave."

We heard noises outside, and Marcel said, "Oh! They're back already."

Fraya said, "You stay here, and I'll take some treats out to your friends." She prepared another plate of churros and more mugs of hot chocolate and took them out to where the wood was being unloaded.

After almost two hours and several wagon trips, we finished our work. Marcel said to me, "You want to have the honor?" He handed me the torch to light the Trojan burial. We all cheered and toasted with our hot chocolates, churros in hand, my friends completely ignorant as to what really was in those ovens. It was not until many years later that some of them learned the truth. But at that moment, it was only Leocadio, Marcel, and I who exchanged knowing glances.

After Marcel thanked my friends for their help, he said, "If you need charcoal in your house, you don't have to buy it. You know where you can get it, and you just come over here."

We said our goodbyes, and Marcel said to me, "I have to take Leocadio back to the ranch. You know what we're going to do."

I said, "OK—good luck."

I took my friends back to their homes and returned to the veterinarian's clinic to see how Kimbo was faring. Raimundo received me with affection, but I was unsettled by the sorrowful expression on his face. I braced myself for the worst.

Raimundo put his hand on my shoulder and said, "I have good and bad news." I scratched my chin in nervous incomprehension. "Which do you want to know first?"

Without hesitation, I said, "The good news first."

"OK," he replied. "Your dog Kimbo will be OK. He will need some time to recuperate, and you'll have to leave him with me for at least a few weeks, perhaps a couple of months. I don't know how long, but the great thing is that he's out of all danger and will live for years to come."

I smiled and said, "That's great—but what's the bad news?"

He rubbed his face. "Well, to save his life, I had to amputate his left front leg."

"Oh, no!" I exclaimed.

He said in resignation, "It was either his leg or his life. I thought you would prefer to save his life—was I wrong?"

"No, no—you did the right thing, thank you." I stayed silent for a few seconds and then asked, "Will he be able to walk with three legs?"

He smiled. "It will take him a while to adapt, but with a little effort and training, he'll be walking. And with the help of a carpenter, we might be able to devise a crutch or something that will make it easier for him to walk without falling. If you remember, the Dictator had as a symbol and a pet a grulla[19] that his driver had hit with his car in Santiago de Cuba. Batista wanted to save it, and a veterinarian friend of mine was the one who amputated its leg and prolonged its life."

The one-legged grulla that became a symbol of Batista's regime

I nodded my head and touched his shoulder. "Thank you very much. I really, really appreciate it. He's alive, and that's all that matters, even if he has to limp the rest of his life."

Raimundo smiled brightly and said, "That's the right attitude."

"Can I see him?" I asked.

"Of course, but he's sedated and will remain so for a few days so that he doesn't hurt himself. If you want to see him, I will bring you inside."

---

[19] *A Cuban crane*

I followed him to the little room that had several cages in his clinic. I saw Kimbo lying in one of the cages.

Raimundo opened the door for me, and I petted the sleeping dog's head. "You'll be OK, my friend," I said to Kimbo. "Thank you—thank you."

Raimundo asked, "What happened?"

I shook my head. "I'd rather not talk about it."

He nodded. "Say no more."

"Thank you very much," I said to him, "I appreciate all that you did. How much do I owe you?"

"Don't worry about it," he said. "I owe a lot of favors to your father. Let's wait until Kimbo gets completely well, and then we'll talk about it."

"Very well," I said, and I returned to my house. I was relieved, now that I knew my dog would be OK. He was young and very strong, and I knew he would learn to walk with a wooden leg without great difficulty.

I couldn't sleep that night. I had horrible nightmares involving the two dead men and their being burned inside the oven. The incident that evening had provoked a search through the drawers of my memory and brought to the surface the images of the young men who had been executed by firing squad the night I removed Che's bag from the regiment. I remembered how their bodies were opened following the execution and their organs harvested. The images clearly had a strong psychological and emotional effect on me and had been hiding away in the recesses of my mind, opened once more by this recent incident.

After waking periodically throughout the night in a cold sweat, each time shivering from head to foot, I decided to

The Dark Face of Marxism

get out of bed and take a hot shower to relax my nerves. I ate some fruit and drank a *cafe con leche*[20], and left the house quietly, as it was still very early in the morning.

I drove to the ranch, where Leocadio told me that everything had gone quite well that night. Leonel was safely en route to Florida and was of all danger. This made me feel much better and more relaxed. If they had been caught smuggling Leonel out of the country, they would have all been sent to the firing squad for treason against the Revolution.

After my brief chat with Leocadio, during which I gave him the news about Kimbo, I left for Marcel's house. I found him sitting by the ovens in a folding chair, guarding the large smoking structures. When he saw me coming in, he left his chair to come to my side. He said with a very big smile, "What brings you to my humble abode so early in the morning?"

"Just came by to see how everything is cooking, and make sure everything is OK," I said. "If there's anything I can do to help, you know all you need to do is ask. Besides, I couldn't sleep all night."

He replied without losing his smile, "Me either. All night, I was worried that someone would come snooping around and find our packages inside the ovens." His expression clouded and said more seriously, "The smell is so horrible that Fraya told me that I have to do something. Somebody will smell it and call the authorities. She asked me what kind of wood I put in—it smells like rubber

---

[20] *A typical Cuban breakfast including a glass of milk with a little coffee*

burning or cow leather. To make her quiet down, I told her that it's possible that an animal accidentally fell into one of the ovens." He shook his head, this time in worry. "After she told me that, I couldn't sleep anymore, thinking that someone would complain to the authorities about the smell."

I said, "Take it easy, man. First of all, you don't have anybody living within several miles of you—you're well out of town." I sniffed the air. "It doesn't smell so bad," I lied. "You can't even smell it anymore."

He lifted his face and sniffed. He raised his eyebrows. "Well, it's not so bad now, but in the early morning hours, it really stank, like the tires of a car burning."

"It could be the resin of some of the trees we brought or perhaps cedar—maybe some seeds. You know how cedar seeds can smell like rotten eggs; maybe we wound up with some cedar seeds in there."

He considered that and nodded his head. "Yeah, that could work as an excuse."

I smiled and said, "You see? I always give you an exit."

"Yes, you do, you do. Thank you."

After we said goodbye, I left and headed towards Marlina's house.

She received me on the porch with a hug and a smile, but that quickly faded when she asked, "You know what happened to Yaneba and her family?"

"Yes, Chandee told me all about it." I sighed deeply to contain my emotions, and we sat down. "But I don't believe it. There must have been some survivors. There has to be something we don't know yet."

She put her right arm around my shoulder. She said sadly as she shook her head, "No, no—not according to

The Dark Face of Marxism

Hector Garcia and the other fishermen with him in the boat." Two tears ran down her face and she stepped in to me to hug me. She saw my pale face and the depression in my eyes. I returned the hug, understanding that she was trying to console me.

After a few seconds, I gently disengaged from her and said, "I want to hear the whole story from their lips." I pointed at my chest. "Something here tells me that Yaneba is not dead, that there's a possibility that some of them survived. Maybe Hector and his friends arrived after the Coast Guard had already picked up survivors. According to Chandee, when Hector and his men got there, the Coast Guard had already left—they didn't see the vessel while it was moored next to Josue's boat."

Marlina shook her head sadly, but said nothing.

"Please," I said, "let me believe it until I talk to them. I cannot accept that Yaneba is dead—not yet. Can you please take me to those men?"

Marlina nodded silently. She wiped her face with both hands. "Wait for me for a few minutes. I have to wash my face and tell my mother that I'm going to leave with you."

"Thank you," I replied. "I'll wait for you here."

As soon as she walked inside, I stood up and started to pace from one corner of the porch to the other, anxious for her to return so that I could discover the truth about the incident. A couple of minutes later she returned, and I was resting against the veranda of the porch.

She took one of my hands. "Let's go to Las Canas, and you can remove once and for all that thorn in your chest. I know you will not be satisfied until you hear from the eyewitnesses of what happened to Yaneba and her family."

I nodded and said, "Thank you."

She touched my face, and we walked to the Mercedes to leave her house. As we drove along the highway, we passed by the small island with the palms where Yaneba and I had made love the night she left. Like a movie running in my mind, all the details returned to me. I couldn't help it, and I pulled over. I even remembered the scene of our running naked to avoid being run over by the large truck, the driver blowing his horn as he had fun with us.

I breathed deeply, thinking for the first time since I received the news that the reality was that Yaneba was dead. I started to tremble, starting at my stomach, and the hair on my neck started to raise. Goosebumps broke out all over my arms, and I shook my shoulders in an attempt to remove that uncomfortable sensation without result. I rubbed my neck with my right hand in a new attempt to rid myself of that involuntary tickling along it.

Marlina looked at me and realized that I was not all right. Trying to remain calm, she asked, "Are you OK?"

I looked at her with tears rolling down my face and said, "Right here, in this particular place, Yaneba and I made love for the last time the night she left Cuba." I rolled down the window and pointed at the middle of the highway. "Right there," and then I pointed at the grove of palms, "and right there."

Marlina grew emotional and started to cry once more. She hugged me again. She said, "Cry—it will make you feel better. Crying will help you let go of that pain through those tears. If you try to hold on to it, it will drown your heart. The pain in your chest will come to be unbearable."

The Dark Face of Marxism

For a few minutes, right there, we remained tightly embracing each other along the side of the road, the motor of the Mercedes still running. We both let go of the pain of the loss of our dear friend, and we wept openly over her death at that moment.

After a while, I told her the full details of Yaneba's effort to indelibly imprint in our memories through the crazy idea of making love in the middle of the highway. Marlina couldn't help but smile when I concluded my story.

"Yes, yes," she said, "no doubt about it—that was my friend Yaneba. No doubts, no illusions, no inhibitions, but with many convictions how to make a reality whatever she dreamed about and how to make certain she will live on in our memories for all our lives."

"Yes, she achieved that. I don't think I'll ever forget for the rest of my life that night." I nodded, feeling more recovered.

We left that place and continued on to the beach house.

When we reached Las Canas, my heart started to pound. Even though I wanted to know the complete truth, in my mind I knew that reality could be brutal. Whatever these men saw is what they would tell me, and if those facts were convincing enough, my hope of ever seeing my beautiful Yaneba again would forever vanish.

I swallowed hard as we passed in front of her house. It was closed up and abandoned. Evidently, Martina had been kicked out by the government.

A little further along, I stopped the car next to a light green house, which Marlina indicated was where Hector lived. From outside, we could see several people through the window sitting inside. They were sitting around the table playing dominoes. We didn't have to knock on the door; as we walked up, one of the ladies came up to open the door cordially for us.

"Can I help you?" she asked.

Marlina replied, "We're looking for Mr. Hector Garcia."

"Please, come in," she said. She held her hand out to us. "I am Mariana, Hector's wife."

We greeted her and followed her into the dining room by the window. She introduced us to the gathering and said to a man sitting at the table, "Hector, these kids want to talk to you."

He stood up to greet us. He was a tall man with straight hair and a pleasant face. He said in a deep baritone, "Well, you found me. What am I good for?"

"Well," Marlina said, "the reason we are here is he wants to know the full details about what you guys saw on the open ocean with Josue's family. I am the daughter of Martin. This is—"

"I know who he is," Hector interrupted. His joking demeanor had turned serious. Everybody at the table stopped playing and watched us with great attention. The two women and three men froze at the table.

Marlina understood that whatever she had said hadn't settled very well with the group. She put her hand on my shoulder once more. "There aren't any problems with him. Everything will remain between just us. He only wants to know the truth."

Hector pushed the table away so that he could come around to us. He raised his right arm and said, "I know you are the Commandantico, and I know Josue and all his family loved you very much. He told me great things about you. I also know you loved his daughter. But things are very hot in this town. I've told this to two people, and the entire town now knows what happened. It's come to the ears of the G-2, and they broke into our home late last night and asked us thousands of questions about Josue, the family. It looks like some informant here in town told them that I have pictures of the MiG shooting Josue's boat and killing the entire family. Of course, I denied that and said that I never mentioned any pictures, that I had seen a plane shooting at a boat, but I didn't even know it was his boat. All we saw was very confusing. We were several miles away."

He leaned back and nodded his head. "Of course, that is what I told them. You have to understand, this is what I should tell everybody. They said that if they hear from one more person anything different from what I signed with them, my entire family and I will be arrested. From last night on, what I tell anyone should never differ from that account. Of course, as you understand, none of these people want to be arrested as counterrevolutionaries and put in front of the firing squad for something we can't help anyway, since they're all dead now. They told me clearly that this would be defamation of the government." He raised his eyebrows sardonically. "It would be contrary to the interest of the people—that someone would die in the middle of the ocean, shot by a military plane. That is the interest to those people—but we cannot say anything! You understand?"

"Yes sir," I replied, "I understand."

He walked over to me and put his arm around my shoulder. He said to Marlina and the others, "Would you excuse us, please? I'm going to take a walk with the Commadantico along the beach."

"Of course," said Marlina. "Please."

As we walked out of the house, he said, "I'm going to ask you an immense favor. Do not repeat what I'm going to tell you to a single soul." He gestured with his thumb over his shoulder towards the house. "Even to her. This has already brought me enough trouble." We walked on the sand to the beach. He said, "If you tell anyone and they come back to me, I will deny it—you understand?"

"Yes," I replied, "I understand perfectly. I only want to know if there's a remote possibility that anyone survived. I have in my heart the feeling that Yaneba is alive."

"No, I'm sorry to tell you this," Hector said compassionately. "If anyone survived the attack, the sharks would have gotten them. There had to have been several bodies to dye the waters of the sea as red as I saw it."

He wiped his forehead with his left hand in distress as he recalled the grisly scene. He shook his head and continued, "No, no—it's not possible anyone survived that ordeal. I don't want to give you false hope. I know that's not what you want to hear, but in reality, that's what happened."

He templed his hands together. "If we only had the connections to somebody out of the country who could make public these pictures. Every day this government commits atrocities and violations of human rights upon innocent people who have nothing to do with their politics. They just want to leave the country and live in peace." He raised his eyebrows sadly and bit his lip. "Maybe if we find a way to be a witness to the entire world of these criminal acts, we can finally put an end to this and the international community will take more seriously what's going on here in Cuba. This is not a government; they are a team of executioners to put down anyone for even the slightest contradiction to the image they want to present to the world."

I stopped walking abruptly and asked, "Are you telling me you have pictures of what happened?"

He looked at me dubiously, clearly reflecting on whether or not he could trust me. He replied, "I used to have them. I destroyed them after the G-2's visit. You have to understand, I'm afraid for the safety of my family. The first thing that came into my mind was that they would search my house, accuse all of us of being counterrevolutionaries, and take us to the firing squad, all for some stupid pictures."

I looked at him in puzzlement. "But you just told me a few seconds ago that if we had the contact, we would be able to denounce these crimes. You don't trust me? Do you know who I am? I'm the one who facilitated their exit from Cuba, for God's sake! You know that—what is holding you back?" I put my right hand on my chest in anger. "I have the contact, in an embassy, who could make public these pictures and create a huge embarrassment for this country. But one minute you tell me you have them, and the next you tell me you don't! Can't you make up your mind, or are you playing with my head?"

He smiled mischievously and said, "Calm down, calm down, Commandantico. What I told you is true: I destroyed the pictures. What I didn't say is that I still have the negatives."

My eyes widened in surprise. "Really?" I asked.

"Really," he answered with a broad grin. "All I can say is that it's very good that you came here today, because I was thinking of destroying the negatives tonight. Even if I don't keep them in the house, it wasn't worth the potential threat to my family, especially since I don't have the contact to do anything with them. But you do." He nodded. "Follow me. I have them in my fishing boat."

We walked along the one of the piers. We climbed down the wooden stairs to the floating platform that connected the pier with the berth to which a rowboat was tied. He shipped the oars, cast off, and rowed us out to his vessel that was anchored about half a mile from the shore.

When we were almost to the ship, he said, "The pictures are unbelievably clear—I have the latest Kodak camera, very professional, with a really good telescopic lens. One of the pictures is so clear that we can see the registration number and Cuba flag on the MiG, clearly identifying the plane as one of the Cuba Air Force's birds."

"Well, it looks like we caught their hands in the cookie jar with this criminal act," I said with a smile. "This will be the best tribute we can give to Josue and his family and the best way we can honor the memory of my lovely Yaneba: by exposing how they were assassinated in international waters—their only crime the desire to leave their country after being denied permission to leave legally."

We reached the ship and tied off at the stern. We climbed up the ladder, and a few minutes later we descended below the deck. I followed Hector closely as we passed several crew cabins and reached the galley. We went inside, and he opened a cabinet. He removed several cans, one labeled coffee, another salt, and finally one labeled cinnamon. He emptied the contents onto a kitchen towel. He pulled out an envelope which he then handed to me. I sat on a stool bolted down to the deck and opened it.

Reality hit me as I looked at the negatives with the light bulb behind them. Hector hadn't exaggerated at all; the pictures were magnificent and showed the events of that dark day very clearly. The tracer lines of the shots from the plane were clearly visible, as was the flying debris from the boat as the bullets struck. One of the pictures clearly showed the name and home port of the boat: "Elena, Las Canas."

Hector looked at me compassionately, knowing that every single hope I held was lost in that moment. He said, "If you can get those pictures out of the country and expose this attempted genocide, this will be the best way to avenge their deaths."

I replied, "My mother is Catholic, and she told me many times that vengeance is not good for your heart. But I believe that every single rule has an exception, and this, I think, will probably be my exception. It might not be good to seek revenge on anybody, but at least it will be sweet to expose these barbaric incidents and how they kill men, women, and children with impunity."

I wiped a couple of involuntary tears from my eyes with the back of my hand. It hit me at that moment that I would never see Yaneba again.

Hector noticed this and said, "Kid, I keep asking myself how that pilot can sleep at night after he did such a thing." He put his hand on my shoulder. "Hide those negatives very well. If they find you with them, we will be two more victims of this regime and its murderous leaders."

I nodded. After I tucked the envelope inside my shirt, we both left the fishing boat and climbed down into the rowboat. It was still daylight, and the sky was very clear. As Hector rowed, I looked down into the crystal waters at the ocean floor. We drew near to the pier, and it was perhaps fifty feet deep. As we drew closer, I could see a lobster pot on the bottom in the seaweed. As the boat continued on its course, I fixed my eye on those lobsters and thought back to the day when Yaneba and I had seen something similar in that area. This time I kept my silence as I remembered those moments of happiness we had together.

I was completely lost in my thoughts until one small white gull with a black ring around its neck snapped me out of my reverie as it landed on my right shoulder. Curiously, it started to preen against my neck.

Hector looked at this in awe. The gull acted like a domesticated bird. I reached up and gently stroked its neck feathers with my fingers. The gull didn't move but crooned as it bobbed its head up and down in response to my caresses. I reached inside my shirt with my left hand and felt the medallion with the image of the Virgin of the Caridad del Cobre. Unseen by Hector, I started to stroke the medallion with my fingers, even as I continued caressing the gull's neck and head with my right hand. It appeared to be very relaxed, and demonstrated no attempt to move or shift its position.

Hector and I looked at each other. He smiled and said, "That means peace, tranquility, and a lot of good luck."

I continued petting the gull. When I stopped, it flew off, but not towards the shore. It flew out towards the ocean, like it was continuing on into the infinite. I turned my head in an attempt to follow its flight, expecting it to turn at any moment and circle back towards the shore. However, it continued and flew out over the deep waters of the ocean. I didn't want to be superstitious, but it shocked me.

"Do you see that?" Hector exclaimed. "No sea gulls fly in that direction!" Hector crossed himself as he stopped rowing. He contemplated the gull's flight in open-mouthed awe.

The little angel on my right whispered that the white bird was a messenger from the Lord, sent to let me know that Yaneba still lived. But then the demon on my left pinched me and murmured that it could also be a final goodbye from her, noticing how depressed I was at her death from her vantage in the other world.

It could even be simpler than that, of course, I thought. My shoulder could simply have served as a resting station for that gull for a few minutes after a long flight. Now rested, it had simply continued on to whatever destination it had in mind.

I shook my head uncomprehendingly. I remember what my mother had once said: "God works in mysterious ways, and sometimes we can't comprehend what He's doing." I smiled, thinking that perhaps one day in the future I would understand the significance of everything that had been happening.

Then something even stranger, with no logical explanation or reason, happened. I still had my hand on the Virgen de la Caridad del Cobre inside my shirt. The image on the medallion was of three fishermen in a small boat as the Virgin hovered above them, saving them from some danger. The boat was precisely like our row boat. The medallion had been given to me as a present from Yaneba, and with that thought an unbelievable feeling of serenity and comfort washed through me, mixed with a bit of joy. It filled my heart and flooded my spirit. In a split second, it removed the frustration and agony I had been feeling all the hours since Chandee had given me the news of the deaths of Yaneba and her family.

I looked around the boat and Hector while still touching that medallion, and the realization came back to me that, after all, the mission of the little gull could have been the healing of my pain. Within a few seconds of caressing that bird, my demeanor and frame of mind had completely changed. I felt re-energized to continue my fight against the evil, injustice, and sorrow perpetrated by this regime. I shook my head violently, thinking I was being too superstitious and perhaps a little conceited to think that, because what was I? A little skinny thirteen-year-old kid, like any other kid in the world. Why would God and the Virgin be so concerned about how I felt and worried about my pain?

Hector continued his rowing in silence. He had been observing me carefully, and when he saw me shake my head in that manner, he said, in a voice strong in conviction and faith, "Many times the most extraordinary things happen to the most humble, innocent, and insignificant people. Maybe this is the way that our Creator has to teach us humility while at the same time showing to us His own humility. That is the blessing and maybe the way of compensating us for who we are."

I stayed quiet and thought about that, analyzing what he had said for a few seconds. I nodded, my fingers continuing to rub the surface of the medallion under my shirt. Hector could see my hand was concealed, but he couldn't see what I was doing, so he asked curiously, "Are you OK? You got a pain in your chest or something?"

The Dark Face of Marxism

"No," I said, "I've never felt better in my life. I'm fine." I took the chain out and showed the Virgin to him.

Hector smiled. "Well, well—you're not so insignificant, after all. You're devoted to the Patroness of Cuba. Now I understand why she protects you." His face grew serious, but his tone still contained wonderment as he asked, "Who gave that beautiful medallion to you?" He had begun to slow down his stroke as we grew deeper into our conversation.

Almost immediately, I replied, "Josue's daughter, Yaneba."

He stopped rowing abruptly, like he had received an electric shock, sliding the oars up out of the water and stowing them in the boat. He climbed onto his knees and clasped his hands together in prayer. After a few seconds he got up and said, "I have something inexplicable right here in my chest—a wonderful sensation of serenity and comfort, and the frustration and hate that have been drowning me since I witnessed that massacre is gone, like a magician had made them disappear! It's like something from another world."

I listened to what he said, my eyes wide in astonishment. He was describing his feelings in precisely the same way I had thought of them. I had goose bumps all over my body. My stomach started to quiver. The same cold sweat I had felt before when I was in danger or under extreme stress hit me, but it was now a completely different feeling. It was like being in a desert and thirsty, and then obtaining a canteen of ice cold water—the same shivering sensation of drinking that cold water hit me, but there was also a sensation of profound strange satisfaction that accompanied it.

Hector looked at me and clasped his hands together once more. "I thank God from the bottom of my heart, because we both have witnessed an extraordinary sign, a contact with another dimension, whatever you want to call it. In forty years as a fisherman, I have never before seen sea gulls fly out in that direction over the open ocean without turning around to head back to shore. I followed that gull with my eyes, and I completely lost her—she never turned either to the right or the left!" He raised his arm and asked, "Where could that gull be flying to in that direction? Only to Heaven. Only the angels could do that!"

I scratched my ear, hesitating in responding. I said with a smile, "I don't want to give you more to think about, but the same thing you just said and your description of how you felt a few moments ago—I felt the identical emotions you described when that gull landed on my shoulder." I pointed to my chest with my index finger. "The exact same emotions."

Hector's eyes widened in astonishment. He said, "Really?"

"Really," I replied. I kissed my thumb in oath and said, "I swear to you, I'm telling the truth."

He shook his head and said, "You don't have to swear, for God's sake, I believe you. But no one else will believe us. They'll say we're both crazy! Well, at least I have you as a witness. What a pity we don't have someone else with us!" He smiled then. "Please, don't ever separate from that medallion, not even for a second. Evidently, she will protect you from all danger."

I smiled and nodded my head. "Yes, I'll be sure to keep it with me at all times."

The Dark Face of Marxism

We had arrived at the pier. Hector jumped out of the boat, full of energy and joy, like some ten-year-old boy. I followed closely. We tied the boat off on one of the posts along the pier, and walked towards the house. Hector put his arm around my shoulder as we walked along the sand, and said, "My God, I feel like I'm fifteen years old again! My wife will enjoy that very much tonight."

I smiled. When we got to the house, he told everyone exactly what had happened, adding in only a little drama. I didn't contradict him in any way, since what he was saying was essentially the truth. He was so impressed with everything, but with nothing more than the gull's landing on my shoulder and preening against my neck for several minutes, as if it had wanted my complete and undivided attention. He wondered why the gull had landed on my shoulder and not his. Marlina and the others were all fascinated with the story. After we chatted for a while, she and I said our goodbyes and left Las Canas, heading back to Pinar del Rio.

On the drive back, Marlina asked, "What about it? Did Hector convince you with his story? You guys took a long time. You must convinced by now, right?"

I replied, "Yes and no. I don't have any doubt in my mind now that Josue's boat and family were the ones that MiG sank in the ocean. But I'm not completely certain whether anybody survived the attack, even though Hector is convinced that no one did, even though he the Coast Guard could very well have brought somebody aboard, and at that distance Hector and his friends wouldn't have noticed. But according to his assumptions and calculations, the immense amount of blood spread out over the ocean is an indication of several victims. That means the possibility is slim."

Marlina shook her head in discontent. "Well, in other words, he left you with the same doubts. We wasted our trip, then, since you're coming back the same way you went in."

I smiled with irony and touched my stomach where I held the negatives inside my shirt. "No, it was very fruitful. Right here, I have the proof of the crime that was committed, so this atrocity won't go unexposed. Besides, coming over here and speaking personally with the main witnesses from the scene served me as a great comfort, and has brought to my soul the tranquility and serenity that I have been needing. God knows better than we do what He's doing and why, and I can assure you that it's not important where Yaneba is, whether in Florida or in Heaven. Wherever she is, it will be better than being in the Inferno the rest of us have been living in for the past few years."

Marlina looked at me compassionately and said, "Well, then, our trip was very successful. You have that tranquility and serenity, and that is very good for your spirit." She looked at me in deep curiosity and asked, "What kind of proof did Hector give to you? And what kind of plans do you have next? If the government is the murderer of our friend and her family, who can you delegate to bring justice when the ones in charge of dispensing that justice are the guilty ones?"

I smiled and looked at her, this time mischievously, and replied with another touch of my stomach, "I have here the negatives of the pictures taken by Hector with a very professional camera. They show every single detail of that

The Dark Face of Marxism

crime, even the registration of the plane that executed it on that target."

I rubbed my forehead with the fingers of my left hand and clenched my jaws. I continued sourly, "I believe that now is the time for the rest of the world to know how these criminals violate human rights every day while under the mask of being humanitarians and a government for the people. I recently made a new friend in the Belgian embassy. I will put these negatives in his hand to take out of the country and spread around the international press, and finally strip that mask off and reveal these bastards' cowardice, perhaps even bring down the cartel image of benevolence."

Marlina asked, "How in the hell will you be able to get into the embassy, where the Cuban government maintains extremely high security? So many people try to escape Cuba through those embassies. It will be a miracle to get inside one of those embassies without being identified and creating a major problem for yourself. I hope that medallion protects you. They are under surveillance twenty-four hours a day."

I raised my right arm and placed my index finger against my temple. I had been thinking of that exact thing. I smiled and said, "I know a way will present itself. I will come up with something."

Marlina asked, "Do you need my help?"

I shook my head. "No, I don't want you involved in any of this. This could become very dangerous, and you're not even a member of any single organization of the Revolution. You would be the first suspect they would examine."

Marlina looked at me and nodded in agreement. She might have been remembering that night when her friend Chantel's life was abruptly ended in the park by a bullet to the head. Perhaps because of that she didn't insist.

We arrived at her house. I stepped out of the car and opened the door for her. She gave me a hug and said, "I don't think you should go to that embassy. Leave things the way they are. Nothing you can do will bring Yaneba back to life." She touched my face. "You are too young to end up in prison for the rest of your life or in front of a firing squad." Her eyes grew moist. "Can you imagine, if that happens to you, how your poor mother will feel for the rest of her life? And the rest of your family? You should think about that before you take that trip."

I knew she was saying that out of compassion, trying to persuade me not to take unnecessary risks and walk into danger. I smiled and touched her face in return as I replied, "Don't worry, sweetie. I've already conceived a plan, and nothing bad will happen to me." I held my medallion. "First, I don't just have the Virgin behind me; I have Jesus Christ as my personal guardian angel. Second, in order for them to do something bad to me, they'll have to catch me with my hands in the cookie jar. That will never happen, because I would rather die than get caught. That is how I am."

She looked me in the eyes, hugged me, and kissed my cheek. "God bless you and protect you from danger."

"Thank you very much for these kind words and for coming with me to Las Canas."

This time, she replied with a smile, "You are very welcome, my friend."

Big Dreams of Reality

My dreams are big and pure like the sea, the sky, and the sun, but based in reality like the ground under my feet and the blood pumping through my heart. They are as big as the ocean, the mountains, and the reflection of the sky. I dream of eliminating on earth the hatred, greed, and egotism of men. My dream is to replace the worst instincts of men on earth for the most beautiful love for freedom, truth, harmony, and the greatest love of all for the Master of the Universe, our own precious God. That big dream also shows me the flags of many countries will truly represent the word "United" in the international identity, one protected under our mighty God. That glorious and happy day I will greet with profound happiness in my heart as the biggest of my dreams will finally be complete, and maybe the dreams of many millions of other people in the most wonderful reality that any man can achieve in his dreams through the course of his life.

Dr. Julio Antonio del Marmol

Chapter 8: The Belgian Connection and Cuban Human Rights Violations

We said goodbye and I left her house, heading for mine. My plan was completely developed in my head.

When I arrived there, I found Mima in a very bad mood. She was very unhappy, since she had received another note from the director of my school with bad news in regards to my attendance and grades. It didn't help that I already had my bag packed to leave for the capital again. She was definitely losing patience with the state of affairs, as she always worried about my future.

"I need to talk to you," she said.

"Mima, I'm in a rush. I have to leave—I had something very, very serious come up, and I have to attend to it at once."

She looked at me and repeated, "I need to talk to you, Julio Antonio del Marmol. I'm very serious, too."

"Mima, why don't we wait until I come back? Please."

"No. Come with me to the library and sit down for just ten minutes with me. This is important."

"OK, Mima." I walked behind her obediently and sat down in the library. I wanted to keep things pleasant with her and not cause her any further stress.

The Dark Face of Marxism

After she closed the door so that my brothers and sister could not hear us, she sat down in a rocking chair.

"Look my son—I know you're involved in many things, and I know your father is behind you a hundred percent. But I see how you're wasting your time—not attend to your schooling, throwing away your future with all this garbage. Why do you and your father insist on wasting so much of your time on this government? The only thing it's doing is destroying Cuba and our society! If you don't go to school, you'll wind up a nobody. That is the end of the whole thing. In order to be somebody in society, you have to be a doctor, an attorney, or something like that—going around with the leaders of this Revolution and doing all this crap isn't going to do that. You're wasting your time miserably!" She took a breath.

I took advantage of the pause and said, "Please, Mima, look at me. I'm not dedicating my time to this Revolution. On the contrary—I'm working to destroy and stop what this Revolution and its leaders are doing to Cuba. Of course, I have to appear to everyone that I'm not doing that, or they'll put me in front of the firing squad, like they've done to many other people." I took her hands in mine and shifted forward to the edge of my chair. "Remember my friend, Yaneba and her family—Josue, Maria, and her little sister, Elena?"

She looked at me in surprise, the question in her eyes. "Claro, I know them. What about it?"

I squeezed her hand. "Mima, every one of them is dead. They were killed."

Mima pulled her hand away as she clapped both hands to her mouth in horror. "How? How did they die?"

I leaned back in my chair and replied, "When they tried to leave Cuba in Josue's boat, a plane from the government, a Russian MiG, shot them to pieces in international waters. Josue's friend Hector and several other fishermen were witnesses. It's a perpetual embarrassment to the government that people continue to flee to Florida, and so they were killed. These men saw it happen from a distance and rushed to try and help them. But when they arrived on the scene, half the boat was already sunk, and whatever was left of the bodies had been devoured by the sharks in the ocean."

Mima winced and uttered a guttural moan of pain. She crossed herself and said, "My God! Poor family and those little girls! God have them in His kingdom! What murderers, these bastards!" She placed her right hand on my shoulder. "You have to walk with great caution, because if these unscrupulous murderers find out what you're doing, they will do the same to you. They won't care about your age or that your father has helped the Revolution with his money and time, putting his family in danger all these years for this worthless political system. In such a short time, it's distorted itself into something a thousand times worse than the dictator we had before. Killing an entire family, just because they would be an embarrassment! That is the most outrageous thing I've ever heard in my life!"

She shook her head in disgust. "Your father never listens to me, no matter how many times I tell him about these ignorant leaders. What can you expect from them, except envy, hatred, destruction, and death! This is the result."

She rested her left arm on the arm of the rocking chair as she rested her forehead in that hand. She looked up into my eyes and said, "My son, I know how you feel, truly, and as I told you before, I'm very proud of you. Don't tell this ever to your brothers and sisters, but you are my favorite son. I don't want them to resent you for that.

"But you have to think of your future, especially if you see yourself in a predicament in the future of having to leave this country. If things don't change very quickly, it will be very difficult to live here, and every day it will be more difficult to abandon the island. Many realized early on how bad this government would become and left already. That was fortunate for them—they were smart—not blind, like your father. I don't want you to give away your life, like other members of our family have, for nothing, for this worthless Revolution."

She leaned back in her chair. This time, she grabbed one of my hands in supplication. "Please, my son, listen to your mother—don't burn your life like a butterfly burns its wings against a lightbulb in the night. If you listen to your Mima, who only wants the best for you, you will be better off."

I replied, "Don't worry, Mima—I will put a lot more attention to my studies and will eventually make myself an educated man, as you and Papi both want. I will make you proud." I touched my stomach. "But I want to show to the world how bad these bastards are. I have photographic proof of how this crime was committed and by whom, and I will see to it that they are exposed all over the world. That will be my greatest satisfaction—to uncover their faces in front of everyone. I have to put these negatives in the appropriate hands."

Mima asked, "Who took those pictures?"

"Hector," I answered, "the fisherman friend of Josue."

Mima shook her head.

"Mima, when we have knowledge of a crime and we don't try to expose it, we are criminals as well."

She stood up, and I followed suit. She hugged me and said, "I know how you feel, my son. I look at you and see myself many years ago. You are a rebel, as are your mother and father, and rebels don't break bread with murderers or with injustice. But please, please, be very careful. If something were to happen to you, I wouldn't want to live anymore. What you're trying to do is extremely dangerous—it's not a game."

I nodded and said, "I know."

Mima kissed my cheek and said, "OK, go. The Lord protect you, my son."

"Thank you, Mima." I kissed her cheek again and took my travel cases from the rocking chair closest to me.

She looked at me in surprise. "Why two cases? Are you planning to stay for long?"

I smiled. I raised one and said, "This one is the ordinary one with my clothing and personal effects." I put it down and raised the other one. "This one is the bridge that will let me get to my destination without anyone identifying me or creating any problems."

She nodded. "You have it very well planned already, eh? Remember what I told you before: in love and war, all the tricks are permitted. Use extreme caution, and keep those secrets in your heart without showing them to anyone. That is the only way you can fulfill your destiny."

"Thank you, Mima."

The Dark Face of Marxism

We said goodbye, and I left the house with a smile of satisfaction as I prayed, "Thank you, God, for giving me such an extraordinary woman as a present from Paradise to be my mother."

I went to Raimundo's veterinary clinic. After I checked on Kimbo's condition, which was improving, I started to drive towards the capital. A few hours later, I arrived in Havana. I pulled into a Shell gas station at the outskirts. It was the only entrance from Pinar del Rio, and it was very busy. I told the attendant to refill my gas tank and service it. I saw a vendor with *fritas*[21], *pan con bistec*[22], and *papas rellenas*[23], and the smell of all that food grabbed me by the nose.

A Harley Davidson motorcycle with a sidecar pulled into the gas station behind me. A tall, black man who wore goggles and helmet was driving.

As I gave the order to the attendant to check my car, I handed my keys to him and said, "Please, when you're done, park it over there. I'm going to go get some food."

I walked over to the vendor and greeted the tall, straight-haired, light-eyed mulatto. "Would you please make a *frita* for me with no hot sauce?"

"Do you want onions and French fries?" he asked.

"Yes," I answered, "without cashew and tomato sauce, just a little mayonnaise and a lot of pickles."

---

[21] *Ground beef with small pieces of* chorizo

[22] *Steak sandwiches*

[23] *A mashed potato with meat at the center, breaded and deep fried*

"Very well," the *fritero* man said. He asked then, "Would you like something to drink?"

"Yes," I answered, "a *Malta Hatuey*[24]."

The *frita* is similar to the hamburger, with spices, oregano, garlic, pimento, and *pimenton español*[25]. The dish is pan fried and served in a Cuban bread similar to a baguette.

The owners of such stands were independently owned and operated. Once done with their daily work, they hooked their carts to bicycles or cars and went out to service people. These stands were seen all over the capital and were common around the island. They paid a small fee to the business owners to set the stands up on the premises, sometimes in exchange for having the landowner supply the Maltas and other beverages.

These independent businesses began to disappear with the intervention and greed of the government to grab every business that produced economy and provided any independence of the citizens from the socialist regime before its slide into open Marxism. Through the usual arbitrary laws typical of socialist governments, in April of 1968, all the *fritas* stands became prohibited nationally. The excuse was that these stands were eyesores in the cities and gave the foreign visitors and tourists a bad impression. Contrary to all logic, prostitution was so promoted that, while the brothels technically no longer existed, the women could be found in five-star hotels all over. They were considered indispensable to the

---

[24] *A popular brand of wheat soda*

[25] *Spanish paprika*

The Dark Face of Marxism

entertaining of the visitors, while the *fritas* stands were thought to project an image of poverty. What was once regulated by the government and more secure hygienically had become an unregulated health risk to the people—just another contradiction of the socialist regime.

As I waited for my food and sipped my Malta, I felt a hand on my shoulder. A voice said from behind me, "What about it? You're not inviting me to a *frita*, my great friend Commandantico?"

I turned around and saw the big, toothy smile of my friend Chopin, his goggles hanging from his arm. I signaled with my left hand to the *fritero* man, and said, "Claro, man—give to him whatever he wants." I held out my hand to him and said, "It's a very great pleasure to see you here. I just arrived in the city—what a coincidence for us to meet!"

He shook his head with a big smile. I looked at him in puzzlement, and he said, "I've been waiting for you for almost forty-five minutes."

That took me completely by surprise, but I didn't want to create a scene in front of the *fritero* man. I only raised my eyebrow and looked at him intently, but said nothing. Chopin stepped close to me, and said to the man, "Please make for me a steak sandwich with French fries, no tomato sauce, a little mayonnaise, and heavy on pickles. No picante or hot sauce. For a drink, please make me a papaya shake."

"Onions?" the *fritero* asked.

"Yes, grilled onions, please," Chopin said.

"Very well." The young *fritero* said cordially.

Chopin half-turned around and put one of his arms around my shoulder. "Why don't we walk over there to one of those tables?"

We walked over were there were several folding tables and chairs with some umbrellas. We sat down, and he said, "I need to talk to you."

The *fritero* arrived with the shake, and Chopin asked, "Could you please give me a straw?"

The *fritero* pointed at a small wooden box and said, "If you look in that box, you'll find some straws in there."

Chopin opened the box and shook his head at his missing the obvious. "Well," he said, "these straws are protected from everything."

I said nothing, but sat there, observing him.

He sipped the shake and nodded in appreciation. "This is very good," he said.

I continued my observation, nodded in agreement, but maintained my silence. He began to grow uneasy at my lack of engaging him in conversation.

"Relax, man." He took a ring from his pocket and put it on the table. It looked like a Masonic signet ring. He pointed at it. "You see this ring? You can't even wear it on your finger today in our country. No Masons, no Catholics, no Christians, no Jews, no Muslims—the only thing that counts in this country is if you are *Fidelista*. If you are not one of those, you are a counterrevolutionary. What a shit hole these Castros have converted our beautiful Cuba into!"

He looked at me, expecting a reaction. I, however, remained silent and continued observing him, only fiddling with my bottle of Malta.

The Dark Face of Marxism

He said, "I've been on this corner for a long time waiting for you. Your friends, the ones watching your back, called me and told me that you were coming in the direction of the capital. Since that's the only entrance to the city, I waited for you here. I didn't want to lose you, and once you were inside, it would be difficult to find you."

I simply nodded.

"Our friend from the Occident told me that you have a valuable package you brought with you from Playa Las Canas. It was also possible you might need help to get it to its destination."

I leaned back in my seat, holding the bottle up and toying with it. I looked at him dubiously, and kept silent.

"I know you're uneasy, but you only need to tell me what you need from me. I'm not going to ask any questions. They only told me to put myself at your disposition, because your contact here is out of the city, and her father is also away on something that will keep him occupied for a while. Before I proceed, let me give you the code you have with your uncle and the General."

He leaned in and whispered the code in my ear, and then sat back down.

I breathed a sigh of relief and said, "Why didn't you start with that, black man? Didn't they ever tell you that you should always start with that? You had me with my hand on my pistol from the moment you started to talk to me. I've had an adrenaline rush for the last ten minutes!"

The *fritero* returned with Chopin's steak sandwich and my *frita* after attending to a young couple who had just approached his stand. Chopin picked up the ring and returned it to the pocket of his pants. As he started to eat, he said, "Did you know I was a captain in the regular Army before? I was in the Army of Camagüey Province. When they started to do the political indoctrination of the Army, I immediately resigned my commission. I would prefer being a *maricon*[26] to being a communist."

I almost spat my Malta and half-chewed bite of *frita*. I regained my composure and continued to eat. He continued with a shake of his head, "No, no, no—seriously! The *maricones* don't interfere in anybody's life or hurt anybody. All they do is present their butts to anyone they like. These communists, though, execute anyone that doesn't agree with them. They sentence even their best friends to twenty or thirty years in jail, like they did my old Commander, Huber Matos. And if that wasn't enough, they intrude into your private life, demanding you give them details about which toilet you put your ass on all day long and how many times in a day you do it!" Chopin paused and then asked me, "You tell me—which is better?"

I smiled and shook my head as I finished my Malta. "What kind of comparison is as strange as that one? Are you actually a homosexual?"

Chopin looked at me very seriously and then leaned back abruptly in denial. "No, no, no! It's only an innocent comparison that I made. Don't get confused, OK? *Una puta vieja con una vieja puta*[27]. They are very different things!"

---

[26] *Homosexual*

[27] *Don't confuse an experienced prostitute with an elderly prostitute.*

The Dark Face of Marxism

I smiled and replied, "Well, it's not because I care what anyone does with his rear end. It's only good to know who is who, especially if you're going to be working with me. If you're a homo, you don't have to hide it from me. I don't care, that's all."

Chopin looked at me gravely and said, "Damn! Again and again, you want to make me a homo! Let's change the subject, please! *Carajo*! What did I make that comparison for! The Commandantico made me maricon in less than five minutes—that has to be the quickest conversion I've ever heard of in my life! This is the last thing I need today."

"Calm down, man," I laughed. I went and paid the *fritero* and returned.

"Thank you for the food."

"No problem," I said. I went to the station attendant to get the keys to my car, paid him for the gas and service, and gave him a tip. I went back to Chopin and said, "OK, where can we go to talk in private and I can tell you what my plan is?"

"You can follow me to my house in Marianao," he said. "We can discuss the whole thing there."

I looked at him askance. "Your house?"

"Yeah," he answered. "Is that a problem?"

I maintained my serious expression, but I wanted to fool around with him some more. Still feigning distrust, I asked, "You live alone?"

He looked at me and shook his head. "No, I live with my wife. What's the problem?"

"No, no, no—I only wanted to know where, just for the record, you wanted to take me after that weird comparison you made." I couldn't hold it back any more and burst out laughing.

He shook his finger at me in recrimination. "You are something else, OK?" He started to laugh as well, once he realized I was just playing around with him.

I followed him closely until we reached the residential area in which he lived. He told me to wait for him, so that he could pull his car out of the garage and allow me to park the Mercedes inside. That would make my car more secure while at the same time not calling attention from his neighbors to my fancy car. He opened the gate by the right side of his house and parked his motorcycle there. He put a very fancy cover over it. He closed the gate and invited me inside his comfortable residence.

He told me he had bought the house for a small fraction of what it was really worth from family friends who had left Cuba. At that time, because the Revolution hadn't strictly enforced who could buy houses, he was able to get away with it. Later, however, if one sold a property in one's name in order to leave the country, one would then have to reimburse the government the full value of that property first before the exit visa would be approved.

He introduced me to his wife, a beautiful, distinguished looking mulatta with corn rows in her hair and very elegant manners.

She held out a hand with long, thin fingers to me and said, "My name is Chia. Nice to meet you."

"The pleasure is mine," I answered as I took her hand. "I am Julio Antonio del Marmol."

Chopin said with pride, "Chia plays the piano as beautifully and professionally as Carlos Anzas. Do you want to hear her?"

"*Claro!*" I said.

The Dark Face of Marxism

Full of pride, Chopin virtually pushed her to the piano to play. She gracefully acquiesced and sat down to play for us some Classical melodies, popular Cuban music, and then some by international composers. This acted as a sedative for my nervous system, and I was able to relax and better coordinate what I had been planning to do. After she finished playing, Chopin took me outside and to the left side of the house, where he had a small stand much like the frita stand. It was different, however; this one had a large compartment at the bottom and a sink on top. It looked like the stand used by oyster vendors.

I asked in surprise, "What the hell is this for?"

"This is my second job," he said. "My undercover intelligence work. I can move wherever I want, and I don't attract anyone's attention, especially not the government's. Nobody knows what I've been doing, and it gives me the perfect excuse to be anywhere at any hour, even late at night, selling oysters."

I slid the door at the bottom and looked at it. "This is a good hiding place, as well. You could transport just about anything in here!" There was also a bucket that was used as a catch basin for water draining from the sink when he was rinsing off oysters. Oyster stands like this, like the fritas stands, could be seen everywhere, but more so in the capital than anywhere else. The difference was that the oyster stands were seen more often near movie theaters, bars, and night clubs—any place where people would hang out at night, when typically people would want to get an *ostionaso*[28]. Before couples went to bed, they often

---

[28] *A shot for your brains*

desired the reputed aphrodisiac properties of oysters to cause a nice date to end in a trumpet fanfare for both instead of whisper or for a man to still be able to satisfy his wife after a long day at work. I smiled mischievously and said, "You know, this could be my exit if things get too hard and complicated at the embassy. Since I'm so small and skinny, I could fit perfectly in this compartment. After all, the oysters will be working for me."

Chopin nodded in agreement and removed the bucket. He gestured to me. "Get in; let's see."

I climbed inside, and he slid the doors shut for a few seconds. He opened them again and with a big smile handed me the bucket, saying, "Put that in your lap. Let's see if that fits down there with you inside."

I put the bucket on my lap and he closed the door again. He opened the door and tapped his temple. "Great idea! I don't even have to throw away the bucket."

I climbed out of that hiding place and said, "The only thing I don't know is if vendors will be prohibited in that area."

"Don't worry about it," he said. "I can stay a short distance away, even if they don't let me in. The good thing is that you will know that I will be there waiting for you if you have to run for any reason. And you'll have a safe place to hide if things get too hot for you."

I nodded. "Yes, securing an exit in advance is very important to surviving."

Chopin put his hand on my shoulder and said affectionately, "Let's go inside. I want to show you something that could be vital to your survival. From now on, you should have it with you at all times for your personal security."

"Very well," I replied, and we walked back into the house. I followed him to a small room at the end of the hallway adjoining the garage. We entered the room, and he instructed me to sit down.

He pushed a heavy, dark-stained antique hutch away from the wall just far enough that he could slide behind it. The hutch had a television, a radio, and a record player with several 33 rpm albums and 45s separated with chrome headings so that one could read what each album was. Behind it was concealed a wall safe. He opened the safe and removed a small box about nine inches long by six inches wide. He brought it to where I was seated and placed it on top of the glass-topped table before me.

He opened the box, pulled out a ring box, and then pulled out a small magnifying glass. He removed a silver ring mounted with an onyx in the center from the box. On top of the onyx was the old Cuban national crest with two swords crossed above it.

He said as he showed me the ring, "You have to be very careful. This is a lethal weapon and very delicate."

He showed me a small, almost indiscernible button on the side of the ring. It was conveniently placed to be activated by one's thumb. He demonstrated it, and when he pressed the button a very thin needle sprang out of the center of the two swords on the crest.

He explained that the ring was a symbol of the Cuban anti-communist resistance. The two swords were symbolic of the good and the bad—the Revolution had been done for good, but it had turned bad. A virtually imperceptible drop hung suspended from the tip of the needle; the magnifying glass was needed to see it. It was like venom from a snake's fang, so small that it might represent an eighth part of a drop of water.

"This is enough to put any man to sleep," he said. "Once it gets into his bloodstream, he should become semi-conscious in only ten seconds. Less, depending on his weight and, more importantly, his metabolism. It is a sleep he will never return from, and he will be dead inside of twenty seconds. That is why you can only use this if your life is in danger.

"This is the most powerful and rapid poison in the world. It is extracted from the yellow lip snake of Mexico. Ordinarily, a bite from this snake causes your flesh to fall away and death happens in a matter of hours unless you get an anti-venom. They concentrated it so that the necrosis happens more rapidly and liquefies the heart as soon as the blood carries any of the toxin to it."

He turned the ring over and showed me a small opening beneath the onyx. "This is the reservoir for the venom. It holds enough for fourteen injections."

He closed the small compartment and placed the ring on the glass table. He took a pair of long metal syringes with glass tubes in them out of the larger box. The needles were covered. Inside the same box were two long glass containers, corked at one end.

"The one with a single X is the refill," he said. "Think of it as the spare bullets for your pistol. The one with the double-X is the antidote. Sometimes it takes too long for the antidote to go through the digestive system if you administer it by dipping your finger in it and sticking that finger in the victim's mouth. If you really want to save somebody, you don't take that chance—you use the syringe to inject the antitoxin directly into the victim's bloodstream. You have to do that as soon as he loses consciousness—if his metabolism is very fast, you can't lose a single second. The faster the metabolism, the quicker the poison will kill him.

"Even though it is very rare, I have to advise you that, in some cases, people have accidentally poisoned themselves. I want to make sure to tell you this. If, by any chance, this happens to you, the most important thing is not to lose your calm. The other thing is to make sure that you both suck the antidote off your finger and also give yourself an injection. Remember that the same way the poison is administered by the needle in a single shot, the antidote is administered in the same amount as the poison."

I nodded my head and said, "I understand you perfectly, but I have a single question to ask you." I showed him the ring and the button, which could only be activated by the thumb. "In order to release the poison, you have to press this button?"

"Yes," he answered, "if you don't press that, the needle doesn't come out, so the poison doesn't get released."

I stepped back and scratched my head. "If this works the way you're telling me, how is it possible that somebody injects himself, unless he's doing it deliberately? The ring is on the finger, and there's only one digit that can push the button—unless you use the other hand. How can this accident happen?" I shook my head. "I'm sorry, can I put the ring on?"

"Sure, go ahead."

I put the ring on my right hand. I waved my hand around as if I were going to hit somebody with the needle nonchalantly. After a bit, I switched it over to my left hand

and simulated attacks once more. I said to Chopin, "The left hand is a lot easier for me to casually touch someone while in conversation or something, like I hadn't intended to. I think it's more casual and more effective to make it look unintentional."

Chopin grinned broadly. "You and I, we have a lot of things in common. I feel a lot better with it in my left hand, even though I'm a right-handed guy. Thinking about it, I don't like picante sauce in my meals, and I realized that you ordered yours without any, as well."

I smiled. He took the Masonic ring out of his pocket and let me look at it closely. It also was a poison ring—the only difference was that the one he had only had the capacity for seven injections. It was one of the first ones made when they started to develop them, and he hadn't wanted to change it due to the Masonic emblem on it. I was about to remove the ring I was wearing and hand it back to him.

He raised his arm and said, "No, no, no." He pushed the ring box and the larger box with the syringes, antidote, and extra venom towards me. "This is for you. They want you to carry this for your personal security and protection. They wanted me to explain this very carefully to you and then give all the materials to you."

"Very well," I answered. "Thank you very much." I smiled and added, "I didn't want to offend anyone, but with all my respect to anyone who managed to stick himself with this ring, only an imbecile or someone very clumsy could do something like that. But please, I want to ask you to not tell that to anyone, just in case someone has actually been through this and thinks that I'm just trying to put them down."

Chopin grinned again broadly, showing his perfect white teeth. He replied, "You see? Another thing in common we have: that is exactly what I told your uncle when he gave me my first ring! You don't have to worry about it—what you just said to me, I've already said aloud long before you."

After a few hours of planning for the next day, Chopin suggested that I spend the night at his house. This would help me avoid attracting the attention of his neighbors by my presence, and we would have another opportunity to review the plan before we headed towards the embassy in the morning.

The next day, I had an early breakfast and a shower. I opened the second bag, selected some of my younger sister's clothes, and dressed myself in them. I then put a white wig, glasses, and a prosthetic nose with a wart on it, and Chia helped me with the final touches on my make-up and disguise.

"Not even your mother would recognize you!" she exclaimed.

I practiced walking back and forth like a little old lady with her cane. Chia said, "Remember, even if you get scared and want to walk faster, maintain your pace at all times. You don't know if someone is observing you or not."

When we felt we were ready, I climbed into the white and mint green '58 Ford Edsel. Chopin hooked the oyster cart up to the car. We drove towards the embassy and reached the street on which the Belgian embassy was located. Chopin slowed down as we saw a long line of people waiting to get inside the embassy.

Despite the early hour of the morning, we were astonished at the number of people in line. It was surrounded by a high iron fence with tall hedges in front of the fencing. As we slowly passed by so that Chopin could scout the area, we noticed two guards on duty at the gate checking the tickets of everyone seeking entrance and organizing the line. We also noticed parked on the opposite side of the street from the embassy a car with three men inside. They were obviously monitoring movement into the embassy.

Chopin asked, "Does anybody aside from you know that you're coming here today and know what you're planning?"

Immediately I answered, "No—nobody knows specifically what I'm planning to do."

Chopin scratched his head in puzzlement. "It's very strange," he said with a shake of his head. "Something is going on here. Though, lately, there have been incidents with people violently breaking into the embassies, shooting and killing guards. But I've never seen the G-2 hanging around any embassy like this. They put Cuban soldiers on guard because it's an embarrassment for people to get inside the embassy that way. The rioting shows too much desperation, too much urgency for people to want to leave the country, and it would reveal to the outside world the level of repression going on here."

He jerked his thumb over his shoulder. "That car doesn't look like regular police or even secret police. It looks like the State Security, so it looks like the G-2 is hunting." He smiled ambivalently. "Well, if they're looking for you, all I have to say is good luck to them. Looking at you right now, my God—goodbye Charlie, if they expect to see you in that embassy."

We drove around the block. Chopin found a parking space about half a block away on a parallel street. We could see the embassy from where we were, but were out of sight of the G-2 car. He parked and walked around to make certain that the oyster cart was all right. While he did so, I remained inside the Edsel.

I thought about the question Chopin had just asked me: had I mentioned to anybody any of the details of what I had planned to do? The only person I had given any details at all was my mother, and although I had not told her specifically what I was going to do, she of all people had my absolute trust.

I shook my head—if Chopin's suspicions were correct, I couldn't think of who I might have told. I never mentioned anything to Hector—I had only told him I had a friend.

"Oh, my God!" I said softly aloud. "Marlina! I told her specifically that I had recently made friends with the Belgian ambassador. I told her that I would put the negatives in his hands." I was still talking to myself when Chopin opened the door.

"Hey—what's going on, kid? You talking to yourself? Don't get so stressed that you get whacked out on me."

I was surprised by this interruption. "No, no—I was just thinking about loud about who might know about what we're going to do."

He got back out of the car and closed the door. He looked once more at the embassy in thought. He leaned in towards my window. "I'm going to walk to the embassy and explore the conditions more closely. You'd better stay here in the car. I will be back shortly."

"Very well," I replied. I watched him walk towards the embassy. I remained there, consumed with concern about the possibility that Marlina was an informant for the government. I tried to calm myself down and remove those thoughts from my mind, reminding myself that the extreme security we were seeing could be the result of some other situation that we both had nothing to do with.

I needed to make sure I wasn't driving myself crazy needlessly. When you're guilty of something, it's easy to think the worst.

I shook my head and looked towards Chopin's reflection in the rear-view mirror of the car. He had nearly reached the embassy. I watched him speak to people and the guards at the gate. A few minutes later, I saw him point towards us, and my stomach dropped through the floor. I wondered if I needed to get out of the Edsel at once and leave. He was gesturing his hands towards the guards as if he were describing something. Even though I could see him, I could hear nothing of his conversation.

About ten or fifteen minutes later, I was so nervous that I was about to open the door and get out of there. I saw a covered construction truck with a few workers sitting in the front seat with the driver. They drove up to the gate. While the guards searched the truck, I could see them speaking with Chopin. The driver handed Chopin a business card. After a few more minutes, the guards finished their search, opened the gate, and the truck drove on through into the gardens beyond. I watched Chopin speaking to people in line, and then he started to come back. As he did, he waved in a friendly fashion to the G-2 sitting in their car.

When he returned and stopped by my side, he said, "I'll tell you in a bit what's going on. Forget about our plans. Someone definitely blew the whistle to the G-2 about whatever you might be trying to do. The guards told me that since noon yesterday a car has been stationed outside the embassy. There's also another car on duty behind the building keeping an eye on the gate that the ambassador normally enters and leaves the embassy. It's very strange."

He walked around to the driver's side, opened the door, and sat down. He started the car and began to drive off.

"But not everything is bad news," he continued. "I offered them free oysters. They told me it would be no problem to park the car here and push my cart over to the sidewalk next to the embassy. I told them it would only take me five minutes to unhitch the cart from the car. They said, 'No problem, *compañero*.' I promised them that, if I had a good day, I would grease their hands." He smiled. "It's unbelievable what a little grease, a few oysters, and a smile can buy in the way of important information."

We drove around behind the embassy. Sure enough, there was another car, identical in make and model, with three additional men inside, camped out on the rear gate.

"I have a plan," said Chopin. "I think you'll like it very much. I think I can manage your entrance to the embassy without trouble."

He held out the business card the construction driver had given to him. "We might have to grease some other hands, but this might work." He held it out to me. It read, "Remodeling. All Types. Bathrooms, Rooms, Anything

Custom Made. Commercial and Residential. Workmanship Guaranteed. Pereira Constructions."

I looked at him in bewilderment. "What the hell does this have to do with us?" I asked him.

Chopin smiled and replied, "Look on the back of the card, and you will see the private telephone and address of the owner of that company."

I turned the card over, and there was a handwritten address and telephone number on the back. The name on it was Ricardo.

Still smiling, Chopin said, "These guys told me that they are working on the remodeling of the private bath of the ambassador, and it's very possible that tomorrow evening they will have it finished. They just have to install a Roman bath that they've been waiting for—it finally arrived from Rome. They are supposed to pick it up at the Port Customs. They told me how beautiful it was, and I mentioned that I was thinking of installing one like that in my house in Miramar. Since, as you know, it's such a rich area, they looked at me and wondered how a black man like me could be living there. They must have thought I'm *Fidelista* and gave me his card."

I smiled and shook my head. "But you don't even live in Miramar—you live in Marianao!"

He replied with a mischievous smile, "Well, they don't know that, and I will never tell them. Will you? Tonight, we will call our friend Ricardo and make him a proposition that he might not be able pass on. Of course, we have to offer him enough greasy oil to fry a banana with."

"What do you expect to get out of this?" I asked skeptically.

"Well, maybe our friend Ricardo will get you in that box for the bathtub. That would be the perfect ticket for you. No one will even see you enter the embassy, and if things get too hot in there for you, I will be waiting for you with my little door at the bottom of my oyster cart. Even the G-2 won't be able to see you, because the line of people will be blocking their line of sight to my cart. I'll put it in a way so that the doors are on the side of the bushes by the gates."

This time, I was the one who grinned broadly and I patted him on the shoulder. "My God, that is a genius idea. Well, of course, that is going to be if your friend Ricardo will accept the notion of becoming one of our accomplices."

Chopin stretched himself as he drove along. "Commandantico, with enough money, the monkey not only dances, he'll walk a tightrope. The most important thing is to see what his needs are without telling him too much of what we're planning to do. We also need to discover his true feelings about the government and this Revolution." His expression was optimistic. "My friend, we might find a patriot, and he might even do it for free, just for the satisfaction. But if we're not lucky enough to find that patriot, we'll offer him money until his eyes pop out of their sockets."

I leaned back. "Do you have so much money hidden, black man?"

Chopin nodded slightly and smiled. "Ah, a little bit. Not much. Some."

I smiled. "Well, let's cross our fingers and hope that Ricardo goes along with our business proposition."

We were near Chopin's house. He said, "I will call him a little later to make an appointment, and maybe we can go to his house so that we can talk to him privately."

Chopin arranged the meeting for early that evening. We drove towards Old Havana, where Ricardo lived on Aguila Street, close to the Malecón. The building we pulled up next to was in bad shape. The tiny apartment where Ricardo lived with his wife and three kids was on the third floor. He certainly wasn't living like to those who hired him for remodeling jobs. I thought to myself that it was like being in the home of the blacksmith and finding a wooden knife.

In order to speak to him away from his family, the three of us had to sit on the tiny terrace overlooking the traffic along the old Malecón. Even here, so many people had left Cuba that one noticed how much lighter the traffic along the Malecón was compared to former times.

Ricardo was of medium height, about fifty years old with salt and pepper hair. He was chubby with thick eyebrows, and he had a kindly demeanor. He offered us something to drink, which we politely declined. He asked in curiosity, "What is the great business proposition you told me you had over the phone?"

Chopin answered the question with one of his own. "How long have you been living here?"

"A few months only. I was finally able to sell my house in the suburb of Fontanar. I sold it to my wife's relatives for less than half the price I paid for it. At least, I'm not leaving it to the parasites in this goddamned government."

Chopin looked at me and then looked back at Ricardo. "Oh—you leaving Cuba?"

The Dark Face of Marxism

Ricardo nodded. "Yes, that is what I'm hoping, very soon. But I'm continuing to work, because I'm still short on money to complete the payment for the visas for my family. I want to take my parents and my wife's parents, as well as my wife and children."

Chopin looked at me once more with a smile. I had remained silent, letting him handle the entire transaction. Chopin asked, "How much money do you need to complete them?"

This time, Ricardo answered with a frustrated smile, "About thirty-two hundred dollars."

"Well," Chopin answered, "I think we can help you with just one day's work. You won't have to be here much longer, and it will expedite things for you."

Ricardo looked at Chopin in doubt and suspicion. "How is that?" he asked cautiously. "Can you please explain to me?"

Chopin moved to the edge of his seat and said in a low voice, "You told me today that tomorrow morning you will go to the port to pick up that Roman bath you're installing in the embassy for the Belgian ambassador. Is that still true?"

"Yes," he said with a nod. "What does that have to do with anything?"

Chopin put his hand on my shoulder. "Well, all you have to do is let my little friend here get inside the box for that bathtub before you take it over there. Since he's so skinny and small, your workers will not realize that there's something different inside that box when they unload it at the embassy."

Ricardo looked at him askance. He thought about that in silence. He pointed at me and asked Chopin, "Is the government looking for him or something? What's going on? Did he kill somebody?"

Chopin smiled. "No, no, no—it's nothing like that."

Ricardo asked, "He wants to ask for political asylum?"

Chopin replied a little more seriously, "No, it's not that. It's something else, a lot less important and complicated."

Ricardo shook his head. "It cannot be of such little importance when you offer me so much money and he has to be smuggled inside the embassy in that box." He waved his hands. "Forget about it, man—forget it. I don't want to get involved in this. What if the soldiers search the box? I have to think about my wife. I just want to work until I can leave the political fiasco of this Revolution behind me. Let's hope that the rumors going around the capital aren't true—that very soon the government will completely close all the exit visas and make it so that it will take years before you can qualify for one. I don't want to get stuck in this swamp of human bowel."

He stood up, shaking his head and waving his hands in negation. "Forget it, man. If this gets complicated, this could be a big, huge shit. You guys don't want to tell me what's going on, or I might be able to consider it."

I interrupted, seeing that Chopin was losing the negotiation. "Plain and clear: this government killed my girlfriend and her entire family when they tried to leave Cuba, including a little four-year-old girl. They shot them in international waters just because they tried to leave after being denied visas. I have the proof with me. A fisherman friend of theirs took pictures while it all was happening. I want to expose the crime to the rest of the world as soon as possible. The only way to get that done is to give the negatives to the Belgian ambassador—he and

The Dark Face of Marxism

I know each other already and have good relations. This is the best way to get into that embassy without the guards recognizing me or anybody being able to prove that I was there. There's another way, but it's extremely risky. This is a once in a lifetime opportunity for us, because you are going to bring that box in tomorrow."

I said all of this in one breath, my face contorted with my passion and the pain of all the details as Hector told me his story. My eyes were moist with emotion and I looked straight into his eyes. "It's up to you—if you want to help us, we will help you. It's not a payment. If you don't want to help us, I understand, but I believe in my heart that those of us who see a crime of this magnitude and do nothing about it become accomplices to those criminals."

Ricardo had remained standing in his intention to cut the interview short. He saw the pain reflected in my face, listened to my emotional plea, and sat down once more.

"You know what's going to happen, kid, if they find you inside that box?" he asked me. "I can always say I didn't know you were in the box. You're willing to risk your life?"

"Yes, sir," I replied. "I'm more than willing to do that."

He looked into my eyes. "I just have a question for you. Suppose everything goes well and the guards don't open the box but you have problems inside the embassy after we leave you in the bathroom. What are you going to say about how you got in there?"

I had been leaning back in my chair, but now I sat forward and looked him in the eyes in deadly earnest. "If they do open the box, you will do exactly what your workers will do, since they don't know anything. You should act completely surprised, just like they will. Ask me in front of them how the hell I got inside the box. I will say to whoever finds me that I sneaked inside the box at customs in the port before you picked it up." I raised my finger and pointed at him. "I give you my word of honor."

Ricardo remained silent for a few seconds. He said to me, "I really appreciate your honesty. You took a big chance, because I could pick up that phone after you guys leave and get you in a lot of trouble, just to keep myself in the clear."

I nodded and said, "Yes, I know. My question is if you would be able to live the rest of your life with that on your conscience. Not to mention that some of my associates might get out of control because of what you did to us and develop a personal vendetta against you and your family. That's the last thing I want. I don't like violence." I turned to Chopin and asked him, "Do you have dollars?"

Chopin shook his head. "No, only Cuban pesos. The dollars have disappeared lately, and it's been very difficult to find them anymore. Whoever has any wants an enormous amount of money for them."

"I have dollars," I replied. "If Ricardo agrees, you can give him the equivalent in Cuban pesos, and I will ensure that, in the next few days, I will send the dollars to you by courier and you can exchange them with Ricardo. That way, he can get the visa for his family."

Ricardo remained silent during this conversation. He edged forward in his seat and put his hand on my shoulder. "I thank you very much, but even if you don't have the dollars you say you have, with all the risk this involves, I will do it with satisfaction. I know now what you feel in your heart, and there's no doubt that all of these leaders are going to become communists. They are all bastards like their Maximum Leader." He held his hand out to me and said, "You got a deal."

I took it in a handshake and said, "Thank you very much. But you don't have to worry about it. I have that money, and you will have your visas."

"I know, kid," he said. "There's no lie in you. I can see that in your eyes." He clearly felt some shame at having to get the money from me.

After we set the time to meet the next day, we said our farewells and left.

"You know," Chopin said, "you took a big chance when you told Ricardo, a man we don't even know, what we were going to do tomorrow."

I nodded in agreement. "I know very well the risk I took. That is why I let him know what would happen to him if he betrayed us. I have to ask you for forgiveness. I should have consulted with you, as we're taking this risk together. But I saw that the deal was falling apart and he didn't want to continue with the negotiations. I didn't have any alternative at that point but to play my last card and tell him the truth. We won't know whether we won or lost the game until tomorrow morning. If he is not waiting with the G-2 for us tomorrow, then we will know if my decision was great or not."

Chopin smiled nervously and shook his head. "No, no—that humble man has been working all his life and now he sees himself being practically kicked out of his country, leaving behind everything he worked for. He's a dignified man. He won't betray us. And if he does, it will be another huge disappointment, like this Revolution." He pointed at his crotch. "I could even make a bet and put my chorizo on the table!"

I smiled and shook my head. "Let's hope that won't be necessary, or you will be a sorry-assed black man with no chorizo."

For a second, he took his hands off the wheel to clasp them together. "Please, Lord, listen to my prayer!"

"You'd better put those hands back on that wheel," I said, "or we might both lose our chorizos!"

He grabbed the wheel with a smile. He looked at me and said, "I want you to know that no matter what happens tomorrow, it's been an honor to work with you. You may be very young, but you've got the testicles of an elephant, and I am a witness to that."

"Thank you," I said. "But it's not really a question of having balls; to me, it's a question of having convictions. When you start something, you should finish it, even if it costs you your life. When somebody embraces something with his heart, it isn't precisely honorable if he abandons it before its conclusion because of some obstacles in the road."

Chopin grinned from ear to ear, and his white teeth flashed in the darkness of the car's interior. "You see? That's another thing we have in common—I cannot leave anything undone in life, even if it costs me my testicles. Even though it might sometimes be smart or wise to retreat and recoup more strength to come back and conclude it later—but that is only when it is absolutely necessary, and you don't have any alternative."

I nodded. "I absolutely agree with you on that. Yeah, you're right—we have some stuff in common."

We both smiled and laughed. We hoped that the next day would be a fruitful one.

Early the next morning, I dressed once more as an old lady. We went to meet Ricardo in an abandoned warehouse. On our way there, I felt a knot develop in my stomach. Like Chopin was probably doing, I started to wonder what we could expect when we arrived there. We traveled in troubled silence, our nerves keyed up to an almost unbearable pitch, prepared for the worst while praying to the Lord that Ricardo would keep his word.

When we arrived at the location, we could see that Ricardo was by himself in the construction truck—exactly as we had agreed. Chopin grinned in relief and looked at me. "With your last card, you evidently won the game. Congratulations!"

We both smiled in satisfaction. The relief was almost overwhelming.

Ricardo opened the back of the truck, and we could see that he had already loaded the bathtub inside. Chopin pulled out a razor blade and cut a thin line in the blue tape holding the edges of the box together. The packing material was wood shavings, so they removed enough of the shavings to give me a space to occupy the box. Chopin put the removed shavings in a sack and locked them in the trunk of his car. I settled myself inside as comfortably as I could. They went over the plan with me once again, wished me luck, and closed the box back up. I heard the sound of the transparent packing tape running over the edge to conceal the fact that the box had been opened.

As we had agreed, Ricardo went to pick up two of his men and take them to breakfast first, in order to give Chopin time to get his oyster cart into position. If everything went without a hitch, I would walk out of the embassy and make my way to the Edsel. It would be unlocked, and I would simply sit in the passenger seat and wait for Chopin.

It was completely dark inside the box. I was completely covered under the wood shavings in case the guards insisted on opening the box for a search. I heard the engine of the truck start and then felt the jarring of the gears being engaged and the truck moving off. The truck stopped a couple of times as he picked up his workers. A more prolonged stop of perhaps thirty to forty minutes marked the planned breakfast—I couldn't be certain, as I had no light to check my watch by.

The engine started up, and the truck went into motion. Here we go, I thought. We were on our final route to the embassy.

A while later, we stopped. I heard voices, one of which was Ricardo's. He seemed to be speaking with the guards at the gate. Then came the sound of the door rolling up along the roof as the back door opened. The voices became more perceptible.

A voice I didn't recognize—I assumed one of the guards—said, "I'm sorry, *compañero*, but our orders are to inspect every single thing that gets brought in here."

Ricardo's voice replied in a submissive, respectful tone, "It's only the bathtub that we're going to install now. The box isn't even opened—it's in exactly the same condition from when we picked it up at Customs."

The voice sounded a little less authoritarian and more apologetic, "I know, *compañero*, but we've got cameras here. If I don't do this, I could get in big trouble. These are my orders, and I have to obey them. Either you open it, or I have to."

Ricardo replied, "It's no problem—I'll open it for you. I just want some of the embassy personnel to witness it. What if it comes broken, or something is wrong with it? They'll have to realize that is the way we received it, and so I don't have any responsibility."

"Don't worry—you tell them we opened it, and we are responsible."

As soon as I heard that and the sound of Ricardo cutting the tape, I tried to squeeze myself further in to try and hide completely under the portion of the bathtub formed for the faucets. The tub was vast, perhaps eight or nine feet long, and so took up most of the truck's storage space. The space I was squeezing towards was also near the far end of the truck, so my hope was that I would be so far out of reach that any search would give up before they could possibly find me. My heart started to pound so loudly in my ears that I thought that the guards would hear it.

From my position, I could see the light as they opened the box. I saw two dark hands, probably the guard's, pulling some of the wood shavings out of his way. It started to make a mess, however, so he resorted to thrusting his hands deep inside and moving them from side to side to see if anything was hiding in there.

He continued to creep closer and closer towards me. I no longer had any place to go. But, to my surprise, he stopped perhaps an inch before he would find me. I was overjoyed to see him pull his hands out. His search had actually covered me even deeper in the shavings, doing me a favor.

I was even happier to hear him say, "It's all right, compañero—you can fix it up now. You don't have anything to worry about. Nothing is broken, I touched everything. It's all in order."

I thought about the heart attack Ricardo might have had at that moment as he wondered where I had gone. Little did he know about my contortion act as I had avoided the searching hands.

This time, I saw a pair of white hands redistributing the shavings to their original configuration. Finally, I heard Ricardo's voice say, "Oh, I'm so glad that the bathtub is undamaged. That was my biggest worry, because it not only would waste my work day, I would have to explain it and deal with the responsibility for it being cracked or whatever."

The dark inside the box returned as he closed it back up. "It's not necessary to reseal it," I heard him say. "It's only a few yards to where we're taking it."

I heard the door slide closed, and the engine started back up. It jerked into motion, trundling inside the embassy grounds. It stopped again a few minutes later, and the door slid open once more. I heard the steps of several people inside the truck, and Ricardo said, "Be very careful, OK? Let me tape it after all, so it doesn't fall out of the box on you guys and get scratched."

Someone with a broom swept the leftover shavings out of the truck. In the distance, I heard someone give instructions about where the box was to be taken. One instructed them that the freight elevator was down the corridor and to the left.

Ricardo pleasantly thanked the people giving instructions, and I felt the box come to rest in the elevator. Ricardo urged his men to caution, and I felt the lift in my stomach as the elevator went up. Then I was picked up, and I heard Ricardo's voice say, "OK, we're in the master bathroom by the private office of the ambassador."

This was a signal to me, but it sounded like instructions to his men. "You guys go and bring the tools, caulk, and the small boxes with the faucets. Please don't forget to park the truck on the same side by the garage, where they tell us to always park it."

"Very well, boss," one of them replied respectfully.

I heard the top of the box flip open and light flooded the interior.. I heard the footsteps of the men leaving to follow their instructions, their voices as they determined who would be in charge of moving the truck, and the jingling of keys as Ricardo handed them off. Ricardo tapped on the box and said, "The coast is clear. I'm going to the bathroom."

The door closed.

I got out of the box as quickly as I could. I brushed the shavings out of my clothes and wig. I adjusted myself carefully in the mirror as more shavings fell onto the marble floor. I retrieved my cane and cleaned it of the clinging shavings.

I double-checked myself in the vast mirror in that luxurious bathroom. It was so large that it looked more like a gym's bathroom than a private one.

I hurried out of there, still trying to brush shavings out. In my rush, I didn't notice that my brushing had moved the wig askew slightly to the left.

I got close to the door to the ambassador's office, which went through a small hallway with closets on both sides. It was very dark there, but I saw a beautiful office at the end of it with elegant furniture and exquisite décor. I could see the ambassador seated behind the modern glass-topped desk speaking with a beautiful woman in her late twenties. She was a brunette with very long hair and, from her profile, a beautiful face. I waited patiently, hiding in the hallway's shadows until his conversation was finished.

Finally, they were done, and the voluptuous woman stood up and said goodbye to the ambassador. He stood up and walked her to the door, stepping out of the office and into the main corridor. I could hear them continuing to chat through the open door. I left my hiding place and hurried over to his desk. I placed the card he had given me at our first meeting, positioning it where he would see it as soon as he sat down. I wanted him to see it and have some time to remember before I showed up in front of him in my current disguise. It would also give me a little time to explain to him who I was before he summoned his security and unnecessarily complicated things.

I returned to my hiding place in the shadowy corridor and waited patiently. I saw him come back and settle himself comfortably in the executive chair. He picked up the card and turned it over, surprise written all over his face.

That was my opportunity to leave my hiding place, and I walked over. He watched me walk in with a look of utter astonishment.

He asked me in confusion, "Who are you? What are you doing in my private quarters?"

I put my index finger to my lips with my left hand to motion for silence. My cane was in my right hand, and his eyes were glued to it. Of course, in his position he had to wonder if it was a weapon and I was an assassin. I replied softly, "Mi amigo Abdul Marcalt, this is the card you gave to me on Pierre's patio at the French embassy. Before you do anything you might regret, do you remember?"

There was still doubt on his face, but the card before him spoke loudly. It was his own card, with his own handwriting on its back: Please extend every courtesy and preference to the holder of this card and his own signature.

Dr. Julio Antonio del Marmol

Chapter 9: The Lightning and the Old Lady

I rested my arms on the back of one of the two chairs and leaned forward slightly. His eyes remained fixed on the cane in my hand—a potential weapon.

"My name is Julio Antonio del Marmol, the Commandantico." I pointed my finger towards the card. "Do you remember now? This is just a disguise. Your embassy is being watched by the G-2, and you personally are probably being watched very closely as well. They have the assurances that you are a dangerous foreign enemy spy, working for either the Mossad, MI-6, or the CIA. My recommendation to you is to walk very carefully."

He grinned broadly as soon as he recognized me under my disguise. He held his hand out to me as he said, "Oh, don't worry about it. They don't have any basis for those suspicions, and they can't corroborate them. They know it, and I know it. They've never caught me doing anything to substantiate those doubts. All they have is an unproven theory. I'm very happy to see you—it's great that you're here. Sit down—sit down, please. What a magnificent disguise! I'm sorry, but I've already pushed the panic button." He raised his hand to calm me. "Don't worry, though—it's not a problem. I'll take care of it." As I took a seat, he picked up the phone and began to dial a number.

The Dark Face of Marxism

I had no sooner sat down and leaned my cane against the arm of the chair than the doors to the office burst open and a squad of soldiers entered, weapons drawn and safeties off. "Mr. Ambassador, are you OK?" asked the leader

The ambassador had the receiver to his ear with his left hand and waved the guard off with his right. "Yes, yes—I'm very sorry. I accidentally brushed against the panic button. Everything is absolutely fine." He held up the receiver to show them. "I was just calling you guys to let you know it was a false alarm."

He paused as a tinny voice spoke from the receiver. He signaled for the guards to wait a moment as he spoke into the receiver. "Yes, yes—it was only a false alarm. I accidentally touched the alarm button. I guess I've been working too hard and am a little clumsy today. Thank you for responding so promptly." He motioned the guard over. "Please come here—your superior wants to speak to you."

The guard walked over to take the phone. As he did, he glanced over at me. "Yes, Chief. Yes, everything is in order. The Ambassador is attending to an older lady. Yes, he is alone with her. Yes, yes. OK, we're coming back down." He handed the phone back to Abdul.

Abdul said once more, "Thank you very much. A very quick response!" He held the phone up to his ear. "What's that? It's OK, you're very welcome. It's always good to praise a job well done."

The guards left, and before he closed the door, the leader said in a very courteous tone, "I'm sorry for the interruption."

I looked at him from the chair and nodded silently with a smile. The ambassador also smiled as he said, "If anyone has to apologize, it's me. Thanks again for the prompt response."

The leader smiled and waved. "That's OK, Mr. Ambassador. We're only doing our duty."

Once the door closed, we were alone again in the office. That was apparently not enough for Abdul. He stood up and walked over to the doors and double-locked them to ensure our privacy. He pushed a button on his intercom. A feminine voice replied to the buzz, "Yes, Mr. Ambassador?"

Abdul replied, "Please see to it that no one interrupts me. I will be busy for at least the next few hours."

"Very well, Mr. Ambassador. Anything else?"

He thought about it for a moment. "Yes, as a matter of fact." He asked me, "Would you like anything to drink?"

"Either a Jupiña if you have it or a tomato juice."

"Which do you prefer?" he pressed.

"A Jupiña."

"Very well. Please bring a Jupiña for my guest and one double Bacardi añejo on the rocks for me, please."

"Right away, sir," the lady replied.

"Thank you," Abdul replied.

Before he took his finger off the button, we heard her reply, "At your service, Mr. Ambassador." He looked at me and smiled, this time in sincere satisfaction at seeing me there. "I don't know how I can compensate you adequately for the information you provided to us. Please let me know immediately how we can transmit funds to you. What you sent to us inside those cigars...." He raised his right hand in excitement. "That was ingenious! Was it your idea?"

I smiled. "Yes, but there was nothing extraordinary or genius about it. It was the product of necessity, and I didn't have any other option but to improvise. Thank God everything went well—even better than I had hoped."

He shook his head. "I think you're too damn modest. What you did that day and the way you behaved was just unbelievable. Very original. I still ask myself what you put in those cigars that gave Pierre and his friends diarrhea for several days." He laughed.

"By the way," he continued in the manner of a small boy planning some mischief, "speaking of those Habanos cigars—we have a lot to talk about. Thanks to you and that information you gave us, the insurance company is completely rejecting the claim. The Cuban government won't receive a single cent for any damage to the port or anything else. The investigation into the incident will continue for a very long time. The only people who will receive any compensation will be the civilians who were seriously injured or who lost family members in that explosion."

"Those are the only ones who should receive compensation," I replied with a smile, "not the murderers who perpetrated it."

He nodded his head in agreement. I placed my hands inside my clothes, removed the envelope of negatives, and held them up. "If I'm not mistaken, you just asked me if I want any type of compensation for my work."

"Yes, yes," he said, "whatever you want."

I put the envelope down on top of the desk. "I want you to take these negatives out of the country and publish them in the most famous, most widely read magazines around the world, so that every newspaper and magazine around the world pick them up. I want to remove the blindfold from the eyes of the world so they can see this criminal government for what it is. They are not only political criminals, but common criminals who kill men, women, and children."

Abdul snatched the envelope, opened it, and held the negatives up with the fluorescent ceiling lights behind them. He shook his head in disgust, and his face bore an expression of revulsion. I waited patiently as he scanned all of them.

When he finished, he said, "Did someone in your family die in this?"

I pressed my lips together to hold my pain in as I remembered the details Hector imparted to me. With moist eyes, I replied, "My girlfriend and her entire family. The worst part is that I helped them get into that boat to leave Cuba. I bear a double guilt."

He shook his head and put the negatives down on the desk. "From the bottom of my heart, I'm very sorry for this. I guarantee you that in a few days, perhaps even hours, these negatives will be publicized in every major newspaper and magazine around the world. I will be proud to expose these atrocities which violate every basic code of human rights." He sat back in his chair. "Actually, this is part of my clandestine work. You just made my job very easy, kid."

I put my head down to conceal the two tears running down my cheeks. "Thank you."

He had already noticed them. He pushed a box of scented Kleenex tissues across his desk to me. I reached out and took two tissues in my right hand. I blew my nose with one and wiped the tears away with the second one.

There was a knock on the door. I was about to stand up, but he waved me back into my seat. He got up and walked over to the door. When he opened it, a young, very pretty lady with long black hair and almond-shaped eyes stood there with a tray in her hands.

"I'm sorry for the delay, sir," she said, "but they informed me that they had run out of the añejo Bacardi. We only have in stock the carta blanca, so we had to send out to the next store for what you wanted. I didn't want to substitute what you ordered."

She started to enter the office.

"Thank you very much, Sonia," Abdul replied, taking the tray from her hands at the door. Understanding that he didn't want the intrusion, she backed away and left.

He closed the door with his foot, returned to his desk, brushed the negatives and envelope to one side, and placed the tray in front of himself. He went back to the door and re-locked both security locks. He came back to the desk and leaned back in his chair. He took a long sip of his Bacardi, while I took the Jupiña, poured it into a glass of ice, and took a sip.

He looked deep into my eyes and shook his head. "I still can't believe you're doing what you are at your age. You are extremely brave. You see the suffering of those subjected to the cruelty and greed and lack of respect by this totalitarian regime. It has no respect for any religion or the desire for freedom in the human soul. Such a man as you doesn't want to live under a regime that tortures, persecutes, and murders so many people, nor wants to submit himself to that dictatorship. He also suffers in his own flesh by witnessing all of this."

He looked at me compassionately and clasped his hands together. "Really, you made a great impression on me when I met you. You could be the most beautiful example for the youth, not only in your country, but around the world. Those young men have the dilemma of either accepting a dictator or putting their lives on the line if necessary to stop him in order to defend their freedom, the principles of the establishment, and freedom of religion."

I looked at him and observed his demeanor. I stroked my chin, and noticed the sincerity and level of conviction in his eyes which matched his words and tone. I raised my arm and saluted him. "Thank you. I only do what I believe is correct and perceive to be my duty: to defend the freedom and principles that we have all been taught by our ancestors and for which so many men and women have fought and died for throughout human history."

Abdul nodded and smiled. "Yes, unfortunately not everyone has that position. They won't put their lives on the line for those principles, as you and I do. So long as people like you and me are in the world, however, dictators like Stalin, Hitler, Mao, and now Castro will never succeed in swallowing the world. We will stop them."

We looked at each other, smiled, and nodded in perfect sympathy with each other. Abdul leaned forward and leaned on his arms as they rested on the desk. "After our previous meeting at Pierre's house, I ran a check on you. You really puzzled me, and I wanted to know who you worked for. Nothing came up—you don't show up anywhere in any part of the world as working with any intelligence group. No matter who I ran it through, CIA, MI-5 and 6, Mossad, Interpol, the Sûreté, the West

German BND, Scotland Yard, and even as far as the Vatican—no one has any record of you. Who the hell do you work for, kid?"

I looked at him in deadly earnest. "You know better than to ask me that question. I read a long time ago that curiosity killed the cat. But we've established a certain bond between us. I feel like I can trust you, and after you publish those prints, I will trust you a lot more. To remove a little of your curiosity, I will say that I don't work for anyone. That was one of the conditions I established when I started working in espionage. You asked me at the start of this conversation what compensation I wanted—I understand that. All of you guys in the intelligence work for a salary. Exposing your lives every day has no price, and there is no doubt in my mind that behind those paychecks, you are all patriots with convictions, and you do what you do because it's in your heart and mind. You want to preserve what we have and protect our society. I don't want to sound offensive or disrespectful, but the only problem is that some of your men have weaknesses and personal ambition, and those men can be very easily bribed when the enemy puts in front of them a check a thousand times larger than the ones you receive." I pointed at my chest. "With me, that risk doesn't exist," I said with a little pride. "I don't get a check for what I'm doing."

He nodded. "Well, what you just said is logical," he said a little dubiously. "The problem is how to know whether the information you risked your life to obtain will end up in the right hands and correct the problem you want to fix."

I reclined in my chair and crossed my legs. "How do you know," I asked, "that the information you put together will end up in the right hands?"

He nodded. "Well, I have absolute trust in my contact, and I can see the results of my work, sometimes even on the front page of the newspapers."

I smiled and replied, "Me, too. But I have to tell you, sometimes the results you expect are not satisfactory for you. Is that not true?" He nodded. "You might be expecting better results." I shook my head. "It's the same with me. My contacts are absolutely trustworthy. They not only have my total confidence, but they provide me with perhaps the same physical and psychological training to survive and defend myself that you received. The only difference is that my name, as you said, is not on any payroll anywhere. I'm untraceable. It makes me practically a ghost, which means I can't be sold to anyone. Without that pink slip, there's no property title, as it were. No substance to me. If anything happens, it's their word against mine. That doesn't sound too good in this day and age, especially in a business transaction."

He leaned back in his chair and grinned broadly as he shook his head. "I hate to admit it, but kid—you're right! I really hate to ask you this, because it's a pretty stupid question, but my contact wanted me to ask you the next time we had a one-on-one opportunity to speak."

"Shoot—maybe to a stupid question we can find a savvy answer."

He shook his head ruefully as he sorted the negatives and returned them inside the envelope. He put the envelope to one side and rolled his eyes. "Well, my contact spoke to our superiors in the intelligence agency about those Habanos cigars. Since Castro has complete trust in you, they would like to know if you would deliver to Fidel some cigars containing a minute quantity of thallium salt—a chemical that will make him immediately lose all his hair and beard when he smokes one. You won't have anything to worry about, because thallium is untraceable. Even if they get suspicious of you and check the cigars, they won't find anything in them."

I looked at him in stunned disbelief. I could not imagine how a beardless and bald Fidel Castro could possibly be of benefit. It seemed so childish and stupid, and I burst into laughter. I raised both arms and said, "I'm sorry!" I was almost crying from the laughter. I leaned on his desk and took another Kleenex. When I regained my composure, I asked him, "What do you guys expect to accomplish with this?"

Abdul made a motion of washing his hands. "Not me—I told you at the beginning it was a stupid idea. I'm only the messenger, remember."

"Yes, yes—I know you're thinking differently, but they had to at least tell you what the objective of this would be."

Abdul shook his head and rolled his eyes again. "According to them, when people see Castro without his beard and completely bald, his mythos will disappear for even his most fanatic followers."

I leaned back in my chair. I simply couldn't believe what I was hearing. I shook my head slowly. "Abdul, my good friend . . . Mr. Ambassador. In my short life, I have never heard such an outrageous, irrational, absurd, and incoherent plan. It's a magnificently stupid idea. My answer is no. Their devotion won't be destroyed simply because he loses his hair. It will only be destroyed the way it was with me—by discovering that he and almost all his fellow leaders are bandits without scruples, disguised as Robin Hood, but without even the feather in his hat."

I tapped the envelope with the negatives. "In showing to the young men around the world what cowards and murderers these men really are, you will more assuredly destroy that mythos—or at least put a huge dent in it. This is a tangible contradiction of what they appear to be. This is why I risked my life to come here today."

Abdul raised his right hand and replied, "I'm in complete agreement with you. The publication of those pictures will not only be an international scandal with its violation of human rights, but it will also be a kick in the ass of the image of benevolence to the poor this government has constructed. After this conversation, the first thing I will do is call my contacts and make this my top priority."

Abdul handed me back the card I had used to announce my presence. "Preserve this card in case you need to see me in an emergency. I see you didn't use it this time, since nobody called me." He pulled out another card and wrote something on it. "This is my private address at the Country Club on First Avenue in Miramar. I've also written down my personal phone number."

"Thank you," I replied, "for your confidence."

"The thanks are to you from all of us," he said. "By the way, when you come across those excellent cigars again, I want you to remember your friend Abdul. Without the medication, of course."

I smiled. "Of course, of course. The next time I see you, I will make sure I have a handful in my pocket." I stood up and held my hand out to him.

He raised his hand to halt me. "I want to ask you something, if it's not too much risk to you. We need the exact location in the military camps of whatever they have in the way of fighter plane stations and whether they have any bombers. It is of critical importance for our next move. Do you think you can help us with this? We know they've been hiding these planes and moving them around."

I looked at him, considering it. "Let me see what I can do. I'll look around, and if I can find it, I'll get it to you somehow."

"Thank you very much." He asked curiously, "Before you leave, I need to ask you something that's puzzled me from the moment I saw you in my office: how in the hell did you get in here?" He pointed at the monitor for the security cameras in one corner of his desk. "I did not see you come through any door. An old lady would attract my attention, since we don't have many elderly come through here."

"One day, I will tell you," I replied mysteriously. "Not now. At least, not until my sources are clear. But remember what I told you before—I'm a ghost."

Abdul smiled and asked once more, "How do you intend to leave? The same way you came in?"

"No, no—not at all," I said confidently. "Never repeat in the casino the same trick that won you the game."

He looked at me in puzzlement. "Then how are you going to get out of here without calling attention to yourself?"

I shook my head. "I will get out the same way everyone else does: ordinarily. I don't believe the Cuban guards are too worried about people getting out of here. They're more concerned about who comes in."

He stood up as well, walked around the desk, and adjusted my wig. "It's a little bit twisted to the left. I've noticed it the entire time we were talking, and I didn't want them to notice that your hair under that wig is darker. Normally, women want to look younger, not older."

"Thank you. It's not a good quality wig."

He leaned in to me and put his right hand on his shoulder while with the left he pointed at the TV monitor in his desk. "You could not pick a better time to leave," he murmured quietly. "Several people are leaving the offices right now. They've finished the processing of different documents and passports. If you hurry a little bit, you'll be able to mingle with them by the elevators."

I looked at the monitor, which showed that, by coincidence, several families were indeed walking towards the elevators. After we said a hurried goodbye, I picked up the cane and left the office, heading towards the elevators. In the hallway, I mixed with the group I had seen earlier in the monitors. I also passed by Ricardo, who was bearing a small box of marble tiles on his shoulder. We exchanged glances without a word or sign of acknowledgment. Ricardo's two workers were also coming out of the rear door of the bathroom with the large cardboard box of the bathtub, heading with the empty container towards the service elevator.

The bell of the elevator rang, and a well-dressed gentleman courteously stepped back and said, "Please, lady, go ahead." Even though it was a large compartment, it was a large group, and we had to squeeze in to let the last couple in through the doors just as they closed.

My exit will be a lot easier than my entry, I thought. I thanked God that everything had so far worked better than planned. It appeared that my mission was complete, and I hoped that Abdul would be able to perform his part so that the Cuban government would be fully exposed for one of their many crimes.

The pressure of the people in the elevator jostled my wig askew once more. I later discovered that one of the elastic bands was overly stretched, and so wasn't holding the wig in place the way it should have. As I moved about, it also moved. The motion was so slight that I couldn't even feel it. Brushing against someone's clothes or getting jostled by an elbow moved it so much that it became badly twisted without my knowing it.

The group left the elevator, and I maintained my old lady's pace, quickly falling behind by the group.

Fortunately, by the time I reached the gate, the guards were distracted by a woman who was protesting her position in the line with two other people, and so they didn't even look at me. The one on the right opened the gate. As soon as I reached the sidewalk, I met Chopin's eyes. He was serving oysters to some customers, and his eyes widened. The customer had his hand out to receive the cocktail glass of oysters, but Chopin repeatedly tapped his temple with it. The customer was puzzled by this behavior, but Chopin's glance to me was urgent.

I could not continue looking at him, and so I continued on my way without stopping. The well-dressed gentleman who had let me into the elevator approached the oyster cart with his wife, and my view of Chopin was completely obstructed. The guard who had opened the gate for me also looked at me strangely. Out of the corner of my eye, I noticed that he was tapping the shoulder of his partner and pointed at me. The other guard was obviously too busy and fended off the urgent tapping, so I continued on my way. Without running, I walked with slightly greater urgency, but clearly Chopin was trying to communicate something to me, and I got nervous. Without rushing too much, I tried to walk faster. That block was the longest I had ever walked—it seemed at least ten miles long to me at that moment.

I looked at the tall trees on the corner which marked where I was to turn to my right. The hedge surrounding the property boundary of the embassy were quite tall, well-trimmed oleanders, and the property adjacent had much smaller hedges. I could see with great joy in my heart that I was soon leaving the embassy property and would shortly be around the corner, away from the eyes of the embassy guards as well as those of the G-2 men, and safely in the car.

Not once did I look back during that long walk. My training had taught me that, in a situation like this, should I ever look back, as it signaled to the enemy my insecurity and would put me in danger by making me look guilty. Even if someone were to call you, you should not respond immediately, as that person might not be calling to you specifically. The delay in answering would also give you time to think about how to reply.

My heart was pounding, and I was only a few yards from the corner. I breathed deeply and smelled the jasmine growing on the other side of the fence. Finally, I reached the corner and turned right.

I hadn't even walked a few steps from the corner when I heard a voice at my back saying, "Lady, lady—please stop. We wanted to ask you a few questions."

I continued to walk, ignoring the voice without turning around or acknowledging that I had heard the call.

The second time, the voice yelled very firmly, "Lady! Are you deaf or what? I told you to stop! We are from the State Security!"

I ignored him and continued to walk without replying. I could hear rushing footsteps of the man trying to catch up with me. A hand clamped down on my right shoulder. I turned around and raised my right hand with the cane, and hit the shoulder of the man with all my strength a couple of times. The man was of middle height with reddish, wavy hair. His face was pockmarked with a bad case of acne, and he screamed in pain.

"Why are you hitting me? I only wanted to ask you a question!"

I looked at him like I didn't know what he was saying as I fixed my glasses with my left hand. I screamed in a high-pitched voice, trying to make it sound as female as I could as the man flashed his G-2 badge at me. "What are you doing to me?" I screamed at him.

Two more men came up. One was short, fat, and moon-faced with a paunch. The third was thinner, taller, and heavily muscled like a bodybuilder. His skin was bronzed as if he spent a lot of time in the sun. The other two men were trying hard not to laugh, but they clearly were amused by what I was doing to their friend. They came close, but carefully kept their distance as they showed me their badges.

I waved my arms and said, "I don't care! What if you are police? What did I do?"

The pockmarked man showed more aggression, and screamed at me, "What are you doing with that wig? Let me see your ticket for the waiting line at the embassy!"

I held my hand to my ear. "What? What?"

He screamed even louder, almost in my ear. "The ticket to the embassy! Let me see!!" He grabbed for my purse. I raised my cane and swung it at him again. This time, however, he ducked back out of the way. I grabbed my purse and clutched it in the fashion of an elderly lady.

He screamed again, "What the hell are you doing with that wig?" He seized it and disrespectfully twisted it to show that it was a wig.

I fixed it and threatened him once more with the cane. "What kind of policemen are you?" I said. "You tried to steal my purse."

"No, no," he protested, "I just needed to see if you had your ticket in it. If you don't, we need to take you with us to our headquarters. Nobody saw you go in to the embassy, and with that wig, you are very suspicious. We have to corroborate your identity and what you were doing at the embassy." Convinced I was deaf, all of this was screamed combined with gesticulations in his attempt to communicate.

The other two men could no longer hold the straight faces and burst out in laughter. The last swing I made at their friend caused him to nearly jump into the bushes to avoid it, and that was the last straw. The moon-faced man said to the pockmarked man, "I think you're wasting your time. This old lady is as deaf as a post. I don't think she understands anything you're saying to her, or if you're lucky, very little."

The pockmarked man took handcuffs out of the container on his belt. In a threatening manner, he yelled, "We have to arrest you and take you to headquarters to prove your identity. The guards told us you were very suspicious, because they not only didn't see or remember you coming in, but it's obvious that twisted wig of white hair and dark hair underneath! What are you trying to do—make yourself out to be older than you are?"

I cursed the low quality of the wig. I had gotten it a long time ago from the trash. It was originally a Marilyn Monroe wig that my sister, Disa, had worn one Carnival. I had saved it, thinking it would one day be useful, but now I had to think quickly how to get out of there. I could not let them take me to the G-2 headquarters. If I went there, I would never get out alive.

I brought my cane down and signaled a peaceful surrender, and hung it on my right arm. As a last resort of trying to impress them, I showed them the first business card with the ambassador's name and number on it. I had hoped that his message would sway them away from giving me any further hassle. I handed it to the pockmarked man, who took it very cautiously. He read it and handed it to the moon-faced man, who then gave it to the muscular man. They looked at each other. I thought at that moment it might me my last card to get out of that situation, but unfortunately, it complicated things more. Clearly, the G-2 had the ambassador classified as a dangerous spy, something of which I was unaware. I had thought it was known only by the top leaders.

They went a short distance away and circled up to converse. I could not hear them. The moon-faced and pockmarked men both came over to me. The moon-faced man screamed at me, "You have to come with us!" He took me aggressively by the left arm while the pockmarked man took me forcefully by the right. They were ready to drag me, if necessary, to their car.

I couldn't wait any longer, and needed to take drastic measures. My life was in immediate danger. The one man was holding me just under the shoulder of my left arm, and so I pressed the button on my ring and jabbed him in the neck. The moon-faced man, when he felt the prick on his neck, let go of my arm and exclaimed, "Ouch!"

I raised my voice to cover his exclamation, "Look, you hurt my arm! Why are you using such powerful force on me?"

He exclaimed once more, but his voice was lower, "You hit me with something."

I didn't acknowledge it, and simply yelled, "Ow!" I looked at the other guy. "Let go! Let go of my arm, you're hurting me!" I showed him the marks I had on my arm.

At that, the pockmarked man held me even more firmly and screamed, "If you don't behave, I will put you in handcuffs and keep you in them all the way to headquarters! Turn around!"

He released my arm to open up his handcuffs, and that gave me my opportunity. I immediately used it. I grabbed my cane and put it on the ground. Using it, I made a half turn and faked losing my balance. I landed against his chest and jabbed him as I grabbed him to avoid falling.

He immediately let go of the handcuffs and exclaimed, "Ouch!" He started to unbutton his shirt. "What did you do to me?" He exposed his chest, and there was a small mark that looked much like a mosquito bite, but only a little blood at the injury.

The muscular man had been walking towards the car to bring it over. When he heard the commotion, he turned around and saw the pockmarked man's shirt unbuttoned. He walked over and examined the small puncture mark. He shook his head and said, "It's only a scratch, man! Maybe it was her nails or something."

Both of them went over to the moon-faced man and examined his neck. They saw an identical wound there, and the small man said, "Yeah, yeah—she did this to me!"

I was only a few feet away, watching them. Mentally, I was counting: One Pinar del Rio, two Pinar del Rio....

All three turned almost at the same time and looked at my hands, wondering why I had done that to them. This time, worry was plainly on their faces. At that moment, the moon-faced man started to convulse. He tried to say something, but his voice was inarticulate. His two friends looked at him in wonderment. He continued his convulsive dance like he was in some kind of voodoo ritual. Then he dropped to the ground, salivating profusely from his mouth. Slowly, the drool became foam as he lay at their feet. The other two looked on in terrified wonder, completely mute. Then he fell from his knees onto his back and began to convulse violently.

Before the other two could do anything, the pockmarked man began to do the same dance. When he fell onto the sidewalk and started to convulse, the muscular man shook himself out of his shock. Understanding what was happening, he pulled out his pistol and pointed it at me. "What did you do to my friends, you goddamned old witch lady?"

I remained a few feet from him as everything developed, observing them silently. I took a step towards him, looking directly into his eyes. Full of panic, he cocked his pistol, preparing to shoot me.

Suddenly, from around the corner, Chopin appeared at full speed with his oyster cart. He hit the G-2 man so hard that he landed on top of the cart. "Excuse me, *compañero!*" he exclaimed. "Excuse me!"

The pistol flew out of the man's hand and landed in the grass. The muscular man was lying flat on top of the oyster bar. He looked up, and his eyes bulged out of their sockets in terror as he saw Chopin very directly and deliberately advancing on him with his own ring. Even as he struggled to free himself of the cart, Chopin stung him right in the neck with his left hand. He knew now what that meant, but before he could do anything, Chopin used the element of surprise to lean over and snatch the radio off of his belt.

We could hear a voice on the radio saying, "X-9, X-9. Do you have the old lady under control, or do you need our help?" There was a mocking tone in the voice on the other end. "You're taking a long time to seduce an eighty-year-old woman. Do we need to call a national militia emergency team? Over. X-9, X-9, are you there?"

From behind the oyster cart, Chopin yelled, "Grab the pistol!"

The muscular man tried to move towards the pistol, but I hit him in the neck with my cane. I scooped up the pistol and gave it to Chopin. Chopin put the pistol against the man's temple. The man yelled, "Watch out! It's got a bullet in the chamber!"

Chopin said, "Not another word. Don't even move, unless you want your brains all over the sidewalk. You answer your friends, and if you do anything we don't like, that's it. Understand?" He held the radio next to the man's face and pressed the button.

"X-9 here, acknowledging," the stricken man said.

"Yes, X-9," the other voice laughed. "Finally, you got the old lady under control?"

"Yes, yes, everything is under control. We'll see you in a little while."

"OK, out." The man laughed again. "Watch out with that old lady, OK?"

"Out," the muscular man said.

I removed the antidote syringe out of my purse and prepared to inject the moon-faced man. "What are you doing?" Chopin asked. "We don't have any time to waste. Get in the car, before the other guys come out."

I didn't pay any attention to him. I injected the two unconscious men. I rolled them underneath the hedge. There was a lip, and the inert forms dropped down by the roots of the bushes and would be completely unseen from the sidewalk. After I was done with that, I brought the syringe over to Chopin to inject the third man, who was now beginning to convulse. Chopin shook his head. "No, this man saw my face and will recognize me later." The convulsing man looked up at me, the plea in his eyes. The salivation had started.

I looked at Chopin and shook my head regretfully. "It's up to you. If he saw you, he has to go. He also saw the oyster cart and your car. The other two only saw me in my disguise."

Dr. Julio Antonio del Marmol

I helped Chopin roll the still-convulsing man to join his two comrades. Chopin opened the small door under the cart and tossed the oyster water into the bushes. I climbed inside the cart. He handed the bucket to me and closed the door. Just as the door closed, I could see the other G-2 car pulling around the corner and driving slowly towards where the other men had been parked. Chopin took the handles and rolled it towards his car. He hooked the cart up to the rear of the Edsel and murmured through the door to me, "Don't worry, I will drive very slowly. But I don't want those guys to see you inside my car and have anyone remember you."

We drove by the confused G-2 agent questioning the gate guards, who in turn were pointing down towards the corner where the altercation with me had occurred. The guards came out to the sidewalk, following the G-2 to see what could have happened to the other agents. The three men stood in the middle of the block, their hands spread in bewilderment.

Chopin's vendor cart

The Dark Face of Marxism

Chapter 10: Cuban Counter-Intelligence Hits and Misses

On the way back to Chopin's house, I jolted along most uncomfortably in the oyster cart. There were no shock absorbers and perhaps only the kind of springs used on motorcycles rather than in a car. My head hit the wood of the cart's cover several times, and once it cracked against the bottom of the sink.

At last, the cart stopped, and I could see through cracks in the wood that we had arrived in front of Chopin's house. "Thank you, Lord, for letting me get here in one piece," I said softly.

I remained in that cramped position inside the cart without moving, cradling the empty water bucket on my legs. I heard the car door open and close and then his footsteps approaching the cart. Through the cracks, I could see his legs, but he did not open the door. He stood outside, and I could hear him moving bottles around.

I heard him say, "Don't get out of there until I say to. The neighbor on my right is outside in his garden, and he is a *miliciano*[29]. He's watering the garden right now, so be patient until I disengage and roll the cart safely out of his

---

[29] *Militiaman*

line of sight. Brace yourself, because I'm going to have to jerk the cart up and down."

I had to wonder if this would cause me any greater pain than I was already enduring.

"I will try to push it with my hands up the driveway. Hopefully, I'll be able to make it with your added weight. I'll let you know once we're through the gate and in the mews next to the house. Then it'll be safe for you to get out without being seen."

"Very well," I said softly. "Don't worry about me. Do what you have to do."

"OK," he murmured even more softly this time. He then said in a louder voice, "Hey, how are you doing? We really need a little rain, eh? We haven't even had a sprinkle all month!"

Another voice answered from a distance, "Yeah. How lucky we are that we live in the city and can use a water hose on our gardens. Just imagine those poor peasants in the country who are entirely dependent on that rain! I wouldn't want to be in their place, watching their crops withered by the sun."

Chopin continued his conversation to distract his neighbor. As he spoke, he worked at disconnecting the cart from his car. The chain clattered as he removed it, and the cart shook violently as he worked it loose from the hitch. It felt then like he was pushing it up the incline of his drive. "Yeah, it's unbelievable how those poor farmers have to live and eat only whatever the land produces. We're very lucky!"

I felt the oyster cart stop momentarily. Chopin was apparently having a difficult time getting it up over the lip at the top and into the mews. "Damn!" he swore, and he grunted in his effort.

His neighbor said, "Hold on, for God's sake, *chico*! I'll help you!"

Chopin immediately replied, "No, no—I've got it, thanks. Don't worry about it, I can make it. If I can't, I'll call Chia."

I could see the legs of his neighbor appear. He was not taking no for an answer. He might have wanted to help him out of goodwill, and before Chopin could call to Chia for help, I felt the tremendous force of the cart moving forward, this time faster. After it stopped, I heard Chopin say, "Thank you very much."

As they said their farewells, his neighbor said jokingly, "God, what do you have inside that cart? Rocks?"

Chopin laughed nervously and replied, "Something very similar. The shells of the oysters I sold all day."

"No wonder! You probably sold a lot today!"

"Yes," Chopin answered, "it was a very good day."

Silence fell as I heard the gate close. A short time later, Chopin opened the door on the cart, and Chopin said, "You can get out. The coast is clear."

I climbed out of the cart.

Chopin said, "You should go and change your clothing as soon as possible. We have to get you out of here immediately as a security measure, just in case something we left behind could make the State Security unleash their dogs and find us here together. We should never allow that to happen. We don't want to give them any reason to find out what we've been doing together today."

I smiled in surprise as we walked into the house. "I don't have any idea what you're talking about. I just came only a few minutes ago to your house and asked your wife where you were. She told me you were already due back before going to your other job inside the FOCSA Building."

He smiled as he caught my drift. He patted me on the shoulder. "Oh, yeah—that's true. You came to ask me if I wanted to go with you to Carlos Anzas' house tonight. You didn't feel very comfortable going over there by yourself, given the Maestro's sexual orientation."

"Of course, chico," I replied. We walked into the room where I had left my travel bags with my uniform packed inside. I started to change out of my disguise.

"While you change, I'll go and get a five-gallon can to burn this disguise. Just in case."

Chia was walking by and asked, "How did everything go?"

"No problems," I replied with a smile. "Everything went precisely as we planned."

"I told you!" she said.

Chopin turned and looked at me in disbelief as he left the room. He rolled his eyes and smiled slightly as he continued on his way out. I was sure he appreciated my keeping my mouth shut and not going into any detail about our ordeal and the close shave we'd had with the G-2. I didn't want to unnecessarily worry her and thought that Chopin would have plenty of time later in private to fill her in on as many details as he wanted her to know. A few minutes later, he returned with an aluminum can. It looked like the ones used in houses to hold leftover food to be deposited in the backyard for the *sarcocho*. It was the best way to keep the house from stinking with discarded food rotting in the trash.

After I put all of the women's clothing, including the defective wig, into the pail, Chopin handed it to Chia and said, "Put some alcohol on top of all of this. Put it out on the patio and burn it immediately. Don't waste a single minute."

Chia hugged me, and we said our farewells.

I walked with Chopin to where my Mercedes was waiting for me in the garage. He handed me a card and said, "Here is where you can send me the money for Ricardo."

I took the note and tucked it into my shirt pocket. We hugged, and I said, "Thank you very much, my friend. You've been a great help."

Chopin replied, "Just walk very carefully, kid. Don't forget—you are swimming in very dark waters filled with sharks. Please watch your back."

I nodded and said, "Thank you, brother. God bless you."

He stepped back with a smile and said, "Thanks for what? Wait until we go to Carlos Anzas' house, and then you can thank me!"

This time, I smiled and gave him an amused salute. I got into the car while he opened the garage door for me. I slowly backed down the driveway towards the street. I pulled into the street and started towards the Avenue. Several cars passed me, all the same color, each with several men. They were coming from the opposite direction from which I had come. They looked like G-2, all right, and so I slowed down so as not to call attention to myself. I also wanted to watch them to see where they were going.

I winced and a weight settled in my heart as I sadly saw that the cars stopped in front of Chopin's house. They got out, and several men started walking towards his house, while the rest stayed outside on watch. I gulped and massaged my forehead with my fingers as I continued to drive slowly along.

I hoped that Chia had obeyed Chopin and was burning those clothes.

I was at the intersection and had no alternative but to turn away from that scene. If I stopped, I would call attention to myself, as the agents were watching both sides of the street. I mingled in with the traffic, still worried about the well-being of my friends. I drove into the city, trying to put some distance between Chopin's house and myself. My presence anywhere near that area could complicate things far more than they already were.

I drove to the Malecón and decided to go to Che's safe-house in Boca Siega. Since I was already in the capital, I wanted to see if there was any additional information I could get from Che if I was fortunate enough to find him there. Every time I got close to Che, I discovered a new machination he was concocting.

I reached Boca Siega at last. To my surprise, no one was there—not even security around the premises. The house was completely empty. I parked on the side of the driveway, went up, and rang the bell. It was very strange— even if Che weren't around, he normally maintained some kind of security force there.

I rang several times without any answer. I turned around to explore the terrace in the back. There wasn't anyone around at all. I felt very uncomfortable with this.

The Dark Face of Marxism

As I was about to leave, it crossed my mind to check the beach area. I sat down on one of the terrace chairs, in the same area where I had only recently been sitting with Che. I was frustrated, as I had lost thirty minutes for nothing. I thought about returning to Chopin's house as a casual visitor and discover what had happened after I had left. My common sense, however, told me that anybody could have seen me go there before. I had to worry now about that *miliciano* neighbor, and going back there might cause more harm than good.

I decided to eat my worries and starve my curiosity by leaving things the way they were. After all, Chopin knew how to take care of this kind of situation. He had been trained for it. I looked at the waves crashing on the sand on that beautiful beach. I removed my beret and raked the fingers of my left hand through my hair.

I looked at one of the tables next to me and saw something hanging on the back of one of the chairs, close to the table. It was one of the tables the escort normally would sit at when Che was having meetings out here with people. I got up and went to investigate.

To my surprise, it was an M-3 semiautomatic rifle. I also saw a small Thompson submachine gun that I hadn't noticed before hanging from another chair. It occurred to me that the guards might have left in a rush. It was Che's custom to hurry people whenever he moved around, and perhaps in the rush they had forgotten these weapons. Especially in that house, there were so many weapons that a forgotten gun was quickly replaced.

I picked both of them up and walked to the Mercedes. I put the M-3 in the trunk and the Thompson in the front seat. I pulled a shirt out of my travel bag, and covered the submachine gun with it. I walked towards the side of the house nearest the beach. There were some rocks and coconut trees a short distance away, and I sat down on a large rock. I watched the waves once more and went back in time in my mind, pondering how many people throughout the history of the island must have before me enjoyed the wild, tropical beauty I was observing. There was a possibility that it wasn't that many at all, since that beautiful island had, according to the books I had read in school, lain submerged under the ocean for many millions of years before surfacing. It was possible to my mind that Cuba might not even have been populated before Christ, and the only privileged ones to enjoy her beauty were those who had arrived after Christopher Columbus made the mistake of thinking Cuba was India—perhaps some of the Caribes who had lived here before then, but I didn't know when those natives had arrived on the island in their own wanderings from, according to my history books, Mongolia.

    Distracted by my thoughts, I could see from where I was sitting one of the soldiers of Che's escort that I recognized. He was tall and mustachioed with wavy hair. He opened the door of the house. He was wrapped around the waist with a towel and was drying himself off with one hand. With his other, he was buttoning up his shirt.

    I looked at him from where I sat as he walked out the door and towards the Mercedes. It looked like he recognized it, and he walked around it, clearly looking for me. When he saw I wasn't immediately around, he walked back towards the terrace. I was about to yell to him to alert him but the noise of the ocean behind me was so loud

I chose not to. Instead, I stood up to walk towards him, but something on the beach caught my attention.

I saw a man with SCUBA gear on the beach. He was in the process of removing his equipment. He took a sealed bag off of his belt. He opened it up and removed a pistol. He also took out a silencer and began screwing it on to the end of the barrel. Another man joined him on the beach and began to do exactly the same—then another, and then another, each only a few seconds apart. The four communicated with hand signals. It looked like a military squad of some kind, and the house was the target. The one who arrived first appeared to be the leader. His wetsuit had green and red lines on either side, while the rest of the team wore unmarked black suits.

He signaled to the others that he had seen one individual—from the location he indicated, it must have been the escort I had seen go around to the terrace. They split into regular intervals, and like geese in flight maintained a formation as they approached the house.

I was completely caught by surprise and petrified, since I didn't know who these men were. I had no idea what to do. The only thing I knew for sure was that the men with silenced pistols had hostile intention; they were not here to collect shells or drink coconut water.

I ducked back down and tried to camouflage myself in the bushes. My eyes remained glued to the men as I pulled my pistol out. I carefully cocked it and used the rock as a support to settle myself more comfortably. I would also be able to use it as cover, should those men start to approach me and I needed to defend myself. From my vantage point, I could observe the guard attempt to pull his pistol as he noticed the men approaching him. They shot him several times, and he collapsed on his face over one of the beach chairs. The leader of the group advanced on the guard and delivered the coup de grâce. He signaled to the others, and three of them entered the house while one remained outside on guard duty.

A few minutes later, the three men came back outside. The leader had a rolled up tube of paper in his hand. From my distance, I couldn't see precisely what it was. It was easy to distinguish the leader from his wetsuit.

The roll of paper was put inside a sealed bag that the leader removed from a zipped compartment in the right leg of his suit. From a similar compartment in his left leg, he pulled another sealed bag, and also put that over the roll, double ensuring that the documents remained well-protected. The rest of the squad remained on watch while he worked.

When he was finished, he started to walk back towards the beach, but one of the men raised a left hand to stop him. The man pointed to the leader's left. I looked in the same direction and saw two couples walking along the beach in our direction. They were kicking an inflatable ball, laughing and happy, and completely oblivious to the danger they were about to encounter. The four men ducked down to use the beach retaining wall as cover. From my place of concealment, I was able to see everything, and I prayed to the Father and the Son, reaching under my shirt to touch my medallion. I thanked God for nudging me to decide to leave the terrace, or I would probably have wound up being another corpse lying on that patio, all because I was simply in the wrong place at the wrong time. I looked down at my uniform and knew without any doubt that this was an operation carried out by the anti-communists. Had they found me there at Che's house, it would have been my last day alive.

The men in the back held their positions, motionless and silent. They watched the couples get closer and closer, still playing with the large beach ball. I wondered how I could let these people know of their danger and get them to turn around and leave. I knew that those men would not hesitate to kill them if they felt they would be discovered. At the same time, I knew they weren't about to harm civilians unless absolutely necessary. However, they probably had a timetable they were adhering to for their mission, and they simply couldn't wait there forever for these people to finish playing with that ball. Those civilians could easily wind up becoming casualties of war.

I continued watching the men, and from their signals and continual checking of their watches, I could tell they were getting nervous. They needed to rendezvous with the yacht or submarine that had dropped them there, and the clock was ticking. I could find no solution that didn't involve leaving my hiding place and compromising myself.

They were very close to the retaining wall by now. The kicked ball bounced against the wall, and one of the women went to fetch it, practically on top of one of the men.

"Get away from there, you idiot!" I muttered under my breath.

They had been playing around, laughing like they had all the time in the world. One of the women said, "Let's go for a swim in the water! Look at how crystal clear the water is right here by this sand dune—the sand looks like sugar!"

I watched the leader jerk his head up, and he began to signal to the others to go ahead and take the civilians down and giving the plan of attack. I knew I had to do something now, and I reacted rapidly to try and save these innocent people's lives. They had no idea what was going on, nor what was about to happen to them.

I wasn't thinking clearly—just acting on instinct. I jumped over the rock towards the beach with my pistol in my hand. I kept one eye on the people and one eye on the men, and fired my pistol twice into the air. The girl who was about to enter the water stopped, and the man with the ball dropped it. Everyone looked in my direction in surprise. The four men ducked behind the wall, seeking cover.

I knew I would be an easy target, since I was in plain view. I no longer had the men in sight, as I was walking towards the couples on the beach. I began to signal as if I had men around me myself behind the rocks. I needed to buy some time and confuse the armed men so that they would hold their fire.

The couples had been headed at an angle towards the men; now, with my jumping out at them, they were moving towards me and away from the squad. I was hoping to draw them away while at the same time making it appear I had others in concealment and was oblivious to the four men. It was vital to persuade that team to hold on until I did what I was going to do with the couples. I wanted it to appear to them that I had no knowledge of them and had nothing to do with them, so that they would remain in concealment and simply wait for everyone to depart.

The Dark Face of Marxism

It worked; they did not open fire nor reveal themselves. I yelled at the top of my lungs to the couples, "Comrades! Please get out of here! You are trespassing in a prohibited military zone—no civilians allowed!" My pistol was still in my hand at my side.

One of the young men said, "I'm sorry, *compañero*! I live a couple of miles from here," he pointed back towards where they had come, "and I had no idea the military had sealed this beach."

I didn't bother to reply to that, and simply said, "Get out of here, quickly, please! Behind you guys are four snipers pointing at your heads." I added in a very firm tone of voice, "Do you understand?"

They looked at me in terror, at my pistol, and the men each grabbed his girl's hand and they bolted out of there. I let them pass by, and walked briskly fifty or one hundred feet after them. As soon as I felt I was no longer under direct observation, I jumped over the retaining wall of one of the nearby residences. I sat down there and watched the beach, waiting to see the men leave. I made myself comfortable under a planter with a large mango tree in it. The couples were still running in fright and were rapidly disappearing in the distance.

After about ten or fifteen minutes of the beach remaining empty, I finally saw the leader of the infiltration team walk with a man close behind him. At a short distance, the other two walked in a similar formation. I kept my pistol in my hand, just in case, and waited until they left. The leader remained on guard while the other three put on their tanks and the rest of their gear. Then they kept watch while the leader got himself geared up.

They entered the water and slowly disappeared under the surface.

I remained there for three hours. My training told me that there was the possibility that another team would come in to double check the work of the first team or support them in case of trouble. I didn't want to be treated like another *Fidelista* and wind up with a bullet in my head.

While I waited beneath that mango tree in the beautiful residence, I remembered something my mother had told me: appearances could be deceiving. Many times, things that looked one way would, in the end, wind up being something completely different. This was a perfect example of that saying. It would have been the greatest irony had I been found by those men at Che's safe-house and then killed, effectively, by the people for whom I had been risking my life. They would have had no idea that I was on their side and was actively working against that government.

After a while, it seemed to me that it was safe to leave my hiding place. I started to rise up onto my feet and looked towards Che's patio. I could see a 1959 VW minibus, light purple and white, enter the driveway. I tried to see what they were doing as I walked toward the patio, keeping to the bushes as much as possible. My eyes were glued to the new arrivals. Five men, all dressed in civilian clothes, got out. From the way they walked at once to the terrace, it seemed like they knew the layout very well.

The driver got out and everyone followed him very closely. They had something in their hands, but I couldn't see exactly what. As they came close to the body of the guard, they spread it out between them; it looked like a potato sack. They lifted the body and removed his belt. Then they put one sack over the feet and the other over his head. They tied it together in the middle using his belt. Two of the men picked the body up, supported by a third man taking the middle. The other two men remained on watch as the group walked back to the minibus. They deposited the body inside the vehicle; they then entered it themselves after checking the area to make sure all was still clear. The engine started up, and it drove away at high speed.

I sighed in relief. Had I walked over there a few seconds earlier, it would have been trouble for me. This gave me even more worry; I wasn't sure if I should wait longer now because of this fresh development, or if I should get the Mercedes and get out of there immediately. My indecision made me hesitate for another half hour, though it felt like hours to me.

The sun was beginning to set, casting multicolored rays in the blue of the sky as the day ended. Some dark clouds moved rapidly as the sea breeze began to blow, adding some shadow to that tropical sunset. I had to hold my beret against that wind. Since I never liked indecision, I determined to get out of there now, regardless of the consequences.

Still holding my pistol in my hand against my right leg, keeping the weapon out but somewhat concealed, I cautiously approached the house. At a brisk pace, I entered the door of the patio. As soon as I was inside, I stopped and scanned the area. All was quiet, like nothing had happened there. Everything was still save for the breeze through the palm trees. The wind was increasing in strength, and the sky was darkening, heralding some rain setting in. This time, I walked very slowly along the terrace and towards the front of the house. Watching every angle, I walked onto the driveway and found my Mercedes where I had left it. I climbed inside and got out of there.

I was already on the highway towards the capital, and after fifteen or twenty minutes I had to pull over. Extreme pain in my abdomen told me I needed urgently to urinate; the adrenaline rush had completely disguised that need from me, and now it wasn't a request. My body demanded this relief.

I walked about forty or fifty feet from the car, looking for a tree. I urinated for the longest time I had ever spent doing so in my life, and I closed my fly once finished. I turned my back to the tree, and leaned against it. I rested my head against the trunk and squeezed my face in both hands. I mumbled to myself, "Every day I like this business of espionage less and less."

I remained so for several minutes, until a sprinkle started to spatter over my face. It increased over the next several seconds, becoming a steady rain with large drops. I ran back to the car to seek refuge and drove back towards the capital.

After I entered Havana about thirty minutes later, my stomach started to growl loudly. I hadn't eaten all day, and now after my long relief earlier, it was like I had a cat and a dog fighting in my stomach.

I drove slowly because of the rain and took the Malecón to the Hilton Hotel. I felt I had earned an excellent meal after that extremely stressful day. I looked for 23rd Street as I drove, where I was to turn right. Just before I reached there, traffic was stopped. It looked like there had been an accident: several police cars and ambulances had completely blocked the road.

The Malecon in Havana

At first glance, I saw a large crane hoisting a car off the rocks and out of the deep ocean, water streaming out of the vehicle. It started to move towards a flatbed truck, waiting to receive the wrecked automobile. It was obvious what had happened, especially when the large hole in the old wall was taken into consideration. Clearly, the car had flown over the wall, taking a chunk out of it, and landing on the rocks about thirty feet below.

I waited patiently behind a couple of other cars while the crane did its work. For a moment, that car looked familiar. I could see that it had diplomatic license plates. By the front bumper, there was a piece of metal on both sides. One was bare, but the other had pieces of the flag still attached to it. As the crane rotated the car to settle it more firmly on the truck's bed, I could see that it was the Belgian flag.

I raised my left hand to my mouth and said, "Oh, my God. No—please!" I no longer cared about the rain, and got out of the Mercedes. I looked around me cautiously. There were several police cars and three ambulances. One was already leaving, one other was starting to move with the assistance of the police, and the other was still there. I started to trot towards the police line as the second ambulance left. I drew near one of the police cars. I greeted them and introduced myself to a tall, dark-skinned police officer with a thick mustache and wavy hair that just covered his ears. I asked him, "What happened here?"

He replied, "Looks like the ambassador's chauffeur lost control and flew over the wall. The chauffeur might have had a heart attack. At any rate, he had no vital signs. The ambassador is in very bad shape and has just left." He pointed to the third ambulance. "His assistant is in that one."

"Which hospital did they take him to?"

"The *Hospital Clinico Quirurgico*[30]," he said.

"And what about the assistant?" I asked.

"She looks OK. Some bruising and stuff, but she appears to be in good spirits. Her legs might be broken, but she's conscious. She was the luckiest of the three of them. Not so much the ambassador—when we pulled him out of the car, he was bleeding everywhere, ears, nose, mouth.... He was unconscious, but still breathing."

---

[30] *Clinical Surgery Hospital*

I thanked him and walked over to the remaining ambulance. I thought Sonia would probably not recognize me without my disguise, but I might at least be able to find out what had happened. I did not think this was any heart attack but an attempt by the government to eliminate Abdul and make it look like an accident so that his death would not create an international incident. When I reached the ambulance, the paramedic was about to close the doors in the back. I yelled, "I need to speak with that lady before you take her away!"

The two men noted my uniform and respectfully opened the doors and motioned me ahead. I entered the ambulance and looked at Sonia. Her eyes were bruised, her head was bandaged, and both legs were splinted. I gently took one of her hands, and she opened her eyes.

She moaned, "Oh, God—I hurt all over. I think my legs are going to explode." She tried to remove her hand, but I held on.

"Wait a minute, I'm your friend," I said as I gently squeezed her hand. "Take it easy. I'm a very good friend to the ambassador. You won't recognize me, but we've spoken before. I was in disguise. I only want, for your safety and Abdul's well-being, for you to tell me how this accident happened."

She started to laugh but grimaced in pain. "This was not an accident. Someone intentionally pushed us off the street and shoved us against that wall. After we crashed, they stole the diplomatic pouch we were supposed to take to the courier at the airport tonight."

"They just told me that your driver had a heart attack and lost control of the car."

She rolled her eyes. "Heart attack? Please—our chauffeur just passed a physical last week and runs five miles every morning. He is not only the chauffeur; he is also the ambassador's personal bodyguard."

I squeezed my chin. I didn't want to tell her that the driver was dead. Instead, I asked, "Why the hell did the police tell me that, then?"

Her eyes opened wide in shock. "The police told you that? It's a lie. Why don't you go back and ask them where the diplomatic pouch is? That is what they should be concerned about—that was stolen from us. And I told the police that! Oh, my God—I wouldn't even be surprised to discover that it is in the hands of one of those policemen, and that they aren't even the police they represent themselves to be."

That struck a chord for me, and I stroked my chin in thought. I wondered whether this all could be because of the negatives I delivered to the ambassador. Or, perhaps, his enemies had previously planned this attack, since Che had assured me that they knew for a fact of Abdul's ties with the American CIA.

I squeezed her hand again and said, "Listen, take care of yourself. I hope you get well soon. I have to tell you something: thank you very much for the Jupiñas you brought to me today when I was speaking with the ambassador in his office."

She looked at first puzzled, but then I could see she remembered. "What?"

I looked at her with a smile. "You remember the old lady?"

She clapped a hand to her mouth and then grabbed my arm with her other hand. I wished her well, asked her once more to take care of herself, and told her that I would see her soon.

I stepped out into the street and inquired of the paramedic where they were going to take her. He let me know that she was going to the same place as the ambassador, as that was the nearest medical emergency hospital in the area.

I immediately started to hunt for the wavy-haired policeman I had been speaking with before. I went up to a group of them and asked about the man I had spoken with before, and described him to them. One of them answered, "No, we don't have anyone like that. In fact, we can't wear our hair that long—it's against our uniform code. If our sergeant saw anyone that out of code, he would have to write him up at once."

I spent the next fifteen or twenty minutes looking for that man, but he had disappeared. This confirmed the suspicions Sonia had imparted to me. I had to ask myself how a policeman that was not even a paramedic could diagnose a heart attack or be able to make any other medical assessment. Heaven knew who he was; possibly G-2. If I ever found him, the only thing I wanted to ask him with my pistol held to his head was who gave him that medical report. But he had vanished like magic, and I gave up. I needed to get back to the Mercedes, since the congestion was now being relieved. I drove towards the Critical Surgery Clinic.

The Critical Surgery Clinic

Soon after, I arrived and entered the emergency room. I went up to the front desk and asked about the ambassador's condition. I was told that he was in surgery to remove a clot in his brain. I was invited to sit down and wait on a diagnostic from a doctor. The nurse said, "Unfortunately, we've been having a very busy day. There have been a lot of accidents and cases today. It's probably because of the rain."

I went out to the hallway and sat down to patiently wait for the nurses and doctors to do their work. After two hours, however, my patience was wearing thin. Part of my problem was hunger; my stomach was loudly protesting the fact that I still had yet to eat. The cat and the dog, I felt, had progressed from fighting to killing each other.

Politely, I stood and went back to the desk. There was a different nurse on duty now. I asked, "What's happened with the Belgian ambassador and his assistant, Sonia? I was told someone would keep me informed, and I've been waiting two hours now. So far, no one's come out to tell me anything."

This nurse was a cute brunette with short hair. "I'm sorry," she apologized profusely. "With the change in shift, they forgot to tell me you were waiting. Let me take you to the doctor. Follow me, please."

Feeling bad about my long wait, she took me to one of the examination rooms where a doctor was. We introduced ourselves to each other, and she said, "He is a very good friend of the ambassador."

He rubbed his face. "I'm sorry. They didn't make it."

"What?" I exclaimed. "You must be confused. Do you know who I'm talking about? I know the ambassador was in bad shape, but I spoke with Sonia right after the accident. She had some bruising and broken legs, but she was otherwise in good spirits and very alert."

The doctor walked over to me and put his hand on my shoulder. "I'm sorry, but this kind of trauma is very typical in a severe impact or high drop like this. Sometimes, there is some internal damage, bleeding, and the patient dies a few hours later. There's nothing we can do about it."

Suspiciously, I asked, "May I please see the bodies?"

"Sure, come over here." I followed them closely to the morgue. There were three bodies lying on metal examination tables covered with white sheets. The first body he showed me was, sure enough, Ambassador Abdul Marcalt. I shook my head. The second body was Sonia.

As the three of us stood by Sonia's corpse, I could not believe that only a few hours before I had been sitting in the ambulance speaking with her. Now she was lying there dead on that cold metal slab.

I felt a pain in my chest. The young doctor noticed my distress and tried to comfort me. "I'm sorry," he said as he shook his head compassionately. "Such a shame, for a beautiful woman to die so young. From what they told me, the drop was between twenty to thirty feet, possibly more. That kind of impact could easily rupture one of the arteries in the heart. We won't know until we perform the autopsy. They all arrived at the same time, and they were all in very bad shape when they got here, except for the driver. He was already dead. He probably suffered the least, since he died at once. Did you want to see the driver's body?"

I raised my arm. "No, thank you very much."

I left the hospital full of pain and disappointment. I had a picture in my mind of those dead bodies. To make things worse, there was an extremely high possibility that the negatives that Chopin and I had risked our lives to deliver to the ambassador had been in the stolen pouch. It was very likely that the courier had left the airport without knowing what had happened to the ambassador.

When I got to the hospital parking lot, I was filled with frustration. I released my emotions by kicking the Mercedes' rear bumper several times with my boot and slamming my right hand on the top of the trunk. I did this until both hand and foot began to hurt. I stopped not because I wanted to but because my instincts warned me that all I was accomplishing was injuring myself.

I got into the car and drove away from that place. I asked myself at that moment where God was to allow these kinds of crimes to happen with impunity. I had to force myself to calm down after a few minutes of reflection.

I knew I needed to apologize to the Lord, because I realized I should not blame God for a guilt we humans bear ourselves. God didn't put Castro into power; we were the ones who had made the wrong choice. It was our mistake that put the country's reins in the hands of that group of atheist bandits.

The Bible says very clearly that God helps those who help themselves. Given that, I should not blame God for these miseries. In the same way we put them into power, we should put forth our best efforts to pull them out of power in order to bring peace, happiness, and tranquility once more to our island.

This concludes the third part of Rites of Passage of a Master Spy. Julio Antonio's adventures and trials continue in Volume IV, Deadly Deals. For even further adventures of the Lightning, visit our website, www.cuban-lightning.com.

Dr. Julio Antonio del Marmol

Shredded Innocence for the Useful Fools

For years, medical experts have debated the reason why babies are always born crying. The babies come from the darkness of the womb to such a beautiful place full of light and with soft, beautiful music and an environment that is full of promises for their future; that is life.

It is a very simple answer, one unseen by innocent, foolish, blind eyes. It is human nature; it is deception. The baby has been removed from a warm place where it had been living for a while in comfort. Abruptly, it is forced out to a place that is unpleasant, annoying, and full of instability and nasty surprises. Its innocence is shredded by this true reality. This is as close to the broken promises presented by the dark faces of the Marxists as reality can come. It is a little too late once reality finally opens your eyes. It is now the time for you, the baby, to start to cry with all your heart and say goodbye to your freedom and peace, if not forever, then at least for a very, very long time.

Dr. Julio Antonio del Marmol

Photo Credits

p. 27 Cars "stored" in Che's garage
Red vintage car with lineup behind
Copyright: <a href='http://www.123rf.com/profile_jakkapan'>jakkapan / 123RF Stock Photo</a>
Red vintage car
Copyright: <a href='http://www.123rf.com/profile_deusexlupus'>deusexlupus / 123RF Stock Photo</a>
Metallic red vintage car
Copyright: <a href='http://www.123rf.com/profile_deusexlupus'>deusexlupus / 123RF Stock Photo</a>
Black classic car
Copyright: <a href='http://www.123rf.com/profile_deusexlupus'>deusexlupus / 123RF Stock Photo</a>

p. 30 The Mercedes 300 SL
Credit by Stahlkocher at
https://commons.wikimedia.org/wiki/File:Mercedes-Benz_300_SL.jpg

p. 98 Marcello Mastroianni
Credit by Gorupdebesanez at
https://commons.wikimedia.org/wiki/File:Marcello_Mastroianni_02.jpg

p. 106 The FOCSA building in Havana
Credit by Bin im Garten at
https://commons.wikimedia.org/wiki/File:FOCSA_building_1973_Havanna_PD_3.jpg

p. 180 A holding cell at Villa Marista
Credit by Lauren J at
http://www.freeimages.com/photo/inside-alcatraz-2-1551941

p. 284 Chopin's vendor cart
Copyright: <a href='http://www.123rf.com/profile_eugenesergeev'>eugenesergeev / 123RF Stock Photo</a>

p. 311 The Malecon in Havana
Credit by LuisMoro at
https://commons.wikimedia.org/wiki/File:Low_Tide_Malicon_Sea_Wall,_Havana,_Cuba_-_panoramio.jpg

p. 306 Critical Clinic Surgery
Credit by Rjcastillo at
https://commons.wikimedia.org/wiki/File:Hospital_Central_Dr._Urquinaona_I.jpg

The Dark Face of Marxism

Other Works

Cuba: Russian Roulette of the World
The Cuban Lightning: The Zipper

Rites of Passage of a Master Spy saga
Cuba: The Truth, the Lies, and the Coverups
The Havana Conspiracies

Forthcoming
The Deadly Deals
The Evil Rituals
JFK: The Unwrapped Enigma

www.ingramcontent.com/pod-product-compliance
Lightning Source LLC
Chambersburg PA
CBHW031308150426
43191CB00005B/133